TOWARD A MODERN
JAPANESE THEATRE

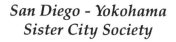

TOWARD A MODERN JAPANESE THEATRE

Kishida Kunio

BY J. THOMAS RIMER

PRINCETON UNIVERSITY PRESS

For Laurence

A nation which does not help and encourage its theatre is, if not dead, dying; just as the theatre which does not feel the social pulse, the historical pulse, the drama of its people, and catch the genuine color of its landscape and of its spirit with laughter or with tears, has no right to call itself a theatre, but is an amusement hall, or a place for doing that dreadful thing known as "killing time."

Federico Garcia Lorca
1934

Acknowledgments

I AM especially grateful for the helpful suggestions given me at all stages of the preparation of this manuscript by Professor Donald Keene of Columbia University, where an earlier version was presented as a doctoral dissertation in 1971. My thanks also go to Professor Marleigh Ryan and Professor Herschel Webb, both of whom made valuable contributions. Dr. Stanley Spector of Washington University (St. Louis) also provided a number of observations most useful to me. Mr. and Mrs. Toshio Morioka of the *Kobe Shimbun* also supplied me with valuable information.

I would also like to express my gratitude to Washington University for a research grant to help prepare the manuscript for final publication. Miss R. Miriam Brokaw and the staff of Princeton University Press have provided expert and painstaking editorial assistance. Nevertheless, errors in fact, or in translations from the Japanese, are entirely my responsibility. All translations from the Japanese are, unless otherwise indicated, my own.

Acknowledgment is also made to the family of Kishida Kunio for permission to quote his writings. Special thanks are due to Professor Hisao Kanaseki and Dr. Kurahashi of the Waseda Theatre Museum, who kindly supplied the photographs of the productions of Kishida's plays. Other photographs were supplied by Mr. Yukio Sugai; they originally served as illustrations for his excellent book *Shingeki: sono butai to rekishi.*

J. Thomas Rimer

St. Louis, Missouri
July 1973

NOTE

THE 1954 edition of *Kenkyusha's New Japanese-English Dictionary* has served as the authority for romanizing Japanese terms. Macrons have been used to indicate long vowels in all words except the most ordinary proper nouns. Japanese names are given in the customary Japanese manner, with the family name preceding the given name.

Contents

List of Illustrations

TOWARD A MODERN
JAPANESE THEATRE

CHAPTER I

Introduction

THE phenomenon of *shingeki*, or, literally, New Theatre, in Japan can be said to correspond roughly with the modern theatre in Europe and the United States. Sixty-odd years of New Theatre activity have attracted little attention outside the country, despite the fact that a considerable body of drama of generally high literary quality has been produced, actors trained, theatres built, and a generous amount of information compiled in modern Japanese literary histories on the movement and its playwrights.

The word "new" suggests an opposition to something "old," and many different styles of drama are currently performed in Japan, ranging from the traditional *nō* and *kabuki* through several hybrid forms which use traditional themes and some modern acting techniques. The New Theatre, however, represents a Japanese version of the same kind of serious modern theatre available in Paris, London, or New York.

The New Theatre movement grew up among a variety of conflicting artistic forces and was influenced not only by them but by the general political and cultural phases through which Japan passed since 1900. Eric Bentley has written that "even more than the other arts—or more crudely— the drama is a chronicle and brief abstract of the time, revealing not only the surface but the whole material and spiritual structure of an epoch."[1] The New Theatre movement provides such a chronicle for Japan, and every confusion of the modern period is mirrored in its activities.

The definition of the New Theatre movement given in

---

[1] Eric Bentley, *The Playwright as Thinker* (New York, 1946), p. 77.

the authoritative *Engeki Hyakkajiten* (*Encyclopedia of the Theatre*) suggests some of the complexities involved.

Until 1910, the works seen on the Japanese stage did not reflect the changes which had overtaken the country. As a result, a desire was felt for a new kind of theatre movement. This movement developed into *shingeki*.

First of all, the New Theatre movement placed itself in opposition to the pre-modern elements remaining in the older theatrical forms. However, as there were other similar movements in Japan at that time trying to add modern elements to the traditional theatre, and since they could not be disregarded, their styles became mixed with those of the New Theatre movement itself.

Moreover, the Proletarian Theatre movement, which had tried to oppose the New Theatre movement and to take the lead itself in developing new techniques was in the end also incorporated into the New Theatre movement.

The intermingling of these varying elements gives the New Theatre movement in Japan its special characteristics.[2]

Many of the points touched on here will later be expanded upon, but even from these short paragraphs, it is clear that the writers participating in the establishment of a modern theatre in Japan faced crucial and complex problems. Much of what they did was a groping in the dark; the general course that the movement took seems clear now only by hindsight.

The history of this movement can best be examined through the career of a representative playwright. For this purpose I have chosen Kishida Kunio (1890-1954), the finest playwright in Japan before the Second World War. Kishida studied in France with the famous director Jacques Copeau in 1921 and 1922, and after returning to Japan did much to

[2] Waseda University Theatre Society, *Engeki Hyakkajiten* (Tokyo, 1963), III, p. 250.

promote the growth of a theatre dedicated to literary and humanistic ideals. In a larger context, however, through the work of Kishida and others, the prewar New Theatre movement did make a crucial contribution towards creating a modern dramatic literature in Japan. The study of this process has social and cultural implications beyond purely literary ones. Concerning this last point, the critic Etō Jun has written with considerable insight concerning the importation into Japan of western literary forms.

> If one observes [the history of modern Japanese literature] from a viewpoint that would differentiate "modernization" from "westernization," he will wonder at this paradoxical process that has induced Japanese literature to *modernize* since the beginning of the Meiji period without necessarily *westernizing*. . . . I am almost tempted to say that the time may come when Japanese writers can express themselves more freely and confidently and achieve their real self-identification only when they are able to realize more clearly the fundamental differences, however subtle, between "modernization" and "westernization."[3]

The question as to whether the "modernization" of Japan also requires its "westernization," and indeed the question concerning the extent to which the two terms may or may not be synonymous, has been an important intellectual and spiritual issue in Japan since shortly after the Meiji Restoration in 1868. Of all literary forms the drama, as exemplified by the New Theatre movement, went furthest in incorporating western elements and abandoning the heritage of Japanese tradition. Thus a study of the activities of the movement may shed light on the means by which one culture can absorb ideas and techniques without losing its own identity, or, rather, can absorb them in the very process of trying to find a new and changing identity. Some

[3] Etō Jun, "An Undercurrent in Modern Japanese Literature," *Journal of Asian Studies*, XXIII, May 1964, pp. 433-445.

tentative conclusions to these complicated questions will be suggested later. Before any discussion of Kishida's work can be presented, however, we must have some background on the early history of the New Theatre movement, in order to show the setting for the "chronicle and brief abstract of the time."

CHAPTER II

Modernization or Westernization: The Movement for a Modern Theatre in Japan before 1925

WHAT was the nature of the movement for a modern theatre in Japan? By 1925, Japan had several thoroughly professional playwrights who wrote works of considerable literary interest, dealing with concerns that would have seemed no less important to a European or an American audience than to a Japanese one. Yet the manner in which Japanese writers first came to take an interest in the theatre, and the problems they faced, suggest that their difficulties were more complex than any their European counterparts had encountered a generation or two before. A brief description of the early attempts made in Japan to alter the nature of the traditional theatre and elevate the function of the playwright will serve to indicate just how difficult these problems were.

In the development of the modern theatre in Europe, the playwrights appeared first. Producing organizations grew up in response to the literary and theatrical challenges thrown down by the authors. It is true that these theatre companies, in turn, stimulated the development of still newer writers, but the fact remains that Ibsen, Strindberg, Shaw, and many others had written many of their plays, usually unproduced and often unpublished, before the advent of the theatre companies that put them on the stage.

In Japan, however, the situation was quite different. The new theatrical organizations there were created in response to a desire on the part of many intellectuals for a new and a meaningful theatre in their country. The organizations

7

were created before any Japanese playwrights of stature appeared. This reversal gave a very different emphasis to the New Theatre movement in Japan and presented it with a different set of problems.

In 1866, when the Emperor Meiji began his reign and Japan opened its doors to the western nations, the contemporary Japanese theatre was best represented by the *kabuki*, one of the great forms of stage art which, although perhaps in a period of decline of the quality of plays then being written, was still a powerful force in popular culture and the dominant form of theatrical entertainment. Any extended discussion of the art of *kabuki* would be out of place here, but the following points should be kept in mind.

The plays in the *kabuki* theatre were stylized to a far greater extent than in the traditional European theatre. It is true, of course, that the *jidaimono* (historical plays) were often based on famous historical incidents, and that the *sewamono* (domestic dramas) were dramatizations of recent incidents; but the manner in which the materials were ordered within the plays shows that the major effect aimed at was a theatricalization of emotion and action rather than any psychological analysis. Of course, if we say that the *kabuki* is an actor's theatre, then we must recognize that Shakespeare's theatre might be described in the same terms. But unlike Shakespeare's, the *kabuki* plays were constructed so as to provide a series of emotional and scenic climaxes, designed as ends in themselves, that do not necessarily represent the inevitable results of the interactions of character and plot. Such a theatre is artistically effective on its own terms, but the principles of dramaturgy involved are far removed from those that stimulated the movement for a modern theatre in Europe. Indeed the better works of even the early nineteenth-century European stage, albeit within a framework of convention, or even of cliché, do pay a certain amount of attention to psychological logic.

8

Kinoshita Junji, one of the foremost of modern dramatists, has written on the differences between *kabuki* and the traditional European theatre in a precise and informative fashion.

There is a great difference in the density of writing in the two forms. In the case of European drama, the speeches are usually written with an ample thread of logical psychology running through them. But in the case of *kabuki*, there are a great many leaps of a psychological and logical nature within the speeches. It is the art of the actor which creates a theatre where such leaps can give satisfaction. And any art that finds such elements essential will naturally be filled with the unexplainable and the surprising.[1]

For Kinoshita, there is a logic in Shakespeare which guides even the passages of greatest bravura, but in *kabuki* the spectator takes his pleasure in seeing a brilliant actor bridge the gaps. Indeed, *kabuki* is a theatre primarily for actors. The companies were often managed by actors, plays were written to suit their talents, then changed to suit their whims. (It should also be noted that the word "actor" should be strictly understood, since men played the women's roles, just as they did in Elizabethan England.)

The function of the playwright under such circumstances was that of a craftsman, admittedly of the highest sort, who knew his company, his actors, and his audience. He would construct elaborate and exciting dramas to exploit all the prodigious resources available to the *kabuki* theatre. The last of the great traditional playwrights, Kawatake Mokuami (1816-1893), was active in 1868, but with him the great tradition of playwriting came to an end. The playwright's view of his own work and its significance within the total ensemble was totally different from that of the mod-

---

[1] Quoted in Shimomura Masao, *Shingeki* (Tokyo, 1956), pp. 24-25.

ern literary playwright, or even of nineteenth-century European playwrights like Scribe or Dumas who, for all their use of conventions, were very conscious of their important position in the triangle of author-director-actor.[2]

The following brief description of the organization of the writers in a traditional *kabuki* company will serve to explain the differences.

There were four grades in the writing groups, with apprentices doing the odd jobs, to learn the theatre system. After this the apprentices were advanced to helping in the actual performance, prompting, moving properties, and helping actors. Next they were permitted to help with the writing, and did stage-management. The chief writer, having been given the plan for the new play by the actor-manager and the promoter, worked out the plot and wrote the main parts, while the assistants filled in the rest, which was edited by the chief writer.

At the first rehearsal, it was the chief writer's duty to read the play to the entire company, and it was necessary for him to give as highly effective a reading as possible, so as to make sure that all understood his ideas. After this the cue-scripts were given to the actors, and rehearsals began, while the stage plans were given to the set constructors by the writer. The design of the programs, posters, signboards was also his responsibility.[3]

---

[2] This is not to suggest that vehicles for actors were not an important part of the western theatre. Take for example the following experience that Eugene O'Neill had as a student.

Augustus Thomas, then the dean of American playwrights and the personification of all that was successful, admired—and hackneyed—on the Broadway stage, took over the class [at Harvard] for a guest lecture. Thomas, with lightning inventiveness and a glibness that revolted O'Neill, proceeded to define the method for writing a sure-fire Broadway success.

"Suggest the name of the star," Thomas invited the class. (Arthur and Barbara Gelb, *O'Neill* [New York, 1962], pp. 270-271.)

[3] Japanese National Commission for UNESCO, *Theatre in Japan* (Tokyo, 1963), p. 61.

10

No modern playwright could conceive of working under such restrictions. True, the results might be as rich as a canvas of the school of Rubens (created by groups in the same way) but it should be no surprise that the results tended toward the pictorial and the decorative rather than the psychological or the spiritual.

The audience for these plays in 1868 was predominantly a city audience, of the merchant class. Others (*samurai*, and sometimes even the nobility) came out of curiosity, but the *kabuki* theatre, like the class that created and patronized it, had a rather bad name.[4] Tanaka Chikao writes that for the elaborate New Year *kabuki* productions, "busy people saved their money to be able to go at least once. But such people were normally sufficiently troubled in their own lives by human and social problems that they surely wanted to avoid any representation of life as they lived it directly on the stage. A play was to represent a world, a beautiful world not of this one. In this sense, *kabuki* can be called a type of fantasy."[5]

With the opening of Japan to the west, the pressures of conflicting civilizations were felt almost immediately, and the theatre began to reflect them. Beginning in about 1870,

[4] These attitudes on the part of the *samurai* and the nobility carried on into the Meiji period. For example, a leading educator wrote in 1882 that *jōruri* puppet plays, also performed in the *kabuki* repertory "were truly the extreme in lewdness and obscenity . . . among *samurai*, such books were extremely despised, and a *samurai* of good conduct would no more pick up such a book than he would a pile of rubbish." (Quoted in Donald Shively, "Nishimura Shigeki: A Confucian View of Modernization," in Marius Jansen, ed., *Changing Japanese Attitudes toward Modernization* [Princeton, 1965], pp. 228-229.) In the novels of Natsume Sōseki and other respected authors of the Meiji period, characters represented as having good "modern" educations often disdained the traditional theatre as vulgar and spiritually empty. Such views were less common by World War I, but were typical twenty years before and indeed were reinforced by the fact that the growing intelligentsia which grew up towards the end of the nineteenth century in Japan associated *kabuki* with the "feudal" ways of the old regime.

[5] Tanaka Chikao, ed., *Gekibungaku* (Tokyo, 1959), p. 13.

11

a variety of attempts were made to reform the theatre in order to make it more responsive to the social and spiritual realities of the time. First were those that strove to modernize the Japanese theatre by making it more contemporary, either in psychology or in subject matter. Second were those that, abandoning the traditional Japanese dramatic forms (specifically *kabuki*) altogether, made use of western dramaturgy to westernize the theatre and to create a new and contemporary Japanese drama.

Modernization involved four distinct experiments between 1868 and 1925.

THE MODERNIZATION OF KABUKI: HISTORY AS EDUCATION

By the 1870s *kabuki* had ceased to be a contemporary theatre. Attempts had been made to incorporate foreign elements, even foreign actors, into the new plays, but the whole mechanism of the female impersonator and the special world of the thief, prostitute, and *petit-bourgeois* that gave the early nineteenth-century plays their special and very real flavor made the new concerns of the Meiji period too difficult to deal with.

Kabuki actors and managers now began consciously to look back and seek out classic plays of the tradition written in periods of greatness. In a famous ceremony at the opening of a new theatre in 1872, Ichikawa Danjūrō IX (1838-1903), the greatest of the Meiji actors, made a speech dressed in white tie and tails rather than in traditional costume. "The theatre of recent years," he stated, "has drunk up filth and smelled of the coarse and the mean. It has disregarded the beautiful principle of rewarding good and chastizing evil. It has fallen into mannerisms and distortions and has been steadily flowing downhill. . . . I am deeply grieved by this fact and in consultation with my colleagues I have resolved to clean away the decay."[6]

[6] Komiya Toyotaka, *Japanese Music and Drama in the Meiji Era* (Tokyo, 1956), pp. 191-192.

Danjūrō and his manager Morita Kan'ya proceeded to do so and they gave *kabuki* a new role: education and morality for a new Japan.

Danjūrō's reforms, such as they were, were centered on the so-called *katsureki* or living-history plays. In practice these plays represented only slight revisions of older texts. Until the Meiji period the *kabuki* theatre, always under the eye of the censor, had changed the dates and historical personages in the plays so as to avoid any overt suggestion of social criticism. Thus the traditional history plays were in one sense fantasies in historical settings. Danjūrō decided to reverse course. He studied old prints and drawings and had consultants who tried to help him represent famous historical incidents on the stage in as literal and accurate a manner as possible. Costumes, properties, and scenery were made to look authentic, and history plays were assigned to their proper eras.[7]

In addition, within restricted limits, Danjūrō tried to introduce a freer method of performance than had heretofore been permitted. He accomplished with a look what other actors had indicated with gestures. In one play he caused a sensation by closing the curtain as the two characters on stage merely nodded at each other, rather than showing the traditional final scene of bravura histrionics.

Danjūrō considered himself a realist, but the kind of changes he proposed, no matter how revolutionary, made no real change in the nature of the drama he was perform-

[7] Komiya reports an amusing incident that shows the sharpness of the public's reaction to Danjūrō's (to them) untoward changes in their favorite plays.

"Danjūrō sometimes suffered for his realism. Often the whole troupe was dissatisfied with him. When in June 1881 he appeared at the Shintomiza in the revenge story of the Soga brothers, he played the younger brother to Sōjūrō's elder brother. Danjūrō was dressed in full armor, while Sōjūrō was dressed in the traditional hitched-up trousers and was barefoot. A critic reported that 'the younger brother was prepared for a fire, the elder for a flood.' Sōjūrō pleaded illness and appeared in only one performance." (Komiya, *Meiji Drama*, p. 202.)

ing. Indeed, his new emphasis on realism could only be detrimental to a theatre like *kabuki*, founded as it was on fantasy, illusion, and spectacle.

His idea to make drama a vehicle for morality and education was perhaps useful insofar as it stressed the fact that the drama could be a serious art form, for this conception would have to precede the development of any new drama of significance in Japan. Yet as Danjūrō learned, when he stressed the older virtues inherent in the plays he only made them seem more remote from a rapidly changing society. The experiment did not please his public, nor was it successful in artistic terms. He had moved too far away from his old audience and he had not been able to find a new one to appreciate his intentions.

SHIMPA: NEW THEMES, OLD TREATMENT

It was becoming clear that *kabuki*, because of both its old-fashioned Tokugawa morality and its stylization was not the suitable vessel into which to pour all the new and conflicting ideas and life styles of the Meiji period. In particular, *kabuki*, because of the censors, had been especially weak in its representation on the stage of the subject which most interested the Japanese in the 1870s and the 1880s, politics. Political theatre has seldom, at least before the advent of Brecht, produced an artistically satisfying style of play, and the political propaganda skits or plays (*sōshi no shibai*) being presented at this time in Japan were without literary pretensions.

The development of *shimpa* (literally, "new-style" drama, as opposed to "old-style" drama, or *kabuki*) is closely connected with the career of the playwright and producer Kawakami Otojirō (1864-1911), a curious and rather ingenious man who had a diverse career. Kawakami had acted in some of the earlier political plays; he then took the style and changed it by dressing up his plays with realistic battle scenes, especially during the Sino-Japanese war. Fired by

14

this success, in 1901 he made a voyage to Europe, Russia, and the United States with his wife Sadako, one of the first women to appear professionally on the stage in Japan, and eighteen others, introducing to the unsuspecting world plays with dubious titles such as *The Warrior and the Geisha.* Komiya indicated that the tour was "something of a national disgrace," but Kawakami viewed it as a great success.[8] After his return, Kawakami was convinced that he must find some artistic means to deal with life in contemporary Japan and that he must use actresses rather than female impersonators for the purpose.

Kawakami and the others who then proceeded to develop the *shimpa* like the *kabuki sewamono* used sensationalist level stories of contemporary life and dramatized them. The plays lost the political pretensions of the earlier *sōshi no shibai.* Actresses were used, but female impersonators were retained as well. Kawakami and his colleagues claimed that the style of *shimpa* was more realistic than that of *kabuki,* but Shimomura dismisses this aspect of the new drama as merely "the realism of train whistles."[9] The emotional attitudes in the plays are not far removed from those in nineteenth-century *kabuki,* and the effect produced, despite an evolved acting style, was a cloying sentimentality. If *kabuki* can be said to have stopped being a contemporary theatre,

[8] Many Japanese at the time were very critical of Kawakami, since they felt that he and his wife were misrepresenting Japanese theatrical traditions. After all, there were at the time no professional actresses in Japan. Sadako had been a *geisha* and knew how to dance, but she could hardly be expected to represent in any fashion the art of *kabuki.* Nevertheless, the trip had an extraordinary impact in Europe. For the reaction there, see the lively account in Leonard Pronko, *Theatre East and West* (Berkeley, 1967), pp. 120-124. For Max Beerbohm's enthusiastic praise of Sadako, whom he puts before Sarah Bernhardt, see his essay "Incomparables Compared" in *Around Theatres* (New York, 1954), pp. 159-160. The only dissenting voice on the question of her talents was, oddly enough, that of Jacques Copeau, who told Kishida Kunio that "her way of doing things was all wrong." (See *Kishida Kunio zenshū,* IX, p. 55.)

[9] Shimomura, *Shingeki,* p. 28.

15

emotionally speaking, in 1870, then *shimpa* might be said to have suffered the same fate by 1910. *Shimpa* troupes still exist today, and when occasionally a fine playwright creates a work for them, the results can be professionally satisfying. But from the point of view of modernizing the theatre, this second experiment was not a success.

SHINKOKUGEKI: EXCITEMENT FOR THE GENERAL PUBLIC

Shinkokugeki, or New National Theatre, was largely the creation of one man, Sawada Shōjirō (1892-1929). The name of the theatrical company was coined in 1917 and represents a later stage of experimentation than *shimpa*. Sawada himself was an actor of some note who had made a considerable reputation with his performance as Iokanaan in Oscar Wilde's *Salome*. Through his participation in this and other productions, Sawada became convinced that the mass of contemporary Japanese audiences were being left behind, and he was determined to "lead from among his public, rather than remain ahead of it."[10] He set out to perform dramas, many of which he commissioned himself, designed to bridge the gap between *kabuki* and modern theatre, but in order to gain the favor of a large audience, he diluted his new plays with sword fights and spectacles; the playwrights who served him were subsidiary to the acrobats. After his death in 1929, the company attempted to add more modern pieces to the repertory, but the results remained close to *shimpa* in mentality. Although the company continues to perform for a certain public today, it can be said that Sawada's catering to public taste produced little of artistic merit.

All three of the movements described above came from within the commercial theatre itself, and they all failed. (Nor, in fact, did the professional companies in Europe provide the impetus for the modern drama.) The various

[10] UNESCO, *Theatre in Japan*, p. 192.

experiments in Japan did, however, serve to indicate a dissatisfaction with the traditional theatre on the part of the actors, producers, and at least some of the audience.

Shōyō: Active Evolution through Amateurs

The fourth and final experiment to modernize the theatre before 1925 came from efforts made outside the milieu of the commercial theatre, as it had in Europe, and was based on the activities of the leading literary critic of the day, Tsubouchi Shōyō (1859-1935). Shōyō was a protean figure in the Japanese literary and theatrical world, who defined the nature of the western novel for the Japanese as early as 1885 in his *Shōsetsu shinzui* (*The Essence of the Novel*). He wrote fiction, and he supported other important novelists like Futabatei Shimei in their efforts to create a distinctive style in modern Japanese literature. He translated the entire work of Shakespeare into Japanese and wrote several plays himself. His career has been well described elsewhere.[11]

Shōyō had a deep interest in modernizing the Japanese stage, evident both in his own playwriting experiments and in his sponsorship of a dramatic company. He was the most powerful and the most effective voice for modernization rather than out-and-out westernization, and his contribution to the modern Japanese theatre was enormous.

SHŌYŌ'S PLAYS

Shōyō was not satisfied with the *katsureki* experiments of Danjūrō. He did not, of course, foresee or expect the decline of *kabuki*; indeed he felt that the form, for all its possible faults, was the form of drama evolved by the Japanese over a long period and that it should continue to serve them well.

As a literary critic, Shōyō's familiarity with the European masterpieces, especially Shakespeare's, convinced him that what would infuse new life into *kabuki* was not the superficial historical accuracy of *katsureki*, but the gradual crea-

[11] Notably in *Ukigumo: Japan's First Modern Novel* by Marleigh Ryan.

17

tion of a new repertory in which the psychological dimensions of the plays would be expanded. Although Shōyō did not consider himself primarily a playwright, he wrote two important experimental plays in which he tried to put into practice his ideas for reforming *kabuki* to give it the kind of contemporary appeal he thought necessary.

The first of these plays, *Kiri no Hitoha* (*A Leaf of Paulownia*) was written in 1884 when he was only twenty-five. He wrote it as a specific reply to those who wanted to do away with *kabuki* and its "excesses" and so, Shōyō thought, destroy the Japanese theatre altogether. Kawatake has documented how Shōyō carefully studied Shakespeare and Chikamatsu, the great Tokugawa dramatist, for three years in preparation for the writing of this play.[12]

The play is in six acts and chronicles the latter days in the career of Katagiri Katsumoto (1556-1615), a famous warrior who served the ruler of Japan, Hideyoshi Toyotomi, faithfully for many years until, after a complicated series of incidents, he was beguiled by Tokugawa Ieyasu into betraying his former master. Shōyō stated that his purpose in writing the play was to try to recreate the atmosphere of tragedy in Osaka castle at that time, and his complex play seems to fulfill his wishes amply. He took hints from *Hamlet* in his composition of certain scenes which, if not historically accurate, do evoke a good deal of atmosphere, even if the effect seems by modern standards a bit overwrought. The portrayal of Katagiri as a victim of circumstance rather than as an out-and-out villain was particularly novel. How the historical Katagiri died is not precisely known, but when the play appeared Shōyō was nevertheless criticized for the fact that in it Katagiri did not die for his supposed villainy. Shōyō replied to the criticism by saying that for a man in Katagiri's position to live was worse than to die.

A Leaf of Paulownia was published in serial form in

12 See Kawatake Shigetoshi, *Gaisetsu Nihon engekishi* (Tokyo, 1966), p. 230.

successive issues of *Waseda Bungaku* (*Waseda Literature*) in 1894 and 1895. The play was well received in literary circles, but the professional actors for whom Shōyō had written it, in the hope of interesting them in his new style of drama, did not find it to their liking. It went unproduced until 1904, at which time it had a great critical and popular success. Shōyō was finally accepted, thirty years after the publication of his text, as a playwright of stature.

More important than this early play, however, was his *En no Gyōja* (*The Hermit*), which he wrote, rewrote, and revised from 1914 until 1921. Several versions of the play were published during those years.

Between the writing of *A Leaf of Paulownia* and *The Hermit*, Shōyō had discovered Ibsen. In a lecture in 1909 on Ibsen's contribution to the world theatre, Shōyō lamented the fact that, although the Japanese had been able to create successful novels in the international style, the low level of the contemporary Japanese theatre represented the greatest shortcoming in all the Japanese arts. Japan, Shōyō insisted, lagged forty years behind the west and had not even been able to imitate, let alone create, western-style drama. Ibsen had led the modernization of the European stage and Ibsen must therefore be studied.

The Hermit is a dramatic legend concerning the Buddhist monk and hermit En no Gyōja, his struggles with the animalistic divinity Hitokoto, and the failure of his disciple Hirotaru to follow his teachings because of his love for a woman. The play is highly poetic and has several powerful scenes, especially those between Hitokoto, who is held prisoner by En no Gyōja, and his mother Katsuragi.

Shōyō is said to have written the play from a sense of deep emotion about his own life in the theatre. Kawatake has written[13] that the play constitutes a kind of spiritual autobiography, with En no Gyōja as Shōyō himself and the

[13] See Kawatake Shigetoshi, *Ningen Tsubouchi Shōyō* (Tokyo, 1959), pp. 205-208.

19

actor Shimamura Hōgetsu (who deserted Shōyō's theatre company, as described below) as the model for the ungrateful disciple.

The first printed version of the play appeared in the August 1916 issue of the magazine *Shinengei* (*New Theatre Arts*) and, in a slightly revised form, was published as a book the following year.[14] The play caused quite a sensation and so excited one Waseda University professor who was then studying comparative literature in Paris that he translated it into French. It was published there in 1920 and was the first modern play from Japan to be rendered into any western language.

Although the play deals with characters and incidents shrouded in myth and legend, Shōyō, perhaps under the influence of Ibsen, gave full play to the psychological rather than the merely colorful aspects of the story, and the shifts of emotions and attitudes of the major characters during the course of the play seem logical, even compelling. Shōyō had come a long way toward modernizing the Japanese drama while still keeping within the bounds and the forms familiar to his audience. Rather than using a modern social drama, like Ibsen, he used a traditional story in which to reflect his deepest anxieties and beliefs as a creative person.

SHŌYŌ'S THEATRE COMPANY

Shōyō was aware that, in addition to new plays, some kind of organization would be needed to mount them on the stage.

As early as 1890, Shōyō, concerned about proper methods of elocution for spoken Japanese, formed a playreading group with some of his younger colleagues. He wrote plays,

---

14 *The Hermit* received its first stage performance in 1926 when it was chosen for performance by the Tsukiji shōgekijō (Tsukiji Little Theatre). This production was a *cause célèbre* in the theatre world, for reasons that do not affect any evaluation of Shōyō's work. See below, pp. 70-71.

dance dramas, made translations, and directed his group in amateur productions. In 1905 he helped with the formation of the first theatre company for modern plays in Japan, the Bungei kyōkai (Literary Society). The society was to carry out a variety of activities, but the staging of plays soon became its most important project. Shōyō, realizing the difficulties of mounting plays in a new style, insisted that the primary purpose of the group should be the training of new actors and actresses. He felt that cultivated amateurs, properly trained, represented the best means to lift standards quickly to a desired level.[15] Although Shōyō had no detailed information (perhaps none at all) on European institutions such as the schools of the Moscow Art Theatre, he knew that his actors needed practice in elocution, movement, and other techniques before they could present themselves to the public as representatives of the new drama. As he had no teachers for his school who had studied drama in Europe, with the exception of Hōgetsu, who had been a student in England and Germany, he worked slowly and simply, using his own good taste and common sense. As various testimonies indicate, the students and other teachers in his school were moved to tremendous efforts by the force of his personality and the range of his enthusiasms. By using women on the stage, Shōyō acknowledged the fact that old traditions he otherwise esteemed had to be abandoned when they impeded necessary change.

By 1910, Shōyō had presented four performances of *Hamlet* (in his own translation) at the school, and in 1911 he staged a Japanese version of Ibsen's *A Doll's House*. These productions were so enthusiastically received that the

[15] Komiya cites the fact that Shōyō "disliked the atmosphere of the professional theatres and considered it necessary to train amateurs, and amateurs as cultivated as he could find, if the cultural level of the theatre was to be improved." (See Komiya, *Meiji Drama*, p. 292.) Shōyō was a partisan of *kabuki* and indeed his translations of Shakespeare, though extremely gifted, were closer to the older style than to colloquial speech. Nevertheless he wished to find colleagues with well-educated minds open to change.

21

management of the Imperial Theatre, the most modern and well-equipped theatre in Tokyo at the time, invited Shōyō's company to appear there. The company also presented *Hamlet* and *A Doll's House* in Osaka.

At this point, the growing success of the company was disrupted by the romance between Hōgetsu and the leading actress of the troupe, Matsui Sumako. Shōyō eventually dismissed Hōgetsu, who went off with the actress to form a company of his own. These ruptures (surely mirrored in the plot of *The Hermit*) caused the dissolution of Shōyō's company in 1913, after a final presentation of *Julius Caesar* at the Imperial Theatre.

Both in his playwriting and in the management of the Literary Society, Shōyō tried to make use of elements in the western theatre to modernize Japanese drama. He wished to work from what he knew toward the development of a natural and truly contemporary art of the theatre in his own country. On the whole, however, his methods were not to prevail. Instead, those who wished to westernize the drama in Japan, rather than to modernize the traditional theatre, began a series of activities which have dominated the Japanese theatre until today.

THE MOVEMENT to westernize the theatre prior to 1925, rather than merely to modernize it, involved the efforts of writers, actors, and directors to reject mere entertainment (the only possible value they found in *kabuki*) for literature. For these men, the playwright was considered a serious artist and intellectual, whose work demanded satisfactory performance on the stage. As more and more actors and writers travelled abroad, the impetus toward westernization grew greater and greater.

Parallel to this movement was the work of a group of writers who tried to turn dramatic literature into political propaganda. The development of a leftist political theatre in Japan provided still another obstacle for the creation of dramatic literature before 1925.

22

THE PLAYWRIGHT AS INTELLECTUAL

Since the time of Shōyō's *The Essence of the Novel* in 1885 and the work of such early novelists as Futabatei Shimei, a new *genre* of Japanese writer developed, close to his western counterpart, who regarded himself as a serious intellectual whose duty it was to observe society and himself with the greatest sincerity in order to write artistic works of merit. By 1900 Japan produced two of her finest modern novelists, Natsume Sōseki and Mori Ōgai, and the list of first-class writing talents was to continue to grow longer as the necessary climate for serious art was created and sustained.

Underneath the competing movements which Japanese literary historians dub Romanticism, Realism, Humanism, and the others, there was one point these writers held in common: a strong and unyielding sense of purpose. They took themselves very seriously indeed. Nakamura Mitsuo, a distinguished critic of modern Japanese literature, wrote "for them, the novel was not merely an artistic representation of human life. Rather, it was a means of searching for a new, true way of living. At the same time, it was a record of this search. This was a hazardous quest, for the sake of which the writers of the Meiji and the Taishō periods risked tragedy in their real lives. They had high, probably exaggerated expectations of the novel, and they dared to believe in them and to live them."[16]

Most of the serious writers of the period concentrated their efforts on the novel or on the development of modern verse forms. Playwriting had not been an occupation for serious writers in Japan, and until they became aware of the work of Ibsen it had never occurred to them that the theatre might be a suitable medium for the expression of their ideas.

As in Europe, Ibsen had a galvanic effect in Japan. Trans-

[16] Nakamura Mitsuo, *Modern Japanese Fiction* (Tokyo, 1968), pp. 7-8.

lations of *An Enemy of the People* and *A Doll's House* made by a minor writer and poet named Takayasu Gekkō appeared in 1901. By the time of Ibsen's death in 1906, however, a variety of writers in Japan were so excited about his work that the following year an Ibsen society was formed for the purpose of studying his plays and his ideas.[17] Shōyō's production of *A Doll's House*, for all its probable imperfections, caused a great deal of attention. Kawatake says that Ibsen's work is responsible for the New Theatre movement in Japan.[18]

Several writers, inspired by what they saw and read, tried to write directly in the Ibsen style. Prominent among them was Mayama Seika (1878-1948); his *Daiichi ninsha* (*Man of First Rank*) (1907) showed influences from *John Gabriel Borkman*, and his *Umarezarishi naraba* (*If He Had Not Been Born*) (1909) was inspired by *Ghosts*. Mamaya did not continue writing in the same style throughout his long career, but his later historical plays and those dramas written for performances by *shimpa* troupes show a continuing consciousness of social issues which may be a heritage from his early interest in Ibsen. Another writer who was attracted to Ibsen was Nakamura Kichizō (1877-1941) who tried to create in his play *Bokushi no Ie* (*The Vicarage*) (1909) a drama in the Ibsen style. Mori Ōgai was an early enthusiast of Ibsen, and his translations of *Borkman*, *A Doll's House* and *Ghosts* were widely read and later performed on the stage.

The kinds of philosophical and social messages contained in these plays were new to Japanese writers, and, in addition, the fact that Ibsen had chosen the theatre as the vehicle for the expression of his ideas gave them the impetus to attempt their own experiments in what was for them a new form. Playwriting, however, like the writing of fiction, has a long history and a necessary technique; thus it is not surprising

---

[17] For a discussion of this group, see Komiya, *Meiji Drama*, pp. 285-286.

[18] See Kawatake, *Engekishi*, p. 395.

that many of these early works were too derivative or ill conceived. Still, there was excitement in the air, and for a time it seemed that the literary map of Japan was to include a whole new branch of dramatic literature.

None of these writers were attracted to the traditional Japanese theatre. Their interest in the drama as a possible form of expression came entirely from their contact with great western writers who had also chosen the medium and not from any experience with the contemporary Japanese theatre. For these writers, as Tanaka Chikao has pointed out, the more they conceived of the theatre as a means to express their literary ideals, the less appeal they found in *kabuki*.[19] Kubota Mantarō, a leading playwright of the 1920s and 1930s, wrote that ". . . among those in the literary movement who studied Ibsen and took an interest in the New Theatre movement, those young writers who seriously wanted a revolution in the theatre found *kabuki* completely beneath their consideration."[20]

In addition, the good writers in Japan at this period, whatever their interest in social concerns, were creating a style of writing which was, if anything, highly emotional and personal. Although they were attracted by Ibsen's strength of purpose and the mordant confrontations between his characters, their own best work was of a very different nature. Edwin McClellan calls this quality Impressionism and stresses that it is "by nature opposed to definition, to intellectual commitment . . ." so that characters are ". . . seen in relation to each particular scene visible at a given moment, and not as fully rounded psychological entities who can be understood only when seen continuously within some intellectualized framework."[21] McClellan is speaking here of the writing of the novelist Shimazaki Tōson, but the concept of Impressionism (a term never

---

[19] Tanaka Chikao, *Gekibungaku*, p. 15.
[20] Quoted in Shimomura, *Shingeki*, p. 29.
[21] Edwin McClellan, "The Impressionistic Tendency in Some Modern Japanese Writers," *Chicago Review*, XVII, #4, 1964, p. 48.

used, so far as I know, by the Japanese critics) serves to explain the great preference among many of the best Japanese writers for a loose and emotional style of composition. To create the kind of tightly worked-out, reasoned, argumentative technique employed by Ibsen in his plays of social concern would have required a tremendous shift of taste and emphasis for these Japanese writers; in fact it would have required a deflection of the national genius.

Writers who experimented with playwriting felt the drama to be merely another literary form, and they tended to write their plays for the page (where they had read their Ibsen) rather than for performance. This attitude was reinforced by that of the literary magazines. Editors took a great interest in drama and printed new plays as a *genre* of literature. Mori Ōgai, for example, was represented as early as 1910 in the *Chūō kōron* (*Central Review*) by his drama *Ikutagawa* (*Ikuta River*), a one-act play that retells the famous legend, found in the tenth-century *Yamato monogatari* and elsewhere, in which two suitors kill a swan at the Ikuta River. In 1915, Tanizaki Junichirō published in the same magazine his important play *Hōjōji monogatari* (*A Tale of Hōjōji Temple*). This play, which centers on the building of the temple by the powerful regent Fujiwara Michinaga, is a good example of Tanizaki's early aesthetic theories worked out in dramatic terms. Such other well-known and respected writers as Arishima Takeo, Mushakōji Saneatsu, Nagata Hideo, Kikuchi Kan, Yamamoto Yūzō, Kume Masao, and Sato Haruo tried their hand at writing plays. Most of their work was experimental, and, except for Yamamoto and Kikuchi, none of them earned any great reputations as playwrights. Still, the idea of writing plays had become a common challenge.

It seemed for a time that the pattern of development taken by the European drama was repeating itself in Japan. Plays were being written, and organizations to produce them were beginning to appear. Many hoped that literature and the professional theatre might join together to create a real

New Theatre movement in Japan. Such an expectation was not to be met, or, at least, not in terms satisfactory to those writers who had looked forward to the possibility with such enthusiasm.

THE CREATION OF A WESTERN-STYLE PERFORMING TRADITION IN JAPAN

Many small theatre companies were begun before 1925, but the major efforts to create a western-style tradition of stage production centered on the activities of Osanai Kaoru (1881-1928), one of the most colorful, talented, and volatile figures in the arts in modern Japan. The range of his interests and enthusiasms was tremendous, and it is he, and no other, who set the foundations for the development of the New Theatre movement in Japan.[22] It was Osanai, in fact, who was credited with the creation of the word *shingeki* itself, when in 1913 he defined the western-style plays he was producing as "neither *kabuki* nor *shimpa*, but a New Theatre."[23] The phrase "New Theatre" had cropped up here and there before, but it was Osanai who gave it life and currency.

All accounts of Osanai seem to center ultimately on his tremendous vitality; this, plus his deep and sincere belief in the importance of dramatic art, made him the idol of the young intellectuals. Tanizaki, in writing of his tangled relations with Osanai, revealed a good deal about the director's complex character. On first meeting Osanai, Tanizaki described him as "a beautiful young man with prodigious talents." (At that time Tanizaki was twenty-four and Osanai twenty-nine.) He first saw Osanai at the opening night of the Jiyūgekijō (Free Theatre), Osanai's company which began performing in 1909.

[22] There are several full-length biographies of Osanai, the best of them by the playwright Kubo Sakae.

[23] See Kawatake, *Engekishi*, p. 389, for a history of the word *shingeki*.

I had seen Osanai from my seat at the Yūrakuza when he made his speech at the opening of the first production of his Free Theatre, Ibsen's *John Gabriel Borkman* . . . he was only twenty-eight then. Everyone's career is affected in one way or the other by circumstances—character, health, or even luck—but each human being, at one time in his life, will have a period of his greatest flowering. . . . I suppose that it is not quite accurate of me to say that the career of Osanai, who fought hard for the theatre until his death, could be summed up in one blooming. And yet I believe that there were few times in his life like the one when, at the end of his twenty-eighth year, he was called before the footlights by a full house at the Yūrakuza. There was no way that I, a real youngster, a mere spectator in my orchestra seat, could have predicted the difficulties he would face, but I remember thinking that ". . . even Osanai has risen to the heights tonight. In any man's life, these occasions do not repeat themselves."[24]

Any judgment on the ultimate value of Osanai's accomplishments as a theatre director must include the electric charge of his personality. Tanizaki's fascination with him can be duplicated in the statements of a score of other writers and intellectuals.

Osanai had many interests, but the two theatre companies he founded, the Free Theatre in 1909 and the Tsukiji Shōgekijō (The Tsukiji Little Theatre) in 1924, were events of the most fundamental importance, for they established the basis for modern professional theatre in Japan.

The Free Theatre was a company formed by Osanai with the help of a close friend, Ichikawa Sadanji, a young *kabuki* actor. Osanai had heard of Antoine's Théâtre Libre and wished to form a similar company to present experimental plays for a limited run and removed from any competition

[24] Tanizaki Junichirō, *Seishun monogatari* (Tokyo, 1958), pp. 226-227.

with the commercial theatre. Osanai had no theatre of his own and so leased the Yūrakuza, a small and well-equipped theatre in Tokyo, to produce three plays a year, with runs of two or three days. The company was later invited, as was the Literary Society, to perform at the Imperial Theatre. Osanai's purposes in organizing the troupe seemed close to those of Antoine and the others. His statement that ". . . a movement for a new theatre must be built on the basis of a new movement in literature"[25] suggested to his friends and well-wishers, at least in the beginning, that he might be able to make a contribution to the theatre in Japan similar to the Free Theatres in Europe. However, the means by which he worked out his plans proved harmful to the playwrights.

THE FREE THEATRE

The Actors

Osanai, like Antoine, wanted to borrow for his productions professional actors who wished in effect to "become amateurs" by learning a new style. Ichikawa Sadanji played the leading role in *Borkman* on opening night (occasionally forgetting his lines, it is reported, because of inadequate rehearsal). As there were no professional actresses available, he used female impersonators from *kabuki* for the women's roles. What a *John Gabriel Borkman* it must have been! Possibly because of his close association with Sadanji, Osanai continued to use *kabuki* actors right through to the last production of the Free Theatre in 1919, even though, as Kawatake remarks, he had come to realize that he would have done better to train young amateurs himself. Contemporary accounts suggest that the actors retained too much of the *kabuki* style in their performances, and that they could never learn to "serve the script" properly. Osanai had the problem, at least until he made his trip to Europe in

[25] Quoted in Shimomura, *Shingeki*, p. 12.

1913, of creating productions of plays he had never seen on the stage in a style of acting concerning which he had no personal knowledge.

The Repertory

Osanai alternated productions of foreign plays with original Japanese dramas, a method that no doubt provided him with the best means of introducing the new experiments in European drama while encouraging Japanese playwrights. From the beginning, however, both Osanai and his audiences at the Free Theatre seemed to prefer the foreign plays. He provided a diet of Chekhov, Maeterlinck, Hauptmann, and Gorky; it is small wonder that those Japanese dramatists who were learning to write in the new style were unable to compete in such exalted company. Tanizaki records his disappointment over the fact that Osanai turned down one of his plays, saying that he thereby lost the chance, as an author, to learn from seeing his play mounted on the stage.[26] Still, Osanai did manage to stage a variety of works, among them plays by Ōgai (the *Ikuta River* mentioned above), Yoshii Isamu, Akita Ujaku, and others.

In 1919, Osanai closed down the Free Theatre in order to have what he called a period of rest and study.

THE TSUKIJI LITTLE THEATRE

In 1923 a severe earthquake destroyed much of Tokyo, including all its important theatres. In 1924 Osanai, with the help of his disciple Hijikata Yoshi, who was independently wealthy, set about constructing a new and proper stage for himself. The building, located in the Tsukiji area of downtown Tokyo, had five hundred seats and excellent lighting and scenic equipment. Photographs taken of his productions show sets and lighting effects fully as sophisticated as those achieved in Europe during the same period.

[26] See Tanizaki, *Seishun*, p. 234.

Itō Kisaku, the *doyen* of Japanese stage designers, began his professional career with Osanai.

Osanai spoke of his new company as a "laboratory," in which various styles of productions were to be tested. He made it clear as well that his theatre was to exist not for the intellectuals but for "all the people." Osanai wrote that "we do not wish to stage our productions for those who lead comfortable lives. One must see plays the way one eats bread. . . . Just as bread should be made as cheap as possible, so must we make the results of our work as cheap as possible, for everyone to see."[27] Discouraged by his earlier experience with *kabuki* actors, he also decided to recruit amateurs, just as Shōyō had done for his Literary Society, and to use actresses. Many of the well-known prewar stage stars in Japan worked with Osanai's company. Osanai's intentions were never met, but a change of emphasis from the Free Theatre was clear.

The Repertory

It was in his repertory work that Osanai made his biggest break with the policies of his earlier Free Theatre. Since the Tsukiji Little Theatre was to be a "laboratory," he decided that for the first several seasons, at least, he would produce only plays in translation and no Japanese plays at all. His decision, so disheartening to those writers who saw in his new company their only chance to see their own work mounted in a professional fashion, was justified, he said, because he found the plays made available to him, including his own,[28] "uninteresting." When Osanai relinquished the

[27] Osanai Kaoru, *Osanai Kaoru engekiron zenshū* (Tokyo, 1965), II, p. 298.

[28] In the early 1920s, Osanai had begun writing plays himself. In 1921 his one-act play *Daiichi no seikai* (*The First World*) was produced at the Imperial Theatre through the help of Ichikawa Sadanji. The play, about a man who cuts himself off from the "first world" of society because of a lost love, is rather thin stuff. His next play, *Musuko* (*The Son*), written in 1922 and the request of a *kabuki* actor, was an adaptation of a short melodrama named *Augustus in*

31

role of encouraging playwrights and decided to concentrate on perfecting his own skill as a director and producer, there were no others to take up the task he had abandoned.[29] The movement to create new and stage-worthy plays of literary value in Japan thus received a blow from which it had the greatest difficulty in recovering. The playwrights were at a loss as to how to proceed. In 1925 an impasse had been reached.

JAPAN AND THE WORLD THEATRE MOVEMENT BEFORE 1925

Interest in the western theatre and drama brought with it a desire on the part of a growing number of writers, actors, and directors to make observations at first hand on the traditions and accomplishments of the European theatre. By 1925 a number of men influential in the New Theatre movement travelled abroad, and the ideas they brought back were of continuing importance in the further development of directing, acting, and playwriting in Japan.

A certain number of figures who were prominent in the early stages of the New Theatre movement had been to Europe (Shimamura Hōgetsu, Shōyō's disciple, and the playwright Nakamura Kichizō, among others); they had gone as students and become interested in the theatre while abroad, and their observations had not been made on any organized basis. The first visit by a professional man of the New Theatre was made by Ichikawa Sadanji, Osanai's partner at the Free Theatre, in 1906, three years before the

---

Search of a Father by a minor nineteenth-century English writer, Harold Chapin. One scene might be from *kabuki* itself: the son, a criminal fleeing from justice, meets his own father but fails to recognize him. Osanai's own failures at playwriting may have caused his attitude of disdain toward the works of his contemporaries.

[29] Osanai did eventually produce some Japanese plays. These productions will be discussed in connection with Kishida in the following chapter.

opening of Osanai's company. At the time he was having some difficulty with his acting career in *kabuki*, despite the fact that his father had been a well-known actor. He was invited by the writer and critic Matsue Shōyō to join him in Europe in order to learn something about developments in the western theatre and to add new elements to his art. When Sadanji left for Europe he was twenty-six; Matsue, ten years his senior, looked after him like a brother and took him to see what he considered the most important theatrical events of the day.[30]

Sadanji's first evening on European soil was spent making a visit to the Comédie Française to see a production of Victor Hugo's *Hernani*, a play in which he had acted shortly before in a somewhat bowdlerized *kabuki*-style version. Sadanji never recovered from this first shock and seemed to remain in a continuous state of excited bewilderment as Matsue, who had a much better grasp of what might be accomplished for his protégé on the trip, took him to meet Sarah Bernhardt and to see productions of Molière and Tolstoy directed by Antoine. Leaving Paris they went to Venice, "about which Shakespeare wrote," Switzerland, "where William Tell came from," and finally Berlin, where Sadanji watched a production of Wedekind's *Spring's Awakening*, an ironic analysis of sexual drives in the young, the meaning of which seems to have escaped him completely. He saw some of Gordon Craig's stage designs in Berlin and a production of Shakespeare directed by Max Reinhardt in Vienna. Up until this time Sadanji had never seen *any* modern plays on the stage, although he had read Hugo, Shakespeare, and a few others in translation.

Matsue then took Sadanji to England to see some productions of Shaw at the Royal Court Theatre (one of the groups which had succeeded Grein's Independent Theatre) and arranged for him to take acting lessons for a month.

[30] A rather complete and amusing account of this visit can be found in Toita Yasuji, *Shingeki no hitobito* (Tokyo, 1952), pp. 120-124.

Sadanji, with no knowledge of English, was badgered by Matsue into courses on elocution and "methods of expression." Sadanji later commented that these lessons had shown him how useless the dialogue in *kabuki* was for expressing the nuances of human emotion. As Toita remarks laconically, Sadanji ". . . formed the whole basis of his later art on what he had received in these lessons of less than twenty days."[31]

Sadanji's activities after he returned home are of considerable interest for *kabuki*;[32] more important, his confused and enthusiastic reports on the European theatre helped give Osanai some inspiration for the specific methods he used to establish the Free Theatre.

Osanai himself visited Europe from December 1912 to the summer of 1913. Unlike Sadanji, he himself had had the experience of several seasons of the Free Theatre behind him. In addition he had a good academic knowledge of the European theatre. A series of accurate and informed articles on such diverse subjects as Gordon Craig, Grein's Independent Theatre, and the German Free Theatre, all published by Osanai before his trip, show that he was knowledgeable and enthusiastic about the latest developments on the continent.

Osanai's trip took him to Russia, Scandinavia, Germany, France, and England.[33] He arrived at a period of extraordinary creativity in the European theatre and witnessed one brilliant achievement after another: the Moscow Art Theatre, Reinhardt's Viennese productions, various German Free Theatres, including a famous repertory company in Hamburg, the acting school of the Swiss Jacques-Dalcroize

[31] Toita, *Hitobito*, p. 125.

[32] See Komiya, *Meiji Drama*, pp. 250-253. Some of Sadanji's reforms were hooted down by conservative *kabuki* audiences. For example, his attempt to use reserved seats, an idea he had picked up in Europe, caused a furor: on opening night, a gang of bullies forced him to retire from the theatre in disguise, and his adviser Matsue retired to a temple in nervous prostration.

[33] Kubo, *Osanai* has some details of the trip. See p. 77 *et seq.*

in Leipzig, experimental French productions in Paris, and the various independent companies in London.

Osanai was still a young man, in the flush of his first enthusiasms. Sugai[34] mentions the fact that Osanai seemed utterly absorbed in the theatre and studied the particular productions he saw with great care, often returning to see them several times. By the time he reached Berlin, Kubo wrote,[35] he was out of money and had to borrow from friends. Yet in his enthusiasm for the theatre, Osanai forgot to examine the civilization, history, and religion from which the European theatre had grown. His education was incomplete.

The novelist Shimazaki Tōson was in Paris when Osanai visited the city, and an entry in Tōson's diary about his meeting with Osanai conveys some of the director's excitement.

> Osanai finally arrived in Paris much later than scheduled, full of various stories about his trip, and especially about the Moscow Art Theatre and the others to which his visits had taken him. His suitcases were stuffed with wigs for women and old men which he had bought in London. I accompanied him to the Paris Opéra while he regaled me with stories of how he saw Chekhov's widow act on the stage and how impressed he had been with the Moscow Art Theatre.[36]

As Tōson indicates, Osanai's chief discovery on his trip was the art of Stanislavsky and his ensemble methods. Osanai was particularly interested in the Russian director's production of Gorky's *Lower Depths* and used his own copious notes on it to recreate similar effects in a version of the play which he produced in Japan late in 1913. (He had previously directed the play in 1910.)

[34] See Sugai Yukio, "Osanai kaishaku," *Osanai engekiron zenshū*, I, p. 502.

[35] Kubo, *Osanai*, p. 77.

[36] Quoted in *Osanai engekiron zenshū*, I, p. 502.

Although Japan's own New Theatre movement was just beginning (Osanai called his company "a kindergarten" after his return), Osanai had unwittingly stumbled on a second stage of the development of the modern theatre in Europe. Ibsen, Strindberg, Chekhov, and the others had already given the modern theatre its basic repertory, and men like Antoine, Graun, and Nemirovich-Danchenko had built up performing companies a generation before in order to realize these plays on the stage. It was on this firm base that the great directors—Reinhardt, Stanislavsky, Copeau, and the others—could build their own interpretations. These men were the central figures in the productions they directed, but in the beginning the author, and not the director, was the most important figure. Osanai, who had learned from Sadanji only six years before what the function of a director might be, now decided that he wanted to follow his spiritual mentor Stanislavsky in creating and directing an ensemble of his own in Japan. There is no question that Osanai's ambitions were laudably high-minded, but his decision was woefully out of step with any possible development of a modern drama in Japan. Shimomura is surely correct when he writes that any movement for a new drama in Japan could be said to have begun only when new plays were being created,[37] and Osanai's undue concentration on what might be described as "the cult of the director" produced a severe aberration in what had been up until then a shaky but not unnatural process of self-development for the drama in Japan.

Osanai, like Sadanji, had learned something but not enough in Europe. And the mistake was often to be repeated. As the European theatre moved into new periods of experimentation, the Japanese visitors who followed Osanai were able to learn only a little of the whole spectrum of artistic activities they might have seen. Each came back with a little piece of the whole, and, in the small and financially restricted world of the Japanese New Theatre movement,

[37] Shimomura, *Shingeki*, p. 60.

the pieces seldom fitted together. The fever for a European experience continued to spread. Osanai was much taken by the Russian theatre, and the English, German, and French stages had their champions as well. England in fact claimed much of the professional career of one young playwright, Kōri Torahiko (1890-1924), who spent eleven years of his short life there. Kōri's was a precocious talent. His play *Dōjōji* (*The Temple of Dōjō*) was performed by Osanai's Free Theatre when he was only twenty-two; emboldened by this early success, he set out for Germany with the hope of making a serious study of the modern drama but left the continent for England when war was declared in 1914. He remained there until 1924, composing and revising his plays, "writing in Japanese and translating, simultaneously, into English."[38]

Kōri wrote several plays on Biblical subjects, but his self-proclaimed masterpiece was the play *The Toils of Yoshitomo*, written in 1922. The play is based on the complex incidents surrounding the Hōgen Insurrection of 1156, which pitted members of the same noble families against each other. The choice of events might have been a good one, but Kōri's use of them is sentimental and historically inaccurate.[39] The last scene transforms Yoshitomo's father

[38] Kōri's English style seems to resemble a pre-Shavian period of theatrical vocabulary. Without wishing to denigrate him unduly, the irreverent may chuckle over these lines taken at random from *The Toils of Yoshitomo* (page references from Kōri, *The English Works*, Tokyo, 1936).

"Well may you curse the chance that blew my sail to the shore of Naniwa this dawn!" (p. 219)

"But Chihaya, with all your love, how much more would you grieve to think that when in days coming they are singing the heroic tales of Genji in the Hōgen years, my name alone should be silent upon their biwa strings?" (p. 239)

"The arrow has scarce grazed my brow, praised be Hachiman!" (p. 230)

[39] Kōri has Tameyoshi commit suicide to aid the cause of his son Yoshitomo. Actually, according to Sansom, he was killed by a minor officer of the clan. See *A History of Japan to 1334*, p. 256.

into a kind of male Madame Butterfly, grasping for the hand of his tiny grandchild Yoritomo as the curtain falls.

Kōri's plays bear all the marks of the melodramatic historical dramas typical of what was being written in Japan at the time and so may serve as a means for English-speaking readers to sample a style which is no longer *kabuki* nor yet modern. If the compromise seems an unhappy one, his English friends, at least, found *Yoshitomo* of sufficient interest to arrange performances at the Little Theatre of London, where it ran for three weeks in 1922. The play was directed by Edith Craig, Gordon Craig's sister, and was also translated into German, Polish, and French.

During his stay in England, Kōri was asked to lecture on the history and significance of the Japanese drama. The information he related is correct in the light of modern scholarship and was probably more detailed than anything else available in English at the time. Yet running through his lecture is a note of disdain for the old and a strong desire for the establishment of a new drama in Japan. Of *nō* he says for example,

> it is rather surprising that in their enthusiastic study most of the English scholars [Yeats and others] have overlooked the fact that nothing is so little original as *nō* poetry, which is mostly a patchwork of bits of old Chinese and Japanese poetry, with also a great deal added from the Buddhist scriptures . . . and all this poetry, which is mostly copied word by word and collected with rather little understanding, weighs down and crushes the essential core of the drama, resulting more often than not in an unhappy incoherence.[40]

Kōri concludes his account with the words that ". . . it is to be regretted that in the course of this long period of history, one fails to find one work of real art, rich and ripe with the fundamental pathos of humanity."[41] False as his views may seem, Kōri's attitude is altogether representative

---

[40] Kōri, *The English Works*, pp. 284-285.   [41] *Ibid.*, p. 298.

of those who were determined to westernize their theatre so as to get as close as possible to their own contemporary definition of "the fundamental pathos of humanity." Kōri represents an extreme case, as he actually made his career abroad, but, with no important exception, all those who went abroad, beginning with Sadanji, saw the western drama as their only possible source of inspiration.

The French theatre had several Japanese devotees, among them Iwata Toyoo (1893-1959), who studied in France from 1922 to 1925.

Iwata made his voyage to France after the death of his mother; when he left Japan he had not yet firmly committed himself to a study of the theatre, but within a year after his arrival in Paris he had made up his mind to try to study the contemporary theatrical scene. His informal memoir, *Shingeki to watakushi* (*My Experiences with the New Theatre*), includes a kind of diary listing the important plays and actors he saw in France, and so chronicles the gradual deepening of his taste and understanding.

Iwata says that his first year was a Russian one: Diaghilev ballets, Bakst settings, and opulent spectacles. The year was crowned for him by his visits to productions of the Moscow Art Theatre which visited Paris.[42] (Iwata imagined himself to be the only other Japanese beside Osanai Kaoru to have seen the company and only after his return to Japan learned that Kishida Kunio had been in the same audience with him.)

During the season of 1923, Iwata saw and came to respect the work of Georges Pitoëff,[43] the Russian actor who, with

[42] Iwata dates his decision to study the theatre seriously from his first visit to the Moscow Art Theatre. He recounts that he tried to find some good books on the modern theatre in French but was told that the best ones were written by English or American authors. He soon found himself, like so many other foreigners in Paris, looking through the shelves of Brentano's Book Store.

[43] In fact Iwata saw his first modern play at Pitoëff's theatre shortly after his arrival in Paris. It was, of course, Gorky's ubiquitous *Lower Depths*.

his wife Ludmilla, staged a variety of first-rate avant-garde productions in Paris at this time. Pitoëff had been credited with bringing to Paris some of the ideals of the Moscow Art Theatre and in presenting to Parisian audiences plays "characterized by simplified and poetic abstractions tending to express the troubled inner landscape of human passions."[44] It was he who introduced the playwright Lenormand to Paris, staged plays by Gide and Jules Romains, and provided the opportunity for Parisian theatregoers to see a steady diet of Tolstoy, Chekhov, Ibsen, Pirandello, and O'Neill.

But Iwata came to revere the work of Jacques Copeau more than Pitoëff's. Copeau, the foremost director in France at that time, is often held to be the greatest in the history of the modern theatre in any country. Beginning his famous dramatic company Le Vieux Colombier in 1913, he stripped away the remaining artifice and frippery from the French stage, continuing a process so well begun by Antoine, and established a repertory company of superbly trained actors[45] who for a period of ten years (during which they made a visit to the United States during the First World War) devoted themselves to the finest and simplest possible presentations of new and classic plays. When Copeau returned to Paris at the end of the First World War, he remodeled his stage into a kind of permanent-unit set, flexible yet sufficiently evocative for any circumstance. Iwata (and Kishida) saw staged on it plays by Shakespeare, Molière, Musset, Beaumarchais, Chekhov, Gogol, and among the young French writers, Charles Vildrac, Émile Mazaud, René Benjamin, Roger Martin du Gard, Jules Romains, and even one by Copeau himself, *La maison natale* (*The House into Which We are Born*).

[44] For a discussion of the achievements of Pitoëff, see Clark and Freedley, *A History of Modern Drama* (New York, 1947), p. 278.

[45] Many of the most famous names in the modern French theatre were involved with the company: Louis Jouvet, Charles Dullin, Suzanne Bing, Valentine Tessier, and others.

Iwata's descriptions of the Copeau productions suggest that he had grasped Copeau's methods and had penetrated into psychology behind Copeau's idealism. Iwata went from an appreciation of Russian spectacle to a love for the simplest of all stages in a process which took him three years; when he heard in 1924 that Copeau planned to close his company, he found himself saying that it was time to go home. Before doing so, he made a trip to Germany, but found the productions of the plays of the German expressionist writers too heavy and old-fashioned for his taste.

In his last year in Paris, Iwata saw other productions of plays by writers who would make the 1930s an important period in the history of the theatre—Pirandello, Jules Romains (especially his *Doctor Knock*), and Jean Cocteau. Iwata took careful notes on all the Paris productions he saw, worked on his French, and collected materials which he used in the dramatic criticism he wrote after his return to Japan. He also became friends with the dramatist Charles Vildrac; shortly before Iwata left for Tokyo, the pair of them spent an evening despairing over the closing of Le Vieux Colombier.

Of all the actors, writers, and directors who went abroad, Iwata remained the longest and developed perhaps the keenest sense of the real accomplishments of a foreign theatre. After his return to Japan, he wrote criticism, made translations, and was involved in a number of projects with Kishida Kunio. He also wrote a short play, a comedy-farce in one act called *Higashi wa higashi* (*East is East*),[46] one of the treasures of the modern Japanese stage. The play tells of the troubles of a Chinese in medieval times who has drifted to Japan and taken a Japanese wife. The conflict of the two cultures is shown there in humorous and theatrically civilized terms.

The First World War brought tremendous changes to

[46] The play is also a linguistic *tour de force*, being written in the language of *kyōgen*, the farces that accompanied traditional productions of *nō*.

the theatre in Europe. Copeau, Reinhardt, and Stanislavsky were still in their prime, but the Russian revolution had brought about in that country the rapid development of political theatre, especially in the work of Stanislavsky's disciple and erstwhile rival V. S. Meyerhold (1874-1940). The postwar political confusion in Germany stimulated the work of the expressionist playwrights there, and by 1920 the worker's theatrical experiments of Erwin Piscator (1893-1966) were well under way. Young Japanese theatre students going to Russia and Germany in this period were much taken with these new methods, many of which had been created in direct opposition to the ideals of the prewar European theatre. This new group of travellers now introduced into Japan another view of the theatre that, clashing as it did with the ideas of Copeau, Stanislavsky, and the others, led to a decade or more of crippling doctrinal warfare in New Theatre circles.

One of the first of these visitors to postwar Europe was Osanai's colleague Hijikata Yoshi (1898-1959), whose chance viewing of one of Meyerhold's productions in Moscow brought an early introduction of the Soviet director's ideas and methods to the Tsukiji Little Theatre. Hijikata had taken an early interest in the theatre, forming a small company while he was still a student. He met Osanai in 1920 and, fired with his new friend's enthusiasm for the theatre, decided to go to Europe for a ten-year period of study. He spent 1922 in Berlin, where he studied with a noted director and scenic artist of the period, Carl Heine. When Hijikata received word of the devastation caused by the Tokyo earthquake of 1923, he decided to return to Japan at once and donate the funds he had set aside for his own study to the building of a new theatre in Tokyo to be used exclusively for the production of modern plays.

Hijikata had seen some Expressionist plays in Germany (Kaiser, Toller, and similar writers were having their plays widely produced there during Hijikata's visit); he returned to Japan through Russia, and while he was in Moscow he happened to see Meyerhold's production of *The Earth in Turmoil*, an adaption and "sovietization" by Sergei Tretyakov of a French play, *La nuit* by the French Marxist poet Marcel Martinet.[47] Hijikata was overwhelmed by what he saw. Meyerhold insisted not on psychology and naturalism, as did Stanislavsky, but on a vivid theatricalism, using aggressive declamation projected on screens to "teach" the audience the meaning of the play; the scenery was a procession of real machines, the actors wore no makeup and used street clothes as costumes.

Many of these ideas had been taken over from the German Expressionist writers[48] (and Brecht among others would go on developing such methods in Germany), but Meyerhold's brilliant success in relating Expressionist abstractions to political propaganda, as Braun points out, created a unique combination of glittering theatricality and a trenchant social message.

When Hijikata returned to Tokyo he worked hard to promote the development of this style of acting and directing. He directed one of the plays in the opening program of the Tsukiji Little Theatre, an Expressionist work by Reinhard Goering, *Seeschlacht* (*A Sea Battle*). Hijikata's

[47] An account of the production can be found in Edward Braun, *Meyerhold on Theatre* (New York, 1969), pp. 187-189. Hijikata so liked the play that he later directed a production of the French original for Osanai.

[48] And something from *kabuki*. Like Stanislavsky, Meyerhold was fascinated with the Japanese theatre. His interest had been stimulated with the visit to Russia in 1901 of Kawakami's troupe (see above), and he attempted to use what he took to be *kabuki* staging methods in a 1911 production of Molière's *Don Juan*. His enthusiastic comments on the Japanese theatre (see Braun, *Meyerhold*, pp. 99-100) are misinformed in details of fact but seem to show that he had indeed caught much of the basic spirit of *kabuki* stylization.

Hijikata himself was evidently unaware of this interest on Meyerhold's part and presumably never studied *kabuki* himself, as far as I have been able to ascertain. Hijikata's accomplishments as a director of abstract and expressionistic plays might have been greater had he possessed the catholic taste of a Meyerhold.

43

rough and abstract methods of direction were quite at variance with those of his partner Osanai, who followed Stanislavsky. Hijikata later wrote that *A Sea Battle* was his "first protest against the decadence of the Japanese theatre of my time; it was the beacon put out."[49] Hijikata had brought the conflict between the two Russian directors to Japan, but the conflict was now within the same theatrical company. In addition, Hijikata, like Meyerhold, tended to view any script as only a springboard for the director's imagination. Again the function of the playwright was bypassed even before the Japanese writers were able to learn the essentials of their craft.

German theatre had also had its exponents in Japan before 1925. Chief among them was Murayama Tomoyoshi (born 1901). Murayama had developed an early interest in theatre and painting. He withdrew from his undergraduate work in the philosophy department of Tokyo University in 1921 in order to go to Berlin, where he remained for two years to paint and observe productions of Expressionist theatre. Murayama was exposed to productions of the plays of such writers as Kaiser, Goering, Oscar Kokoschka (the painter was also a playwright at this time), and Stefan Zweig. The techniques used in these Expressionist plays were extremely subjective: "the faithful portrayal of reality and the pursuit of aesthetic values for their own sake were renounced for unrestrained 'self-expression.' [In the plays,] grammar and syntax were ruthlessly overthrown, articles eliminated, sentences clipped, new words created. In some extreme instances, the dialogue was reduced to bare exclamations—the ecstatic cry was the ultimate mark of expressionist diction."[50]

The early Expressionist movement was basically a spiritual one, but in the work of the young director Erwin Piscator (1893-1956), who began his celebrated Proletarian Theatre

[49] Hijikata Yoshi, *Enshutsusha no michi* (Tokyo, 1969), p. 105.

[50] H. F. Garten, *Modern German Drama* (New York, 1962), p. 105.

44

while Murayama was in Berlin, the German avant-garde theatre took a turn to the left that rivalled Meyerhold's. Piscator took his actors directly to the workers, playing in beer halls and community centers; his success was so great that by 1925 he was offered the best stages in Germany for his experiments. His attitudes toward art and his antipathy toward the methods of a man like Stanislavsky are neatly summed up in a few phrases from his notebooks: "let us consciously create unfinished products. We don't have the time to build formally. So many new thoughts push on to the light. Time is so precious that we cannot wait for the last refined purifications . . . what is most needed is the interim achievement."[51]

Fired with new enthusiasm, Murayama returned to Tokyo in 1923.[52] He wrote plays, painted, and edited an Expressionist art magazine. One of his first commissions was to do the sets and costumes for the 1924 production by the Tsukiji Little Theatre of Georg Kaiser's *From Morn to Midnight*, a story of a bank clerk who absconds with a large sum of money so as to make up in a single day for a life of misery and frustration. Murayama's efforts were successful but he soon decided that a specifically Expressionist and leftist theatre group would have to be created in Japan. In carrying out Piscator's ideas, Murayama, like Osanai, became a spokesman in Japan for the importance of the director even before the plays for his Expressionist repertory were created.

IN A PERIOD of thirteen years—from 1912, when Osanai went to Moscow, until 1924, when Iwata returned from Paris—articulate and determined spokesmen for nearly every significant movement in all modern European theatre had appeared in Japan. Some of these men, notably Iwata, re-

---

[51] Quoted in Maria Ley-Piscator, *The Piscator Experiment* (New York, 1967), p. 74.

[52] Murayama remained a partisan for Piscator's methods and when Piscator published his book *Political Theatre* in 1929, Murayama translated it into Japanese.

mained a long time in Europe and came to know the foreign theatre well. But, significantly, the two most powerful men in the world of the practicing theatre, Osanai and Hijikata, remained abroad only a short time and did not penetrate very far into the real methods of their mentors. Significantly too, most of these men went to study the methods of production of these plays, not the writing of them. They skipped over the most important element.

These extraordinarily various influences, created in half a dozen countries over fifty years, were now brought to bear at one time on a few financially insecure organizations. By 1925, Japan had been brought abreast of Europe in terms of knowledge. But the knowledge had been obtained quickly, and little of it had been put into practice.

FROM LITERATURE TO POLITICS

The first current in the westernization of the Japanese theatre, in which literary values were predominant, centered on an emulation of the ideals of the European theatre before the First World War, of which the work of Jacques Copeau represented a final flowering. Now, however, a series of new writers with dramatic aspirations came to the fore in Japan.

The Playwright as a Member of the Vanguard

The period after World War I brought to the fore in Japan a group of idealistic writers who had taken from their idol, Tolstoy, the conviction that men must develop a social conscience and take practical steps to bring about a concrete social realization of their ideas and beliefs. The most typical of these writers, almost a paradigm of the period, was Arishima Takeo (1878-1923),[53] who, though

---

[53] For an account of Arishima's life, see Nakamura, *Japanese Fiction* and John Morrison, *Modern Japanese Fiction* (Salt Lake City, 1955). One of Arishima's plays in an English translation is included in Iwasaki and Hughes, *New Plays from Old Japan* (London, 1930).

not primarily a playwright himself, infused into the younger generation something of his enthusiasm and of his final sense of disillusionment as well. As a young man Arishima was a Christian but he later rejected religion and became a kind of neo-Socialist, in 1922 turning over his own extensive farm lands in Hokkaido to his tenants. Suddenly his creative energies ebbed away, and in 1923 he committed suicide over an affair with another man's wife in an incident which, like the death of the novelist Akutagawa Ryūnosuke in 1927, was to make a great impression on the literary world of the time.

Following World War I, Japan was presented with a series of difficult economic problems, and Japanese intellectuals who had come in contact with socialist and communist ideas now began working to establish organizations to spread these new ideas. In 1920, shortly before Arishima's death, the Nihon Shakaishugi Dōmei (Japan Socialist League) was formed. Many writers participated. In 1921 the government forced the League to disband but by then Japan's first important socialist literary magazine *Tanemaku hito* (*The Sower*) had begun publishing. Arishima, although he stated that he was "too deeply attached to his own background to accept the ideology of Marxism,"[54] nevertheless had joined the League as an associate member and was a contributor to the magazine, which soon became a rallying point for a variety of distinguished writers and their younger colleagues. The editors declared that "we defend the truth of the Revolution for life,"[55] and the proletarian cast of the magazine was soon quite apparent.

Among the contributors to *The Sower* were three playwrights whose work owed its primary inspiration to the ideals of Arishima. They were Akita Ujaku (1883-1962), Fujimori Seikichi (born 1892), and Kaneko Yōbun (born 1894). Of the three Akita was the most important.

[54] Quoted in Morrison, *Fiction*, p. 163.
[55] See G. T. Shea, *Leftwing Literature in Japan* (Tokyo, 1964), p. 75.

Akita began his theatrical career as a member of the Ibsen society[56] and Osanai presented one of his early plays at the Free Theatre in 1910. He joined the Japan Socialist League in 1920 and was a frequent contributor to *The Sower*. By 1920 Akita, a close friend of Arishima, had become strongly attracted to socialism. His play *Kokkyō no yoru* (*Night at the Frontier*) was first published in 1920, in the magazine *Shinshōsetsu* (*New Fiction*), and was staged the following year by a small experimental theatre group in Tokyo. The play, significantly enough set in Hokkaido, has been described as the "manifestation of a bad dream" and tells a murky story about the problems of human feeling versus the dictates of a social philosophy; it includes masked men, dying mothers, and wailing children. Akita has written that the play was written to reflect his interests in socialism.

When Arishima died in 1923, Akita, disappointed and depressed, became determined to show in his work the necessary relation between the life of the intellectual and the state of society itself.[57] His next play, written in 1924, was entitled *Gaikotsu no buyō* (*The Skeleton's Dance*) and was a fictional retelling of an infamous incident after the 1923 earthquake in Tokyo when a number of Korean laborers were murdered by frightened mobs of Japanese. In order to deal with such political subjects, Akita resorted in this and later plays to Expressionist techniques he learned from the modern German theatre. Osanai, who was at this time becoming more aware of the artistic potential of such drama, produced some of Akita's plays at the Tsukiji Little Theatre.[58]

Fujimori Seikichi was another playwright whose interests in the personality and doctrines of Arishima led him quickly

[56] See above, p. 24.

[57] See Shea, *Leftwing Literature*, p. 115.

[58] It was Akita who accompanied Osanai on his second trip to Russia in 1927, shortly before the director's sudden death. They were invited as state guests of the Soviet government.

into the proletarian camp. He too had joined the Japan Socialist League and wrote for *The Sower*. After Arishima's death Fujimori wrote a play called *Gisei* (*The Sacrifice*) about Arishima's suicide, but when the play was published in installments in the June and July 1926 issues of *Kaizō* (*Reconstruction*), the issues of the magazine were banned. Osanai was greatly impressed with the work and prepared a stage production at the Tsukiji Little Theatre, but this too was forbidden by the authorities the day before the opening.

Kaneko Yōbun, like Akita and Fujimori, belonged to the same organizations and wrote a variety of stories and plays of socialist persuasion, among them a 1922 play, *Sentakuya to shijin* (*The Laundryman and the Poet*) of some distinction.[59] In 1925 Yōbun became the editor of a new leftist magazine, *Bungeisensen* (*Literary Battle Line*), which replaced *The Sower*.

Within a very short time, then, a group of authors appeared to challenge the literary canons both of the older playwrights and of other younger writers who wished to stress purely literary values in their works.

The degree of militancy shown by these writers may be judged by the fact that all became members of a new organization formed in 1925, the Nihon Puroretaria Bungei Renmei (Japan Proletarian Literary Arts League). The founders of this organization were inspired by the 1924 Moscow Comintern meeting where the unification of proletarian writers around the world had been proposed. The purpose of the League was to unite all the leftist writers in Japan into support for a group movement. The League had a drama section headed by Sasaki Takamaru (born 1898), who was later to head several important leftist theatre troupes. By 1925, he had managed to organize these playwrights and to find methods to present their works on the stage.

[59] According to Shea. For a description of the play see *Leftwing Literature*, p. 97. I have not been able to locate a copy of the text.

49

Akita and the others might be considered somewhat transitional figures in the development of the political drama in Japan, but several young writers who began their careers in the early 1920s gave considerable distinction to the movement for a proletarian theatre. The purely literary writers beginning their work in 1925, such as Kishida, were up against considerable competition.

Many of the earlier political writers had received only indifferent schooling, but the younger Marxist playwrights were well educated at the best universities in Tokyo. Murayama Tomoyoshi, mentioned above, had also studied in Germany. Mafune Yutaka (born 1902) studied English literature at Waseda but left his studies in a crisis of personal despondency. By 1925 he was beginning to publish his first stories and plays. Kubo Sakae (1901-1958), who had been a friend of Murayama since student days, studied German literature at Tokyo University and began working with Hijikata at the Tsukiji Little Theatre. His work both as a biographer of Osanai and as a playwright make him the outstanding figure of his generation in the political theatre. Also to be mentioned is Miyoshi Jūro (1902-1958), who after graduating from Waseda with a degree in English literature joined the Japan Proletarian Literary Arts League and began an active playwriting career.

If Shōyō and the example of Ibsen had turned the playwrights into intellectuals by the time of the First World War, the postwar situation turned them into *ideologues*; for these men, the theatre would now state the truth, not explore it.[60] Time would show them the difficulties of combining art and politics, and indeed there were no Brechts

---

[60] The appeal made by the Comintern was clear on the duties of a writer. "In the area of the one great class struggle which is being developed throughout the entire world, the person who is neutral no longer exists . . . for the true artist today, there is no other road to follow than to participate in the fight for the liberation of the proletariat." (Quoted in Shea, *Leftwing Literature*, p. 136.)

among them. But in 1925 most of the talented young play-wrights in Japan seemed very far to the left.

The Creation of Political Theatre
Troupes in Japan to 1925

In the early 1920s, a variety of small companies were created for the purpose of staging these plays. They all operated in great financial insecurity but most of them were able to continue because of the enthusiasm, indeed the passion, of their young members. Although Osanai was unwilling to produce Japanese plays of literary merit,[61] these troupes were actually created in order to produce the propaganda plays of the young Japanese radical intelligentsia.

One of the first of these small theatre troupes, and the most unusual of them, was the Nihon Rōdō Gekidan (Japan Labor Theatre), a small group begun around 1922 by Hirasawa Keishichi (1885-1923), a labor leader who became a writer. The company was based in Tokyo, and like similar groups used mostly amateur actors and sought an audience for its socialist skits and plays among factory workers.

The group had a profound effect on certain members of the professional theatre. Akita Ujaku went to see the troupe perform.

The spectators were all laborers. They cried out "yes!" "that's it!" yelling as they watched the plays. The theatre became a frenzied crucible. Before we set out for the theatre, we thought that there would be little value in their work, but on the way back, we were completely bowled over by what we had seen. We talked on the streetcar coming back. "The way they go about the thing seems

[61] There is some evidence that toward the end of his life Osanai began to take some interest in Marxism and in political theatre (see Shimomura, *Shingeki*, p. 75). The Tsukiji Little Theatre presented more than its share of Expressionist and political plays, but they were almost always directed by Hijikata. Osanai remained true to his principle of creating an artistic theatre in his own productions.

impossible. Imagine making playwrights and actors out of laborers!"[62]

Osanai himself was taken by Hijikata to see the troupe perform and found himself very enthusiastic. He had written of a theatre for the people: here, for the first time, he saw a real people's theatre at work.

The group lasted less than two years. In the aftermath of the Tokyo earthquake Hirasawa and several other important radicals were arrested and evidently murdered by the Tokyo police. The troupe collapsed, but its influence as a source of inspiration continued to remain strong.

Akita Ujaku began his own small company, the Senkuza (Pioneer Theatre), in 1922. Performances were given to invited audiences on the second floor of a Shinjuku bakery, then later on the second floor of a Japanese-style storehouse, which gained the company its nickname of "The Storehouse Theatre." (The storehouse, and the troupe, were destroyed in the earthquake.) The repertory included some of Akita's own work, short plays by Eugene O'Neill, and a one-act play by the then radical literary critic Hasegawa Nyozekan (born 1875) entitled *Ethyl Gasoline*.[63]

Among the members of Akita's group was Sasaki Takamaru, who later, in line with his work as head of the Drama Section of the Japan Proletarian Literary Arts League, managed to organize his own small company, the Torunkuza (The Trunk Theatre), which took its name from the fact

[62] Quoted in Ibaragi Tadashi, "kaishaku," *Gendai Nihon gikyoku senshū*, VIII, pp. 397-398.

[63] *Ethyl Gasoline* is a melodrama of greed. A wealthy manufacturer refuses to stop the production of a lethal variety of gasoline because it is so profitable. His two children leave some in a bottle, hoping he will smell it, think of his own death, and leave his money to them. He does sniff the bottle but dies unrepentant before he has time to make a will. The play, a tentative exercise in the style of Sinclair Lewis, has a couple of effective scenes, in particular an exchange between the manufacturer and a "do-gooder" who comes to reprimand him for his lack of social conscience.

52

that the actors packed all their properties quickly in a trunk so as to be able to travel easily. Although the troupe was to carry out the purposes of the League, its repertory was more humanist than overtly Marxist in the choice of plays, which included *Ethyl Gasoline* and plays by the noted writer Mushakōji Saneatsu, another associate of Arishima. The performances by the troupe have been described as "sham-Expressionist" and rather amateur,[64] but the actors were greatly spurred on by the enthusiasm of their worker audiences.

The history of these early groups is complex and often obscure, but by 1925 Murayama Tomoyoshi and a group of his friends, including Kaneko Yōbun, Sasaki Takamaru, and Senda Koreya (today the dean of Japanese directors and actors), began a new group they called the Zen'eiza (Vanguard Theatre). A year later they were able to rent Osanai's Tsukiji theatre building, where they presented a series of highly successful performances of the Soviet play *Don Quixote Released* by A. V. Lunacharsky.[65] Murayama followed this play with a production of one of Piscator's favorites, Upton Sinclair's *Prince Hagen*, a satire on the financial world and an ironic retelling of the myths in Wagner's Ring Cycle.

Within a period of four or five years the rough enthusiasm witnessed by Akita had been combined with the dedication of the young professionals in the Vanguard Theatre to produce productions of political plays performed with skill and sophistication.

The subsequent history of the various groups performing political plays is a tangled one that, in any case, kept them almost altogether apart from the work of the ordinary

[64] See Shimomura, *Shingeki*, p. 73.

[65] Lunacharsky has not maintained his earlier high reputation, but at the beginning of the Soviet period he was regarded as an outstanding playwright with a strong humanistic outlook. Several of his plays, although not this one, have been published in English versions.

New Theatre groups that continued to stress literary and artistic ideals. Yet the strong inroads into the New Theatre movement made by the political theatre groups were so marked that the period of 1925 to 1940 (when the last of them was closed down by the government) was largely dominated by their activities.

From the point of view of the Japanese playwrights, the irony inherent in the success of such groups was obvious. With a few exceptions (notably the two productions of Lunacharsky and Sinclair), the radical companies made use of Japanese plays. The radical companies now provided what Osanai did not: a place for Japanese writers (at least writers of a certain kind) to have their plays performed.

In both the artistic and the political theatre, however, the directors, not the writers, were the central figures. Indeed, the authors who wrote for the political theatre companies wrote to order, rather like the *kabuki* playwrights fifty years before; this time, their instructions came from their own fixed political convictions and from the powerful directors, rather than from the star *kabuki* actors. But their plays read like circumscribed scenarios. The playwrights were again part of a larger machine.

With the establishment of the Tsukiji Little Theatre in 1924, the age of the experimentation was over and professional theatre in Japan became possible for the first time. The two assumptions of the writers, actors, and directors could now be acted upon.

First, every important figure in the New Theatre movement at this time stood unequivocally for the westernization of the Japanese theatre and opposed any attempt to reform or modernize its traditional forms. *Shimpa* and the experiments of Tsubouchi Shōyō were disregarded. This attitude was as strong among the proletarian writers and directors as it was among men like Osanai, Mori Ōgai, Tanizaki Junichirō, and the other literary playwrights.

Second, the role of the playwright in the performing theatre had been subordinated to that of the director.

54

In 1924, Japan received its first professional theatre with Osanai and its first young professional playwright trained in Europe with Kishida Kunio. The conflicts between them would throw all the difficulties of the New Theatre movement into high relief.

CHAPTER III

Kishida Kunio and the New Theatre Movement in 1925

A NUMBER of good playwrights were at work in Japan during the period 1925-1939. The leftist theatre produced several dramatists of distinction; among those who continued to adhere to predominantly literary ideals, such men as Kubota Mantarō and Morimoto Kaoru stand out for their high level of professional accomplishment. Among them all, however, the work of Kishida Kunio is surely outstanding, not only because of the general excellence of his work, but because his knowledge of the European theatre, greater than that of any other Japanese writing at the time, made him most keenly aware of the disparity between ideals and practice in Japan. He spared neither himself nor others in his criticisms of a theatre that he thought fell short both of its own ideals and of any real appreciation of European styles and techniques that it professed to take as its models.

In addition, like many of his contemporary writers and intellectuals in Japan, Kishida faced the gradual divergence between art and ideology. A great deal of scorn was heaped upon him for his stubborn adherence to artistic ideals in a time of political trouble. In 1940 the Japanese government closed down the leftist theatre companies; only Kishida and his group were not interfered with because, from the government's point of view, their work steered clear of dangerous subjects. Kishida was convinced that his talents as a writer could best be developed through his rendering of individual human character rather than a social or political analysis of a nascent fascism. His attempt to sustain his own artistic views in the face of difficult professional and political situations makes his successes and his failures an index to the development of modern theatre in Japan. Moreover, Kishida was firmly committed to a westernization of the Japanese theatre, and his work did much to make the form a more mature and natural one.

Before discussing Kishida's early career in the theatre in Japan, it might be well to indicate briefly something about his early years and his studies in France.[1]

He was born in Tokyo in 1890, the year after the promulgation of the Meiji Constitution. His father, Kishida Shōzō came from a samurai family of Kishū (the present Wakayama Prefecture) and was a military officer in the Imperial Guard. As the eldest male child in the family, Kishida was expected to carry on the family military traditions.

Although, at the insistence of his father, Kishida attended a military preparatory school, he showed an early interest in literature and by the time he was seventeen he had thrown himself into a study of such French authors as Chateaubriand and Rousseau. He continued his military training, graduating from the Japanese Military Academy in 1912. He was given a commission of sub-lieutenant in the army, but resigned two years later. In 1916 he decided to take up a formal study of French literature at the University of Tokyo.

The faculty at that time included two young professors whose enthusiasm for French literature soon put them at the head of their field in Japan. Both were instrumental in encouraging Kishida's interests, and, later, in helping him publish his first articles and translations. One of them, Tatsuno Yutaka (1888-1964), a novelist and translator (of *Cyrano de Bergerac*, among other works), was in Paris during Kishida's visit to France. Suzuki Shintarō (1895-1970) was becoming well known for his translations of Verlaine and Mallarmé. In addition to the faculty, one of Kishida's fellow-students, Toyoshima Yoshio (1890-1955) was soon to earn a reputation as a scholar of French litera-

[1] For additional notes on Kishida, see Appendix II.

ture and a novelist. He was active in organizing an important literary magazine *Shinshichō* (*New Currents of Thought*) in 1914. Toyoshima was very helpful to Kishida after the playwright's return from France in 1923.

As a student Kishida had developed an interest in French theatre; he had published some translations of modern French plays in the Tokyo University literary magazine and then decided to go to France to see such plays performed. By 1919 he had saved enough money from his translations to begin his journey, and without graduating he left the university, at the age of twenty-nine, and set sail for France.

Or at least for Hong Kong. From there he began to work his way to France on Japanese ships. He got as far as Haiphong in Vietnam, where he remained for three months.[2] Eventually he earned enough money to buy a ticket for Marseilles, and finally arrived in Paris early in 1920.

Kishida was anxious to study the theatre, but he was mostly involved with finding a means to support himself for the first year. As there was a great deal of diplomatic activity in Paris during the period (the Treaty of Versailles ending the First World War had been signed the year before), he was able to find part-time work as a translator for the Japanese Embassy and for the Secretariat of the League of Nations. His translations of Daudet and Maupassant also brought him a small income from Japan that eventually enabled him to travel as far as Austria; later he taught Japanese and made a series of translations into Japanese documents dealing with the Russian revolution and the 1917 Kerensky cabinet.

Kishida's introduction to the theatre took some time.[3] He later wrote that since he had been unable to obtain de-

[2] The play *Ushiyama Hotel*, written in 1929, is based on his experiences in Vietnam. See below, pp. 185-192.

[3] As has been indicated, little European drama was being performed in Japan during Kishida's youth. Kishida recorded that he had seen only five or six productions of any kind before his trip to France. His real education about the theatre began in France, not in Japan.

tailed information in Japan on the actual state of the French theatre, he had to learn over the course of many months who the really important writers and actors were and what kind of plays the major companies were performing. "When I got to Paris, I went around looking at plays like a blind man, foraging in the papers and magazines, picking up the names of prominent writers and theatre companies. I searched through anything I could find to read, old or new; yet even so, I think it took me a good year to get the lie of the land."[4] He soon learned that his early enthusiasms in Japan for authors like Rostand or Hervieu had been somewhat misplaced; writers about whom he knew nothing— Alfred de Musset, Jules Renard, and others—were a stronger influence on young French writers, and Shakespeare, Ibsen, and Molière were of vital importance to an understanding of contemporary theatre.

He read the texts of plays to understand the language and then went to see them; watching the audience laugh in unexpected places, he realized that perhaps he had not really understood the meaning of what he had read. Gradually his French became more fluent and his developing sensitivity toward acting technique enabled him to select the best performances in Paris and study them. Kishida also began to attend lectures at the Sorbonne. His professor took an interest in him and introduced him to Georges Pitoëff and, more important, to the man in France Kishida most wanted to meet: Jacques Copeau.

Kishida described his first visit to Le Vieux Colombier to meet Copeau in rather humorous terms.[5] He was very nervous but was reassured by Copeau's kind attitude. Copeau assigned the actor André Bacqué (well known for his performances of Molière) to look after Kishida, and he was invited to attend lectures at Copeau's school.[6] For almost

---

[4] *Kishida Kunio zenshū* (Tokyo, 1955), IX, p. 56.

[5] See *zenshū*, IX, pp. 54-59.

[6] Jacques Copeau considered the work of his school to be the most important element in his activities at Le Vieux Colombier. Copeau

two years, until his return to Japan in 1923, Kishida attended Copeau's lectures and watched most of the plays in rehearsal. He even recorded that André Gide once asked him for a cigarette—and in English. Copeau's troupe was at its best during Kishida's stay in Paris.[7] He saw productions of Shakespeare, Molière, Beaumarchais, Chekhov, and, among contemporary French authors, Vildrac, Gide, and Jules Renard.

When the Moscow Art Theatre visited Paris in 1922, Kishida attended many performances and, like the Parisians, was struck by the subtlety and finish of the acting ensemble.[8] He later commented that although he was deeply impressed

---

began the school in 1914, using methods and ideas gained from his visits with Adolph Appia, Gordon Craig, and Jacques-Dalcroze, all major figures in theatrical and educational circles in Europe. After the First World War, Copeau put his school on a full-time basis. A select number of students, from ages fourteen to twenty, were exposed to theory of the theatre, theatrical architecture, poetic structure, diction, singing, memory exercises, physical education, French diction, and what Copeau called "dramatic sense." Copeau gave this last course himself and it was this series of lectures that Kishida attended.

Kishida wrote that he found Copeau's remarks always concise and compelling. Although Kishida did not describe any of the contents of the lectures in detail, the general flavor of Copeau's methods can be gained from a description provided by Maurice Kurtz in his *Jacques Copeau: biographie d'un théâtre*: "Copeau, in his technical course in directing and acting, gave his young people extremely difficult passages to read, then cut them short at their mistakes to teach them humility before a manuscript." (p. 111)

Students who succeeded in finishing a three-year course might begin working as apprentices at Le Vieux Colombier.

Along with Copeau, the faculty included Louis Jouvet, Suzanne Bing, Jules Romains, and, for singing, Jane Bathori, the soprano chosen by Debussy and Ravel, among other composers, for the premières of many important French vocal works.

[7] Maurice Kurtz lists Copeau's entire repertory at the time: it was surely the most sophisticated and cosmopolitan in France, perhaps in Europe.

[8] Kishida's comments on the Moscow Art Theatre are in *zenshū*, IX, pp. 61-64.

by the excitement and change in the theatre in France during the period he felt, "that what the Japanese theatre must learn is not the changes but the lasting and vital traditions of the European theatre."[9] Such remained his chief impression from his study with Le Vieux Colombier.[10]

In October of 1922, Kishida suddenly had a severe lung hemorrhage and retired to the south of France to recover. A month later, while still convalescing, he learned of his father's death and left France immediately to return to Tokyo.

Back in Tokyo in 1923, with his mother and sisters to care for, Kishida found his personal situation at odds with his own desires. Although he was still not very sure what he wanted to do, he knew that it would be connected with the theatre. He ruefully remarked that "Japanese painters often say they cannot create in Japan the oil colors of the pictures they painted in Europe. The disparity in nature, which is their model, is too great. But it is more than this. Their whole sense of color seems to become dull when they return home."[11] Kishida felt equally out of place.

He soon got in touch with Toyoshima, who in turn introduced him to Yamamoto Yūzō, a dramatist of some distinction whose plays had been produced by a variety of small New Theatre companies. He was generally considered the *doyen* of the professional literary New Theatre dramatists at the time.

Kishida was grateful for the introduction and wanted to show Yamamoto the manuscript of his first play *Kiiroi bishō* (*A Wan Smile*) written in France. He was afraid that

[9] *zenshū*, IX, p. 184.

[10] Copeau would have considered the lesson well learned. Maurice Kurtz writes that he considered Le Vieux Colombier "not a theatre for intellectuals: the unsophisticated were to come as well. Nor was it an avant-garde theatre, which meant to thrive on its originality and as a temporary attraction for the curious minded. This was no revolutionary movement, since its strongest bond was still with the classics." See Kurtz, *Copeau*, p. 96.

[11] *zenshū*, IX, p. 228.

Yamamoto's interest in German literature might make him feel that Kishida's work was insufficiently solemn, but Yamamoto proved to be a man capable of appreciating several things at the same time.

> it was evening, and as we talked over various aspects of the French theatre, he brought out my manuscript along with the fried fish. It was supper time. He had been too busy to read it before, he said, and he wanted to give it a glance while he ate. It was fine with me. He took the pages up, along with his chopsticks . . . the first . . . the second scene must be finished, I thought. "Um . . ." he muttered, a strange growl which might have been a sign of boredom or of appreciation.
>
> When the third scene was finished he took a short rest. Suddenly his chopsticks began to work vigorously, and behind his glasses, I felt his eyes searching for the proper thing to say. Then the following words came to me as in a dream.
>
> "Among all the plays I've read recently, there has been nothing as interesting as this!"[12]

This dinner, Kishida concluded, convinced him to take up playwriting.

Kishida's future began to look promising, but a month later the 1923 earthquake destroyed all the major theatres in the capital, and the resources of most of the New Theatre companies were wiped out in the disaster. Kishida's career seemed finished before it was begun. He later wrote that the vast changes which came to Tokyo in the wake of the destruction[13] did not touch him profoundly. "These events

---

[12] *zenshū*, IX, p. 192.

[13] After the destruction of most of the remnants of old Edo in the earthquake, a new cosmopolitanism was introduced into Tokyo. For a brief description of the resulting changes in social attitudes, see Maruyama Masao, "Patterns of Individuation and the Case of Japan," in Marius Jansen, ed., *Changing Japanese Attitudes toward Modernization* (Princeton, 1965), pp. 517-519.

were not connected in any intimate way with the problems of my own daily living. I imagine that if I myself had begun a career in the theatre in any tangible form before the earthquake came, then I too would have had a greater shock, and I would have greeted the cries of those who wished to have a renaissance in the theatre with a different and a more profound emotion."[14] Instead he soon forgot about the manuscript he had left with Yamamoto and at the request of Suzuki Shintarō began translating French novels into Japanese, hoping in this way to sustain himself and his family. With these fees, plus the income he earned from giving lessons in French, he was able to save enough to open his own language school, which he called The Molière School (an appropriate choice of patron saint—Copeau had placed a small statue of Molière in the foyer of Le Vieux Colombier).

However, by 1924 two important projects that provided a renaissance for the New Theatre movement were initiated, and Kishida was involved in both of them. The first was the formation of a new magazine, *Engeki Shinchō* (*New Currents of Drama*). Earlier drama magazines had been suspended because of the damage done to the publishing companies in the earthquake. Yamamoto decided that a forum should be created for the best of the new drama, and he assembled an impressive group of collaborators, among them Kikuchi Kan, Tanizaki Junichirō, Kubota Mantarō, and Osanai Kaoru himself. Yamamoto accepted the manuscript of Kishida's *A Wan Smile*, now retitled *Furui Omocha* (*Old Toys*) and published it in the third issue. Kishida was somewhat apprehensive when his very first work was chosen for such attention.

It was scarcely surprising that I was very nervous when the magazine appeared in the shops. Who was reading it? Where? As I didn't know, I felt almost ashamed to go out, which was very foolish. Eventually I

---

[14] *zenshū*, IX, p. 192.

received a few letters from unknown readers. One told me that my work reminded him of Arthur Schnitzler, very nice praise indeed, and I felt relieved. Two or three days later I had a visit from a member of the Cultural Section of the Yomiuri Newspaper. This was quite an occurrence. He asked me to discuss my career and had my picture taken. I meekly answered his questions and sat down in front of the lens. I was then living with my younger sister, so I had her sit for the picture too. Ah, what an obliging country this Japan is! I had become "known" for writing a play like that![15]

Since Kishida's return to Japan he had seen no modern drama produced on the stage. Now his chance was to come, for the second important event in the New Theatre movement was the opening of the Tsukiji Little Theatre, where Osanai, the producer, refused to put on Japanese plays:

And why will Japanese plays not be performed? I can answer this question very simply. We the directors have found no plays written by established Japanese playwrights that interest us. I include my own plays in this category. If on the other hand a play does interest us, we will wish to perform it, no matter what country it comes from. There may be excellent plays by writers who have no reputation; if we find them, we will wish to perform them as well. This policy is by no means based on a dislike of Japanese drama, or a mere wish to copy the west. . . .[16]

Kishida knew of Osanai's views yet hoped that he might be able to contribute to the work of the company because of his knowledge of the French theatre.

Naturally the writers connected with *New Currents of Drama* were hurt by Osanai's attitude.[17] (Some of their

[15] *zenshū*, IX, p. 194.　　　[16] Osanai, *engekiron*, II, p. 44.

[17] See *ibid.*, pp. 299-302 for the text of a roundtable discussion between Yamamoto, Kikuchi, Kubota, and others, all of whom attacked Osanai severely.

objections will be discussed later in a different context.) To answer them, Osanai published in the magazine an essay entitled "What is the Reason for the Existence of the Tsukiji Little Theatre?"[18] The essay, too long to reproduce here, gives three reasons with which Osanai justified his work.

The first was that his theatre existed for the staged drama and not for the sake of the play's text itself. A text is literature and can be read. His theatre was a place not to introduce new plays but to present plays of theatrical value, a value obtained in the presentation of the play and not from the script itself.

Second, Osanai wrote, his theatre existed for the future: for the development of young writers, actors, directors, and technicians, not for past or present ones. He thought that the work of the established Japanese playwrights owed too much to the psychology of *shimpa* and *kabuki*.[19] He wished for the development of a whole new kind of drama, and productions at his theatre were one means of showing the way.

Third, his theatre existed for the people. It did not exist for the writers, nor for what might be called "the theatre world." Nor for the privileged classes. He hoped for an audience of average people.

Kishida wrote that he attended Osanai's opening production with an open mind. Osanai had chosen to present three one-act plays. He directed two of the plays, Chekhov's *Swan Song*,[20] and a play from Copeau's repertory, Émile

[18] *Ibid.*, pp. 48-49.

[19] There is a case to be made for Osanai's criticism of the plays available to him at this time. The English reader may confirm the judgment himself, as plays by Kikuchi Kan and Yamamoto Yūzo are available in English. They are often melodramatic and, although perhaps effective in their way, of limited interest.

[20] Chekhov's *Swan Song* is a short play for two characters: Vassily Vassilyitch Svetkhovidov, an old actor, and Nikita Ivanovich, a prompter in a provincial Russian theatre. Barely more than a skit, it turns on the realization by Svetkhovidov that he is growing old and

Mazaud's *The Holiday*.[21] Hijikata directed the third, *A Sea Battle* by Reinhard Goering.[22] The three plays covered a broad range of theatrical styles, and the widely divergent points of view of Hijikata and Osanai were apparent from

---

has outlived his time. He remains behind after a performance in the darkened theatre, and, in a burst of enthusiasm, tries to recapture his former glory by reciting Shakespeare. Ivanovich, moved, fills in the lines of the other characters for him. The play is really a virtuoso piece for two good actors and is not necessarily typical of Chekhov's longer plays. Osanai went on to produce many of Chekhov's major works at the Tsukiji Little Theatre.

[21] *La Folle Journée* (translated as *The Holiday*) by Émile Mazaud is an effective, if rather minor, mood piece about the vicissitudes of old age. Two old friends meet again: one, Monsieur Mouton, has managed to earn enough money to retire in decent comfort; his friend Monsieur Pique visits him and reveals his terrible poverty to his host. Mouton, chagrined, sends him off as soon as possible, but is ashamed when he later reads a letter presenting an idealized version of what their meeting should have been; the letter, of course, had been prepared by Monsieur Pique as a thank-you note even before he left Paris for Monsieur Mouton's country house. The play was a great success at Le Vieux Colombier and provided Osanai with one of his few excursions into the modern French repertory.

[22] *A Sea Battle* is set in the turret of a battleship before and during the Battle of Jutland in the First World War. The characters, six sailors, have no names. In turn they sleep, talk fitfully, think back over their happy pasts, wonder at the nature of war, and have nightmares about death. The central scene of the play is a long conversation between the First and Fifth Sailors, who discuss the idea of peace and a possible mutiny for the sake of humanity. Later, in the heat of battle all such ideas are forgotten. The Fifth Sailor calls out to his fellows:

> What once has planted must grow,
> Even if it smash us!
> What once has been launched must roll,
> Even if it crush us!
> Whoever holds out to the end
> Lashes the stars,
> If they hang back!

The men begin to feel themselves heroes because of "our vintage

the opening production. (Aoyama Sugisaku,[23] the company's third director, did not contribute to the opening production.)

Kishida was asked by a drama magazine to write up his impressions of the production. His article[24] began a critical battle with Osanai that was to have considerable repercussions on Kishida's own career. His reactions to Osanai's company were to cause him to formulate his own major principles as to how to develop a New Theatre in Japan. He felt that Osanai had made a number of bad mistakes. First Kishida criticized the acting, which (as other contemporary accounts attest as well) was very inept. Why not, he said, choose easier plays if the actors are not more talented? The

---

of blood." All are killed in a series of explosions. As he dies, the Fifth Sailor says:

> The battle continues, do you hear?
> Don't close your eyes yet.
> I shot well, didn't I?
> I'd have mutinied well too, wouldn't I?
> But I suppose it was easier for us to shoot,
>   wasn't it?
> Must have been easier for us. . . .

The play represents an important early attempt at Expressionist playwriting, but Goering never repeated his first success. The play is well described in G. H. Garten, *Modern German Drama*, pp. 128-130. No translation has been published in English, but a typescript of the full text in a translation by Falcone and Morgan is available on microfilm at the Columbia University library in New York. It is from this translation that the extracts above are taken. Expressionist theatre was totally new to Japan and gave the audiences a considerable shock. See, for example, Ozaki Hirotsugu, *Shingeki no atoashi* (Tokyo, 1956), p. 95. The play was repeated a number of times in subsequent seasons by the troupe.

[23] The Tsukiji troupe had three regular directors, Osanai, Hijikata, and Aoyama Sugisaku (1891-1956). Aoyama took up an interest in the theatre while a student at Waseda University and worked with several small companies before joining Osanai. He directed plays and acted a variety of roles for the Tsukiji Little Theatre.

[24] Reproduced in *zenshū*, IX, p. 256.

money spent on constructing the elaborate theatre building would have been better spent in training the actors for a long period, several years if necessary. Second, the choice of plays in such careless translations and productions was a bad one for the purpose of building up an audience, and, third, he thought that the best way to attract an audience would be to put on plays they could understand. Such plays might well be Japanese, Kishida indicated; he recognized that it might prove most practical for the company to stage only foreign plays, but this should be a policy arrived at by experience and not merely decided on beforehand. He later wrote that he found Osanai personally pretentious and dogmatic. Artists must learn how to look at life, Kishida said, for the theatre is not a "hothouse for humans."[25]

Kishida was critical of the opening production, and he was far more so of the second, *Les Loups* (*The Wolves*) by Romain Rolland, directed by Hijikata.[26] He found it completely discouraging. He wrote[27] that even if Osanai were granted his principles he failed to live up to them. Some critics, Kishida wrote, thought that Osanai must have chosen the play because actresses were not necessary and his were bad. Kishida did not deign to discuss the production on this level, but he objected strongly to Osanai's choice of an unstageworthy play from which neither the company nor the audience could learn anything.[28] In style, he continued,

[25] *zenshū*, IX, p. 265.

[26] *The Wolves*, written in 1898, is a play about the French revolution in which an aristocrat who has joined the common people is accused of being a spy for the aristocracy. The man who hates him most finds that the charge is false and tries to defend him, but mob rule overtakes them both. The play is a kind of poster with little individual character development but a strong and very human message. Rolland was basically a novelist, not a playwright, but he told translator Barrett H. Clark that he considered this play the most theatrically effective of all he had written.

[27] See *zenshū*, IX, p. 260.

[28] Kishida seems a bit hard on Rolland, whose play does have a certain force. Still, if we compare it with a play on a slightly similar subject, Shaw's *Devil's Disciple*, written two years before, in 1896,

Rolland's work had nothing whatsoever in common with the three one-act plays previously presented; thus the actors who had worked on the earlier production were given no continuity in their training. No director with any convictions about the real nature of modern drama could choose authors who wrote so differently as Chekhov and Rolland. The real fault, Kishida concluded, lay in the fact that Osanai based his decision to produce the play not on artistic but on political grounds. Osanai had stated as his third principle that he was interested in "the people," and undoubtedly he had chosen the play because Rolland had a reputation for being interested "in the people."[29] Osanai not only was pretentious enough to think that he could make *any* play succeed but he was doing a disservice to his company and to the future of the New Theatre in Japan.

Osanai had indeed set himself up as a personage of unique distinction. "I am not merely a stage director. I wish to make use of my whole personality in my work for the theatre. I am an artist. I also feel myself a philosopher and a social scientist. At the same time I am also a leader of the people and a revolutionary . . . ," he wrote in March 1924.[30] Many were willing to forgive him the grandiose attitude that was, in any case, probably necessary to carry him through all his artistic and spiritual difficulties. Kishida, however, would

---

it is clear that the English writer has been able to introduce real characters to serve as the exponents of his ideas. In terms of the drama created in Europe by 1925, Kishida's judgment seems basically correct.

[29] Rolland wrote a famous series of essays that were collected and published in English as *The People's Theatre* in 1918. In them he investigates the kinds of theatre that might appeal to a mass audience and finds elements of melodrama, historical drama, and pageants that can be taken as models for a new dramaturgy. Although his criticism of French drama is often excellent (of Rostand, for example, Rolland writes that "his success is the rhetoric of life . . ."), many of his remarks betray a somewhat patrician attitude toward his potential mass audience.

[30] Osanai, *engekiron*, II, p. 47.

not grant him this indulgence, for he felt that the New Theatre movement was more important than Osanai.

Osanai was equally unforgiving, as he showed when in March of 1926 he produced his first Japanese play, *The Hermit* by Tsubouchi Shōyō. Before the selection of the play, the staff of the Tsukiji Little Theatre took a poll of its audiences to see which Japanese dramatists were of most interest to them. The results showed that Kishida was far preferred to any other author: he stood ahead of Mushakōji, Tanizaki, Yamamoto, and several others. Tsubouchi Shōyō's name had not figured in the results at all, yet Osanai chose his play and, in doing so, seemed to turn his back conclusively on his colleagues and former friends on the staff of *New Currents of Drama*.

Concerning the production of *The Hermit*, Osanai wrote that avoiding *kabuki* and *shimpa* mannerisms had proved the greatest challenge presented to his actors.[31] He was asked in an interview why he had produced a play with less appeal to a young audience than many other possible choices would have had, but he avoided the issue by saying that his interviewer was raising a literary, not a theatrical, question. "The reason for a theatrical production," he concluded, "is not to explain the contents of a play. If that's what you want, read it at home!"[32]

The Hermit is more than a curiosity; in many ways it was a good choice. But by turning away from the best of the young dramatists, Osanai deprived them of the chance to learn the skills of their own profession by seeing their work performed on the stage. He did later stage several plays by Japanese writers, among them Mushakōji, Fujimori Seikichi, and Akita Ujaku. But he never considered staging a work by Kishida. Many later commentators on the period have expressed their regret that Osanai and Kishida were never able to work together. Perhaps, had Osanai lived longer, the two might have reached some kind of accord, but Osanai

[31] *Ibid.*, p. 209.   [32] *Ibid.*, p. 275.

died two years after his production of *The Hermit*. Iwata has suggested that if Kishida had joined with Osanai and Hijikata upon his return to Japan, rather than remaining with Yamamoto Yūzo and his colleagues, he would have avoided too literary an emphasis in his works and learned much about the practical problems of the theatre; at the same time Osanai and the others at the Tsukiji Little Theatre would have avoided many mistakes. The whole history of the movement might have been different, he thought, since the possibility of their working together was by no means a remote one.[33] Kon Hidemi, however, saw little chance of any *rapprochement*, since Hijikata and Osanai were firmly committed to their own styles of directing and their views on the nature of the theatre were too far from Kishida's.[34] In any case, the failure of the two men to cooperate seriously hampered the creation of a modern Japanese drama.

This brief clash between Kishida and Osanai suggests many aspects of the movement that were in conflict, elements which were to continue to plague the New Theatre movement in the latter part of the 1920s. It was into this theatrical world, with all its limitations, that Kishida came to work.

THE ACTORS

All sources agree that the actors were poor. Even in the case of Osanai's company, far and away the best group producing modern plays, their training was not adequate. Most of them had never been abroad. This was not merely a question of their seeing foreign actors perform but of gaining familiarity with the conventions of European acting necessary to bring to life on the stage dialogue unrelieved by the spectacle of the traditional Japanese theatre. From his

[33] See Iwata Toyoo, *shingeki to watakushi* (Tokyo, 1956), p. 103.

[34] Kon Hidemi, "moraristo Kishida Kunio," *Bungei*, May 1954, p. 34.

71

experience with the Free Theatre, Osanai had learned that professional actors (those trained in *kabuki* and *shimpa* companies) were so wedded to their own stylized techniques that they were not able to perform either in the naturalistic fashion demanded by Osanai or in the Expressionist style favored by Hijikata.[35] Osanai therefore chose many young amateurs to participate in the Tsukiji Little Theatre. (To them he added, of course, a small group of older and more experienced actors with whom he had worked before.) Many of these young people were well educated, but their talents did not necessarily match their background and their enthusiasm. Iwata Toyoo, commenting on the performances at the Tsukiji Little Theatre, wrote that "my biggest disappointment was the clumsy performance given by most actors. Maruyama Sadao [later a famous actor in the proletarian theatre] floundered around like a politician making a speech, and Takizawa Osamu [another

[35] A recent description of postwar *shingeki* acting by a western theatre scholar shows how deep these traditions remain:

> The gulf between the Japanese theatre and its western counterpart embraces more than different social standards and unfamiliar subject-matter. They are two forms built on different aesthetic foundations, and divided by the actor's concept of his relation to the role. The extrovert and presentational style cultivated for centuries in Japan cannot be easily reconciled with plays written for actors trained in a different mode and expected to identify themselves psychologically with their roles. This is the most serious difficulty that the Japanese actor has to face. He is forced, in effect, to relearn the fundamentals of his trade. Japanese actors, on the whole, are more secure in western plays to which the traditional presentational methods can be applied. They are conspicuously successful in the "epic" style, cultivated by Brecht and others, which comes close to, and indeed borrowed from, their own traditions. The "alienation effect" demanded by Brecht from his characters is founded on the premises of presentational acting. But the wholly naturalistic style continues to elude them, with results sometimes disastrous to the play. In Brecht, the [Japanese] actor is moving in a world he knows. (Peter Arnott, *The Theatres of Japan* [London, 1969], p. 228.)

well-known actor who played with leftist troupes before the war] gave the impression of the youth who had surrendered his soul to literature."[36] The only actor who gave Iwata any sense of humanity and simplicity was Tomoda Kyōsuke, generally conceded to be the best performer in Osanai's company. Iwata and Kishida both admired him greatly and later collaborated closely with him.

Tomoda himself had many troubles indicative of the problems faced by the troupe. Despite his intelligence, he had difficulty in memorizing his lines. He defended himself by saying that he could not memorize what he did not understand.[37] Often the translations were at fault, because the translators had rendered into unidiomatic or even meaningless Japanese a text that they did not fully understand themselves. Even when the translation was acceptable, the unfamiliarity of the ideas expressed confused the actors. Iwata writes that he was surprised to see even Tomoda swallowing lines in a translation Iwata himself had made, so he coached him, and the others, until they understood every nuance of the text.[38]

The custom of playing foreign plays and reciting dialogue in the often unnatural rhythm of translated Japanese became a part of the accepted acting style. Osanai had hoped that the constant repetition of good foreign plays would prepare his actors to deal with Japanese texts, but in fact they were afraid of them. Shimomura quotes Tomoda as saying that when he starred in Osanai's production of Mushakōji's *Aiyoku (Desire)* in 1926, he was nervous, since "it was the first time I had worn Japanese clothing on the stage . . . I was very uneasy as it was my first Japanese play. . . ."[39]

[36] Iwata, *Shingeki*, p. 101.

[37] For an amusing description of Tomoda's troubles, see Toita, *Hitobito*, pp. 165-168. At one point Tomoda's wife Tamura Akiko, also an actress in Osanai's company, had to hide behind the scenery to prompt him.

[38] Iwata, *Shingeki*, pp. 118-119.

[39] Quoted in Shimomura, *Shingeki*, p. 65.

73

The Theatre Companies

Several companies resumed activities after the earthquake. The best of them was the Tsukiji Little Theatre. Osanai's troupe worked under optimum conditions for the New Theatre movement in Japan. All the other companies were composed largely of amateurs, untrained and poorly financed. Yet even Osanai's company had little professional experience: Kubota Mantarō remarked that the average age of most of the company was twenty-two or twenty-three. The few older members seemed almost venerable to these youngsters, yet even they were only in their thirties or forties.[40] Iwata mentioned that most of the staff received so little pay that they had to accept money from their parents in order to live. Sometimes a troupe had a patron who, like Hijikata, would underwrite a certain portion of its activities; otherwise, since the admission fees covered scarcely any of the expenses, the members worked, as Iwata put it, "for the pride and glory of it."[41]

Kubota considered that the greatest hindrance to the proper development of drama troupes in Japan at this time was the lack of permanent theatres, although again Osanai was the exception, since he had his own stage and permanent equipment. Other troupes had to engage rehearsal space and a theatre to present their productions.[42]

Even at the Tsukiji Little Theatre, the limited audiences available for the plays meant that productions were usually mounted for only a few performances, usually between three and ten. Successful plays might be repeated later in a season, but probably not more than two thousand persons ever saw any given production. The actors and technicians

[40] Kubota Mantarō, "Hitotsu no kaizō," *Kubota Mantarō zenshū*, XIII, p. 65.

[41] Iwata, *Shingeki*, p. 87.

[42] Often other troupes rented Osanai's theatre, bringing him some extra income. Otherwise the small companies used a variety of small halls and theatres available in Tokyo.

were exhausted by a schedule which called for three or four new plays each month.

During its brief existence the Tsukiji Little Theatre remained the focal point for the New Theatre movement, but after the sudden death of Osanai in 1928, shortly after his return from Soviet Russia, Aoyama and Hijikata, the two remaining directors, split up the company. Hijikata's early interest in German Expressionistic and Soviet plays led him to begin a small new company, the Shin Tsukiji Gekidan (New Tsukiji Theatre Troupe) in order to stage leftist and outright Marxist plays. Aoyama was determined to uphold Osanai's early advocacy of an artistic theatre. He gathered together what remained of the company into a group he called the Gekidan Tsukiji Shōgekijō (The Tsukiji Little Theatre Company). With the artistic resources of Osanai's original troupe now split in half, standards sank even lower. By 1929 there were half a dozen small artistic theatres in Tokyo, all with different principles, credos, and manifestos, struggling to win the support of the same limited audience.

THE AUDIENCE

Theatregoers are a rather mysterious group at any time, in any country, whose identity baffles writers, producers, directors, and actors. Eric Bentley indicated their crucial importance to any theatre movement when he wrote that "drama is a social art. Although it does not require the support of the masses or of any large class, it does require a tradition that lives in some group homogeneous enough to make a crowd in the theatre."[43] Osanai insisted that his theatre was "for the people." And his audience was to have an active function in his work. "The spectators to our theatre will not come, as they did before to other theatres, merely with the idea of being amused. For we are certainly not going to give them that old kind of entertainment. They must look at our plays as students. We believe they must

[43] Bentley, *Thinker*, p. 189.

75

work right along with us. . . ."[44] Osanai's attitude was no doubt admirable for its singleness of conviction but was scarcely calculated to draw the kind of worldly or cultivated audience (assuming that it even existed) that would most have enjoyed his productions. Osanai's attitude may have been the result of his wishing to please Hijikata, his major source of financial support, but in any case, by demanding an audience of serious students of the theatre, he was limiting himself to a small, intellectually curious, but very young clientele.

Susukida Kenji, another of Osanai's principal actors, stated that "the regular audience we could count on for a given production was at the most fifteen hundred, eighty per cent of whom were intellectually inclined students."[45] The leftist theatres had made some attempts to attract a working-class audience, but by the time the leftist troupes gained their momentum in the late 1920s, Shimomura reminds us, they lost that audience and gained an intellectual one. Toita records that Osanai was annoyed when Kikuchi Kan, challenging his remarks about a theatre "for the people," asked him if he didn't really believe that a theatre audience is basically bourgeois.[46]

What were the interests of this limited audience? Learning and culture no doubt, not merely entertainment. Tsumo

[44] *Osanai engekiron*, II, p. 43. A letter by Chekhov to his director Nemirovich-Danchenko, written in 1903, seems to put the whole matter of "the people" into better perspective. "*A propos* of the popular theatre and popular literature," he wrote, "all that is foolishness, sugar candy for the people. You must not lower Gogol to the people, but raise the people to the level of Gogol" (quoted in Cole, *Playwrights*, p. 29). Osanai was apparently of a more divided mind.

[45] Quoted in Shimomura, *Shingeki*, p. 66. Numbers do not tell everything in themselves. Le Vieux Colombier was about the size of the Tsukiji Little Theatre, and Copeau, like Osanai, felt that he had a permanent and devoted clientele of no more than fifteen hundred. Yet Copeau soon raised his audience to about six thousand by the quality of his productions. (For details on Copeau and his audiences, see Kurtz, *Copeau*, p. 115.)

[46] See Toita, *Hitobito*, p. 111.

Kaitarō wrote that one issue of the Tsukiji Little Theatre program carried "the self-congratulatory comment of one member of the audience: 'at long last we have accustomed ourselves to sitting and watching a play in silence.' "[47] Respectful silence, never a habit at *kabuki*, may have signified awe before art, but it may as well have been the signal of a lack of comprehension. Iwata's remarks on a 1927 production of Jules Romains' *Dr. Knock* are most revealing concerning the over-reverent attitude of the audience towards the New Theatre.

I was delighted that the audience laughed in a genuine and spontaneous way. A group of *geisha* from Shinbashi came to see the play. During the very humorous scene in Knock's office, one young *geisha* let out a shriek of laughter as if she were going to faint and kept laughing and laughing. I was extremely grateful for this reaction. The intelligentsia audiences were embarrassed, wondering whether or not to laugh and how they should react.[48]

The audiences did not seek pleasure in their theatregoing in either the superficial or the profound sense. The result was that the natural relationship existing in Europe between artist and spectator was distorted in Japan, so that the development of the relationship was stunted.

Playwrights and their Plays

Most of the talented young playwrights were associated with *New Currents of Drama*, with the exception of the young leftist writers. Some of them had an occasional play staged by some small semi-professional theatre company in Tokyo, but their reputations had been earned through the printed versions of their plays. Unlike some earlier writers, these younger men were no longer content to remain in

---

[47] Quoted in *Concerned Theatre Japan*, Introductory Issue, October 1969, p. 9.

[48] Iwata, *Shingeki*, p. 85.

print. Yet, with Osanai's decision, the printed play remained the only possibility.

New Currents of Drama was forced to cease publication in 1927. The combination of scholarly articles and original play texts was not only expensive to assemble but rather too rarefied to attract the necessary readers. The years of its publication marked the highest success obtained by the literary playwrights. Now other specialized magazines appeared that gave the playwrights an additional chance for a career in print. Several were edited by Kishida himself and will be discussed below. In addition to the specialized magazines, plays were published in *The Central Review*, the rival *Kaizō* (*Reconstruction*), *Josei* (*Woman*), a woman's magazine with good intellectual and literary material, and in *Bungei Jidai* (*Literary Age*), a magazine established in 1924 by Kawabata Yasunari, Yokomitsu Riichi, and others to provide a forum for the literary avant-garde in opposition to the increasingly popular proletarian writing. During the three years of the existence of *Literary Age*, it published a variety of plays, including the works of Kishida. *Bungei Shunjū* (*Literary Annals*) was begun in 1923 by Kikuchi Kan and published some plays by contemporary writers of varying political persuasions. Much of Kishida's work first appeared here. Still, a career on the page was a career by default.

This, then, was the theatrical world Kishida faced: no good theatrical companies to produce his work; conflicting theories of dramaturgy; a small and uninformed audience. Altogether, playwrighting did not seem a compelling career, but Kishida was determined to persevere in the face of difficulties to lift the level of literary dramatic art in Japan.

CHAPTER IV

Kishida as a Man of the Theatre

AT THE TIME of the opening of the Tsukiji Little Theatre, Kishida had come to realize that the level of the theatre in Japan was far below anything he had seen in Europe; indeed, only by taking a charitable view of the situation could he say that a New Theatre existed at all. Kishida's European experience had given him not only very high standards but the strong conviction that the theatre was a social as well as a literary art. He considered himself a playwright, and since he refused to exist only on paper as did many of his compatriots, he involved himself in a variety of activities in an effort to impart his own ideas to the theatre and to lift the standards of the movement.

In many ways, Kishida's knowledge of the European accomplishment was his professional downfall. In his eagerness to see his plays performed on the stage and acting standards changed and improved, he found himself constantly compromising his own personal standards. He did in fact succeed in raising the standards of production in Japan, but at great cost to his own personal art. Yet his convictions gave him no other choice, for he thought that the theatre must establish a communication among author, actor, and audience or it would be nothing at all.

THE CRITIC

Kishida wrote a great deal of dramatic criticism. Soon after he returned from France, the forum of *New Currents of Drama* was opened to him. The magazine ceased publication in 1927, but by that time he was writing articles not only for specialist magazines but for the most important general intellectual magazines in Japan, *The Central Review, Reconstruction, Literary Annals* (of which he became a contributing editor), and, after its establishment in 1934, *Bungakkai (Literary World)*. In addition, he was a frequent contributor to the Asahi and Yomiuri newspapers.

Kishida's critical and theoretical writings on the theatre were often collected and edited for publication in separate volumes. He never, however, wrote any long or systematic book on the theatre,[1] although two collections of his essays entitled *Engeki no honshitsu (The Essence of Drama)*, first published in 1940, and *Engeki ippan kōwa (General Talks on the Theatre)*, first published in 1951, have served later students as textbooks. These books provide a good analysis of the basic principles of the modern European theatre. But a student of the history of this period of the New Theatre movement is less likely to turn to these general books than to the many articles Kishida published between 1925 and 1939. Examined carefully, these occasional pieces provide a good indication both of the state of the theatre and of Kishida's ideas for its improvement. He was a witty and precise writer, and his comments retain their interest even though the specific matters he discussed have since changed.

Kishida's early critical writing after his return from France was largely devoted to an attempt to define the possibilities of the modern theatre in Japanese terms. He had strong feelings that the level and direction of the modern theatre in Japan were not based on any adequate understanding of its possibilities. He struck this note in one of his first essays written after his return, "Mikansei na gendai geki" ("The Incomplete Modern Theatre"), published in 1925.

[1] Kishida himself wrote in 1936 that "I have been looking through my various notes, impressions, and critiques concerning the theatre, but the difficulty in arranging them in any systematic way is due to the fact that I have not written things out in any scholarly fashion. Indeed most of what I have written out has been at the request of others. . . ." (*zenshū*, IX, p. 326.)

We use the phrases "new drama movement," and "modern drama movement." The terms must be clearly differentiated, of course. And are they even applicable to the situation in Japan?

There is no question of Japan's being in any position to advertise the birth of a Chekhov, a Strindberg, a Porto-Riche, or a Shaw. Japan has not yet created an artistic atmosphere conducive to the rise of a modern drama. To be more specific, the Japanese at this time have no clear idea as to what might replace older drama in satisfying their artistic needs.

Both actors and playwrights have abandoned the old and well-developed traditions of beauty in the traditional Japanese theatre. And in their haste to adopt from the modern European drama only its conceptual aspects, they have overlooked its essence as well. Thus we have an arid and tasteless modern drama in Japan.

What the New Theatre movement must do, rather than spending its time defying the traditions of *kabuki* and *shimpa*, is to make itself a full-fledged copy of western theatre. If you don't care for the word "copy," then let us say "correct understanding, accurate absorption." In other words, we must look at western plays (and I am not speaking of clumsy translations) and try to create in Japan what we find enjoyable in them—we must write them, act them, listen to them. . . . I would not deny, of course, that a viable modern drama could evolve from the traditions of *kabuki*. Yet in recent decades Japanese culture as a whole has been influenced by a liking for things occidental . . . and so it is not unnatural that the development of modern drama in Japan should receive valuable inspiration from western theatre.[2]

Kishida continued to stress the relation of the understanding of the real nature and accomplishments of the European example to future Japanese theatrical experiments. He wrote, again in 1925, as follows:

[2] *zenshū*, VIII, pp. 64-65.

What we call our modern theatre in fact lacks a real historical necessity for being. This is because of the rather diluted character of our own modern literary movement. ... Modern western theatre was born out of a real necessity. Japanese modern theatre was born from the accidental influence of the western theatre. The modern theatre in the west could grow on land already tilled by Shakespeare, Molière, Racine, and Schiller. Japanese modern drama, on the other hand, had to be transplanted from fields plowed by Chikamatsu, Nanboku, and Mokuami;[3] handled carelessly, the seedlings may wither, because Chikamatsu, Nanboku, and Mokuami did not prepare the ground to receive any Ibsen, Chekhov, or Maeterlinck. Even if the seedlings don't wither, I suspect their flowers will not be very fragrant, and their fruits will have little juice.

What can be done about the situation? Can we import the soil that Shakespeare, Molière, and Schiller prepared? Or, instead of the soil itself, is there some kind of fertilizer which we can apply? I realize that my comparison is far-fetched, but this soil is the very tradition of western theatre. The fertilizer is a deepened understanding of modern life. It is a great mistake to think that knowing Chekhov's rules, the spirit of Maeterlinck, and so on, constitutes the study of modern drama . . . in fact, what points are there in common between Ibsen and Shakespeare? As a playwright, what has Ibsen learned from Shakespeare? What makes Shakespeare's plays so attractive? What relation has this fact to the essence of the drama? When you can start asking questions like these, you are likely to have reached a more fundamental understanding of western drama. Then it becomes instructive to reflect on the question of why Shakespeare has become a classic dramatist and why Ibsen is a great modern play-

[3] Chikamatsu Monzaemon (1653-1724), Tsuruya Nanboku (1755-1829), and Kawatake Mokuami (1816-1893) were three of the most illustrious *kabuki* playwrights.

wright. You will soon see that what we call our own modern drama is lacking any proper foundation.[4]

Kishida felt that the dilemma of the modern drama in Japan stemmed from the fact that it must base itself on a set of foreign principles. Although the principles provided a practical means for creating a drama close to contemporary life, they were so inadequately understood among theatre professionals that artistic success was impossible.

Yet if the first task of the New Theatre movement was to direct itself toward learning the fundamentals of the western theatre, what value was there in producing Japanese plays? In opposition to Osanai, Kishida thought that the movement could not succeed unless it became a thoroughly Japanese phenomenon. Only then could the talents of directors, authors, and actors combine to produce artistic results. He was convinced that the best and most natural way to create such a drama in Japan was to permit writers to compose plays for stage presentation while learning about western theatre from seeing adequate productions of European plays in translation. Kishida recognized the difficulties in carrying out such a scheme. Foreign plays could help the Japanese dramatists only if they were well translated and correctly produced.

To transpose the words themselves from one language to another is one thing. When it comes to the various problems involved in staging a foreign play, the most important element remains the impersonation of the characters by the actors. No matter how a Japanese may disguise himself, he will not look like a westerner. In his movements and his expressions he may try to imitate a westerner, but he will rarely succeed. To a certain extent, unless the actor's appearance, movements, and expression are "translated" into Japanese terms, their original meanings will be lost to us.

4 *zenshū*, VIII, p. 210.

To take an obvious example, suppose a woman is discussing her unfortunate personal situation. A western woman would certainly never smile; a Japanese woman is likely to. In presenting a translated play, how should this be handled? A smile become an "adaptation," no longer a "translation." Such questions must be raised in staging every scene . . . when somebody says, "I don't quite understand what it is all about, so let's leave it this way," and then flaunts the result as being "the original" is guilty of a crime which ought to be punishable by death![5]

Granted the interdependence of playwriting, acting, and directing, where should a beginning be made? Kishida seems to emphasize first one element, then another in his various essays. For example, in 1932 he wrote:

If the New Theatre movement in Japan is to find a means to rally in the future, a revolution in acting methods will be necessary. Such a revolution might be accomplished by a single person of genius. Or it might come about through the sincere efforts of a group. In any case it is the actors who, through the use of their own talents, observations, and imaginations, must find for us a means to express on the stage, and with a greater liberality than they have exhibited so far, a genuine impression of modern life. If the actor cannot exert this kind of effort, then the techniques of the director will not succeed, and indeed the writer may err in permitting his work to be staged.[6]

In the previous year he had written an essay about the necessary interdependence required between writers and actors in order to lift the standards of theatrical production to a creditable level.

Actors in present-day Japan, rather than looking around to find the kind of Japanese play that suits them perfectly, should as a part of their training perform in as many

[5] *Ibid.*, p. 214.　　　　　　　[6] *Ibid.*, p. 244.

contemporary works by Japanese authors as they can. Writers, for their part, must not give up on the actors but rather choose some objective which they as writers wish to achieve and then give these actors plays written as effectively as possible for these purposes.[7]

THE ACTOR IN THE MODERN THEATRE

Kishida first came to an understanding of the important role of the actor in any total theatrical accomplishment during his stay in France. In a memoir he wrote concerning his early career, he described what, as an author, he thought would constitute an ideal relationship between author and actor.

To an extraordinary degree, literary men in France who wish to take up playwriting always have among their friends suitable actors. When a writer makes a plan for his play, he discusses it with them, and when he begins to write, he will often read it to them, one act at a time, in order to have their criticism and advice. He will often rewrite what he has written. Sometimes he will receive help even to the point of collaboration, and when the time finally comes for a stage presentation, there will be additional revisions and polishing during rehearsals.

Of course a beginning writer will not have anyone so appropriate with whom to discuss his play. When something he wrote is suddenly put on the stage, he must make his requests of those actors in whose hands the play has been placed. The producer and the actors may also make demands on him as well.

Does this method work? To a certain extent, the writer trusts the producer and the actors; certainly in terms of the theatre he respects them as professionals and he knows that as professionals they will not infringe on any aspect of his work that compromises his own artistic individual-

[7] *Ibid.*, p. 227.

ity. . . . I believe my greatest discovery [in France] was this effort made to put a play in its best light for the mutual benefit of everyone.[8]

Kishida's account of selfless cooperation was certainly not typical of French commercial theatre, and his statement no doubt reflects his observations on the extraordinary efforts made by Jacques Copeau to serve his authors. Maurice Kurtz writes,

> Georges Duhamel, distinguished novelist and the troupe's occasional prompter, exhibited what he had learned in playwriting after living in such intimacy with Le Vieux Colombier. He described this attachment in musical terms: a composer creates a harp concerto because there is a harpist he has in mind to play it. "The Vieux Colombier is our instrument." Copeau asked for no better proof of his theatre's influence among writers who had essentially not been dramatists.[9]

Copeau, himself a great actor, was especially anxious to help writers who wished to write for the theatre to realize their ideas in theatrically effective terms.[10]
Kishida returned to Japan to find not only that were the actors unprepared to work properly with authors for an artistic result but that they were generally ignorant of even

[8] *zenshū*, IX, p. 187.   [9] Kurtz, *Copeau*, p. 101.
[10] Kurtz describes how Copeau aided the novelist René Benjamin in the composition of his play *Il faut que chacun soit à sa place*. Of the experience, Benjamin later wrote, "It seemed to me I was entering into convalescence, I breathed, I became free. For the first time, a doctor was soothing me with a kind soul which his sensitivity hid beneath a moody exterior. I found—oh novelty in my literary life!— in this exciting but slippery métier called the theatre, a real man who, with all his heart, tried to make me profit from the experiences of his intelligence. I had a *master*. . . . When I left him, almost nothing remained of a play over which I had been yawning for a year. But I left with the main thing: the happy wish to write one, with the same characters, to whom he had given back their real selves. . . ." (Kurtz, *Copeau*, p. 163.)

the rudiments of their own craft. One comment in his memoir is rather vivid.

Just at the time when the Tsukiji Little Theatre was going to open, a young Frenchman whom I had gotten to know in Paris came on a visit to Japan. He stayed with me for a short time while looking for lodgings. I thought I might take him to see [Osanai's opening production] Mazaud's *La Folle Journée*. He said that he would like to read the text in French beforehand. Unfortunately I did not have a copy. I did know that the play had been staged at Le Vieux Colombier, but for some reason or other, I had missed seeing it. I finally managed to borrow a copy in French and thought to read it myself as well. I had my friend read the text to me aloud. Strange as it may seem, listening to the voice of this young Frenchman, who was of course an amateur, gave me the impression that I was in France and seeing the play myself. I was able to immerse myself in the style and *esprit* of Mazaud's psychological lyricism. Here is where Japanese actors are at a terrible disadvantage. And what kind of translation could be made of such a play? Could the fine nuances of such a work possibly be captured?[11]

It was easy enough for a man of Kishida's talents and experience in Europe to evaluate what he saw in Japan. The important question for him was how to develop better actors. One obvious possibility was to train *kabuki* actors in the new styles. (As we have seen, Osanai himself had experimented with this method earlier in his career.) In an essay written in 1929, Kishida explained why this was impossible.

What abilities do *kabuki* actors lack to play modern drama? The answer is very simple indeed. They do not know anything at all about modern life! . . . It is their very mode of existence that restricts their artistic ex-

[11] *zenshū*, IX, p. 198.

perience and limits their sphere of aesthetic accomplishment. Their style of living is completely in opposition to the temper of modern life.

I am not speaking here on the superficial level of daily activities. Rather I refer to the traditional system originating from their very style of life. They have too many students, who receive an allowance from the theatre and who only act as servants. Even though these students receive an allowance, they rarely make an appearance on the stage. . . . Next is the continuance of the "pedigree," in effect a class system that causes continual difficulties in selecting casts and plays. The students of the most powerful actors are considered as "young noblemen," and regardless of their talent, they receive a high position in the company and play the good roles. The others are blocked from working towards any success of their own. This feudalistic legacy provides a fatal barrier as far as maintaining any real contact with any modern public.[12]

Kishida found that most actors in the New Theatre movement were still too much influenced by older Japanese acting styles quite inappropriate to the plays they were performing. For the playwright, theatrical success involved compromise: he was forced to write the kind of scenes the actors could play. For Kishida, the possible range of characters these actors could create was far too limited.

We require actors who lead the kind of lives we lead; in other words, whose conceptualizations, interests, and perceptions are the same as ours. Thus it is essential that they receive the same education that we have. From a playwright's point of view, if the characters we create are from the *intelligentsia*; we have every reason to ask if any actors today can portray this kind of characteristically modern personality. The greatest fault an actor can have is to lack the capacity to understand the role he is playing.

[12] *Ibid.*, VIII, p. 238.

Perhaps an actor does not need this ability to portray a Saigō Takamori or a General Nogi.[13] But when it comes to playing a company employee with a modern education, or his wife, it is unfortunate indeed if no actors or actresses can bring out these special characteristics inherent in the characters they are playing.

Is it a question of temperament? Of character? Fine. Then we need to have actors with proper temperament and character. . . .[14] (1926)

Progress in any art is slow, slower than an anxious playwright might have liked. Throughout his career, Kishida was to plead with New Theatre actors to take cognizance of their professional shortcomings. In 1926, this theme was already firmly expressed in his writing.

Although there has been an improvement in the fortunes of the New Theatre since the Tokyo earthquake, I do not feel that any proper progress has been made. The movement has continued but not progressed. It can be said, I suppose, that the progress possible in only two or three years need not be apparent to the spectators; but frankly, I see no indication that progress is even desired by the performers themselves.

I do not believe that the perfection of stage technique depends on the firm economic base of the theatre troupe involved. Nor do I feel that it depends on the determined enthusiasm of a few key people. It certainly does not depend on the contents of a particular play or on the methods of one director. Just as a literary movement in any period depends on the appearance of a writer of great genius, so only the appearance of an actor of real talent

[13] Saigō Takamori (1827-1877) and Nogi Maresuke (1849-1912) were two heroic figures in Meiji history; Kishida no doubt meant that actors could represent them on the stage using the same kind of clichés often employed to represent a Lincoln or Washington on the American stage.

[14] *zenshū*, VIII, pp. 217-218.

(or, so as not to be misunderstood, let me say *several* actors) can produce that "new appeal" necessary to inspire real progress. Talent, however, is not all that an actor needs; he needs the mastery that permits him to manifest his talent. If he does not subject himself to the proper training, those talents will dry up.

Why don't the actors today have proper stage voices? Why is it that they walk so badly on the stage? Why do they "listen" on the stage in such a negligent fashion? Why do the lines they deliver have no flavor? Why have they no sense of how to compose themselves on the stage? Why have they no sense of poetry? And of movement? Why? . . . this is too wearisome a list to compile: why don't they know *anything*?[15]

As a playwright, Kishida found little inspiration in the work of actors of such limited abilities.

[As a means of showing young writers] what the New Theatre can be, let me say plainly that the theatrical appeal of the New Theatre is less than that of an amateur company in Europe. To those of us who have some sense of what a play is, the New Theatre brings no fresh inspiration whatsoever. . . .

It is not because nobody can write new plays that we have a famine these days: it is because there are no good actors to write them for! In any country, at any period, have writers tried to create plays for the theatre under such conditions as these?[16] (1931)

In his long 1935 essay "Engekiron no ippōkō" ("One Direction for Dramatic Theory") Kishida came closest to defining what was for him the work of the actor in the composite art of the theatre.

An actor . . . , through his artistic skill, impersonates a character, lives the character's life, and shows it to us.

[15] *Ibid.,* p. 226.   [16] *Ibid.,* pp. 227-228.

... This life can be in the form of a plot created beforehand; or, in some cases, the actor can improvise a story directly on the stage. In either case, his skill consists of his use of words and movements. These skills, along with his use of costume and makeup, provide impressions, both in terms of the senses and of the psychology of the spectators, that form the true, inner movement of the drama.[17]

It was precisely the lack of ability to use these special skills of words and movements that, for Kishida, hindered theatrical development. A year earlier, for example, he had written concerning the way in which Japanese actors delivered their lines. Some actors claimed that movement on the stage was a more important part of their craft than their skill in delivering lines. He took pains to remind them that a balance was necessary.

"Training in movement" may be important, but this can be accomplished after the first essential "training in speaking" has been achieved on a basic level. Almost any "movement" that is isolated from the sense impressions aroused by the lines of the play will not contribute any efficacious result. The New Theatre actors have ignored the proper order of things . . . from the beginning, the movement never adopted any plan to provide any training in speaking, and indeed, the means were lacking to carry it out. Thus actors find that memorizing stage dialogue is an almost impossible task.[18] (1934)

The problems were compounded when Japanese actors played Europeans:

As I have often said, we tend to place too much importance on the "foreignness" of a western play and so neglect its theatrical aspects. As a result the audience only experiences its foreign aspects. Especially in translated plays, the actors work all too diligently to be westerners,

[17] *Ibid.*, pp. 121-122.   [18] *Ibid.*, p. 202.

and the translated text is usually written in a dialogue that does not sound like Japanese.[19] (1934)

Kishida insisted that beauty could not come from mere imitation. No mere copy of reality, especially under such circumstances, could produce art. His statement in the 1935 essay is unequivocal. "Is the theatre an 'imitation?' While it may show this quality in its primitive form, imitation is by no means an art. Unless some kind of beauty is created from the progress of the life we see on the stage, then it is hard to use the word artistic to describe what we see."[20]

For Kishida much of what plagued the New Theatre movement in all aspects of its endeavors arose from the desire to imitate a foreign form rather than to study the form and to take from it a sense of purpose and a sense of beauty that could then be recreated in Japanese terms. For the actors, such a process involved a kind of discipline and training that they seemed unwilling or unable to undergo.

During the 1930s, Kishida did note an improvement in the performances of certain actors and actresses, whom he was quick to single out for praise. Yet on the whole he found himself in a continuing state of disappointment. In 1934 he wrote:

> Our Modern Theatre movement has never achieved its aims, despite some glamorous episodes. No real new drama has been born from *kabuki* and *shimpa*. Doubtless there are many reasons connected with the structure of our society that may be involved. Still I come back to the fact that no actors of real talent have appeared. The New Theatre movement, more than any other endeavor, needed the appearance of people equipped with modern education, modern perceptions, and personal charm. For an actor, questions of technique come after these qualities. Yet there seems no lure strong enough to attract such people into the movement. . . . Judgments on the plays

[19] *Ibid.*, p. 205.　　　　[20] *Ibid.*, p. 122.

themselves must be made on the basis of this problem. The people who want to be professional actors have their weak points, and those who direct them do not always use their best efforts to hide those failings. . . . First of all, the actors are too young. Secondly, there is too much *shita-machi* about them. While this *shita-machi* quality may be appropriate for some plays, it is not suitable for most modern dramas.[21]

Working with these actors was, for Kishida, a compromise. He found a gradual improvement in some of them that enabled him to raise his own standards, but generally his critical position remained constant throughout the period. For him the actor—the human magnetism of the actor—stood at the center of the theatre's appeal; without good actors, the chief means of creating beauty on the stage was missing.

THE NEED TO DEVELOP A CULTIVATED AUDIENCE

Throughout his career, Kishida felt that a potentially larger and more satisfactory public existed, if only it could be located and encouraged to attend and participate actively in the theatre as a discerning and critical element. Kishida's public, like the theatregoing public in Europe and America, was mainly anonymous, despite its small size. Something of the problem involved in identifying his audience can be seen in the following extract from a longer article Kishida composed for the magazine *Reconstruction* when he began writing a regular column in 1932.

[21] *zenshū*, VIII, p. 205. *Shita-machi*, a Japanese word that might be rendered into English as "downtown," refers to a section of central Tokyo. For a Japanese, the word conjures up a whole set of images concerning speech patterns, behavior, and social attitudes. Although the contexts are different, Kishida's comment is roughly equivalent to a statement that too many untrained actors from Brooklyn are appearing on the New York stage.

93

The first thing I wish to ascertain about my readers is how many of them go to see contemporary theatre. Of course, everyone professes some interest in *kabuki, shimpa,* or the New Theatre. However, I suspect there are usually "special circumstances" involved when someone actually decides to go to see a play, pays for his own ticket, and enters the theatre. A potential spectator must think something to himself like, "There's a New Theatre group doing a play by a famous European author. I haven't read it or anything, but it's supposed to be pretty good. I wonder what it's like? Maybe I'll go and see it." Too bad it rained the night he was planning to go. And if he really did want to go, it may be because he didn't want to waste the tickets that someone talked him into buying.[22]

Much of Kishida's writing on the subject of fostering a proper audience is concerned with an examination of what qualities in plays and performances might serve to attract a cultivated Japanese public similar to the kind that attended the theatre in Europe and the United States. Still, he never supposed that the modern theatre would develop into any kind of mass entertainment, at least if high standards were to be maintained. As early as 1924 Kishida took a position that, in one form or other, was to dominate his attitude towards New Theatre audiences throughout his career. "I don't believe there is any real necessity to assume that a play is something to be shown to the great multitudes. It is perfectly satisfactory to say, 'this is a play for people like us.' It can't be helped if you have to say, 'this play isn't interesting at all for others.' "[23]

The implication here is clearly that the theatre is for the cultivated, the literate, and the emotionally sophisticated. The Modern Theatre movement was not intended to compete with ordinary stage entertainment. He insisted however that the plays performed be *entertaining*. At the very least,

---

[22] *zenshū,* IX, p. 153.   [23] *Ibid.,* p. 119.

the spectators must find them interesting. Kishida's most severe criticism of the opening production of the Tsukiji Little Theatre concerned its possible effects on the audience: "Undoubtedly there were various reasons why the performances had to be presented so hastily. But wouldn't it have been wiser to avoid mistakes that produce the opposite results from those intended? In other words, what was the necessity of annoying an audience which was so well disposed, by this kind of performance?"[24]

In an essay written in 1926, Kishida discussed the differences between French and Japanese audiences for the modern theatre.

> Most theatregoers in Japan (I except a few dilettantes) do not show nearly the respect for our classic plays (by which I mean *kabuki*) that the French public shows for their own. And the Japanese spectators certainly pay little attention to modern Japanese plays compared with the respect shown by the ordinary French public for the work of a writer like Rostand.
>
> I would go so far as to say that the level of the audiences for older plays in Japan is about that of those who patronize the music halls in France. The public that in France loves the modern theatre is reduced to going to the cinema in Japan. Of course the cinema has its own proper audience, but I have the feeling that it has enjoyed an increased prosperity because people feel that plays aren't "interesting."
>
> What gives rise to this phenomenon? First of all is the fact that the potential attraction of the modern theatre has not been made manifest. The ordinary public, of course, has been taught to appreciate the theatre only in terms of *kabuki* or *shimpa*, both involving largely the same range of human emotions. When it comes to watching performances of modern plays in translation, the average person is not sufficiently well trained in literature

[24] *Ibid.*, p. 257.

and cannot catch the flavor of these works because the translations are so difficult to comprehend.[25]

The kind of cultivated spectators Kishida hoped to attract were disillusioned by the low level of production of the plays they were able to see. How then could the audience contribute to raising the level of the theatrical performances? Kishida never wrote a systematic essay on the subject, but he made a number of revealing comments.

Early in his critical career he struck the theme that the attitude of the audience toward any theatrical experience was to provide the basis for improvement.

The members of a modern educated theatre audience approach what they see with their common sense; emotionally they are competent to judge whether or not what they see on the stage is the reflection of any genuine emotional experience. They are quite able to compare the writer's ability to apprehend reality with their own. The New Theatre movement must learn to satisfy this audience.[26] (1925)

As long as the New Theatre remained predominantly a theatre in translation, devoted to introducing, perforce out of context, dramatists who had made a contribution in their own countries, the drama would remain an intellectual and not an emotional experience for Japanese audiences.

In addition, Kishida felt that the audience must take an active role in terms of its own response to performances in the theatre.

There are various ways of heckling in the theatre; in the old days in France, there was a barbarous custom of throwing rotten eggs or baked soft apples at bad actors. Later, methods became somewhat less violent and whistling became the form of protest. In this respect, the Japanese theatre appears quite lenient, and our actors

---

[25] *zenshū*, VIII, pp. 215-216.   [26] *Ibid.*, pp. 212-213.

really have an easy time of it. This is why the standards of our stage have become so degenerate. I don't mean to encourage violence, but I think it would be interesting if when our actors bungle, we had the custom of throwing a few *umeboshi* or *konnyaku*![27] (1928)

In an admonition to the theatre audience, written in 1933, Kishida urged them to show their reactions.

If in the course of the play you find it is not interesting, get right up and leave your seat. If you feel sorry to waste the price of your ticket, then you might go up from your seat to the stage and shout, "give my money back!" If something strikes you as ridiculous, look around. No doubt there will be others who agree with you. Make some kind of signal together and start stamping all your feet!

If on the contrary you think that something has been well-performed, applaud as much as possible, just as much as you can without being a nuisance. If you feel yourself too reserved for this, at least give some sign of your appreciation when the curtain comes down. There is in any case no need whatsoever to resign yourself to keeping quiet, wrinkling your brows, with your hands folded or in your pockets, neither applauding nor waving your fists. This is not what art demands of you. . . .[28]

Kishida never found his ideal audience, yet he never wavered in his conviction that a cultivated public would come to enjoy the modern theatre and help it grow, if it could only find in the plays and in the performances the kind of emotional and intellectual satisfaction it had every right to demand. In 1936, in a lecture at Meiji University, he complained that the audiences for the New Theatre were still attending performances for the wrong reasons.

[27] *zenshū*, IX, p. 150. *Umeboshi* are pickled plums, and *konnyaku* might best be described as a rather macaroni-like substance.
[28] *Ibid.*, pp. 152-153.

97

The fact is that the intellectual class in Japan does not attend the theatre. When by chance such a person does go to see a new play, it will be because of special circumstances: he will go "for information," or "for research," or out of embarrassment, since he feels he knows nothing about something that he supposes to be "important." Yet the whole purpose in going to the theatre, or at any rate in going to the theatre in modern times, has been to relax and entertain the human spirit. The commercial theatre may provide sufficient entertainment, but spiritual needs are left completely unfulfilled, and unfortunately [in many New Theatre plays] the spirit is fatigued rather than entertained.[29]

Kishida was certain that modern theatre was capable of appealing to anyone of education and sensibility; the potential audience was thus ever present. What should the spectator seek in the theatre?

What is it we search for in the midst of a play? Not the play but life itself. . . . In order for us, involved as we are in our own lives, to acknowledge the spiritual reality we see on the stage, we must be convinced, first of all, that the play we see is genuine literature and secondly that the actors are themselves involved in modern life. Even if we recognize that the play is genuine literature, if the actors fail us we will be disappointed.[30] (1936)

Kishida propounds a circular argument: the audience, the actors, and the writer are all involved together in a vision of truth: each element has its proper contribution to make but none stands alone. Thus Kishida's appeal to a cultivated audience is part of his larger scheme to lift the New Theatre movement to the limits of the possible in his time.

[29] *Ibid.*, p. 159.   [30] *Ibid.*, p. 162.

THE DANGER OF POLITICS TO THE
ART OF THE THEATRE

Kishida never expressed any interest in contributing to the efforts of the leftist theatre in Japan. Both his temperament and his experiences in France with Jacques Copeau militated against that particular kind of involvement. This attitude no doubt estranged him from Osanai, and certainly from Hijikata and subsequent leftist theatre directors.

Kishida's doubts about the advisability of combining art and politics in the theatre are reflected in some of his earliest critical writing. He took strong exception to Osanai's statement that the Tsukiji Little Theatre existed for all the people.

> The theory that art exists for everyone is a bit too much of a platitude, not just in the theatre but in all the arts. Even if a work of art were created for "all the people," some would respond to the results and some would not. . . . When it comes to any particular work of art, the greatest respect must be paid not to those who do not like it because they do not understand it, but rather to those who *do* understand it but expect something still better. These are "the people" on whom artists must concentrate as a proper audience. Even an art that exists for the few can have an excellent reason for its existence . . . and by rejecting the idea that art exists for a small number of people, one does not automatically insure that brilliant art can be created for the masses.[31] (1924)

Needless to say, "the masses" did not attend the productions of Osanai, whose attitude indeed may have been more that of pious hope than a realistic approach to his public. By 1927, Osanai and Hijikata had moved so far in the direction of a leftist theatre that Kishida was prompted to express his reservations in a more outspoken way.

[31] *Ibid.*, p. 266.

The "proletarian faction" is represented by a group of young writers who espouse communism. Although this group cannot be said to be part of the general movement of literature, they nevertheless have appeared with a certain force on the literary scene. They make use of literary means as a method to propagandize communism. All their plays are colored with certain ideological tendencies, and they emphasize that the theatre should be part of "the movement" before it should be art. They are sure of their convictions and admit no margin of dispute over their theories. They judge as completely worthless all plays that do not fly the communist banner and do not by definition revile and abuse the bourgeois class; and indeed they see the authors of these plays as their enemies and treat them as if they were brutes.[32]

In an essay written in 1931, during the height of the proletarian theatre movement, Kishida stated in precise terms his reasons for opposing what was by then the reigning style in New Theatre circles.

The theatre as an art form has within it elements that can be defined as forms of agitation, and indeed because of the ability of the theatre to promote agitation, it has attracted quite a variety of people. Yet in terms of the strict canons of artistic taste, agitation cannot be regarded as an important element of the form. Raw feelings engendered by blatant agitation have no connection with feelings achieved through aesthetic impressions. The result of agitation is no more than a kind of vulgar excitement. . . .

From the beginning, playwrights with a large public following have filled their works with some kind of agitation, either over some current controversy or on some moral or religious question. Sometimes this helps the artistic effect they are trying to achieve; sometimes it takes

[32] *zenshū*, VIII, p. 221.

the place of that effect. Among the supreme masterpieces of drama, there are none that have agitation as their major purpose.[33]

Kishida did not want the spectator's mind made up for him by the actor or by the dramatist; the spectator was to form his own impressions on the basis of his own artistic responses.

It is scarcely surprising that Kishida, trained as he was in a theatre developed in the great European humanist tradition, would reject a theatre of ideology. For him, the artist himself was the great revolutionary, because he could feel deeply and, through his creative power, serve as a great innovator. "I would tell those propagandists that they need not daub their literature in communist colors. A superior writer will, by the strength of his art, bring a force to bear for revolution, just as great scientists are able to bring about changes in society. Pasteur, Einstein, the others—are they the dupes of the bourgeois?"[34]

Kishida may have seen some of the Expressionist plays staged by Osanai (although, in the light of the comments above, it seems that he did not often attend the productions). He was certainly not aware of major figures such as Brecht, whose work was not known in Japan until later, and he probably knew little of the theories of Piscator, since he remarked in the same essay that he had not read any of the theoretical work of Murayama, who relied heavily on Piscator for his own theories. Had Kishida known work of this caliber, it is conceivable that he might have altered his views; as it was, his own convictions were reinforced by the fact that the evidence available to him in Japan seemed to suggest that first-rate artistic results were impossible, at least at the level at which the leftist theatre then found itself.

In Kishida's 1927 essay quoted above, he mentioned there were several young playwrights in the "proletarian school" whom he considered to be talented, if misguided.

[33] *Ibid.*, p. 241.　　　[34] *Ibid.*, p. 221.

He did not name them, and he did not comment in any of his critical writings on the work of, say, a playwright like Kubo Sakae, whose reputation as a socially concerned writer was quite high by the middle of the 1930s. It is thus difficult to know how Kishida (who, within his limits, was an honest critic) would have responded to politically oriented works of a creditable artistic standard.

THE NEED FOR COMPETENT THEATRE CRITICS

Kishida felt the need for competent criticism of the theatre to guide both the public and those professionals concerned with the theatre to a better understanding of what the medium might accomplish. His comments on the subject, from 1926 on, indicate his continuing dissatisfaction with contemporary criticism.

Some who write literary criticism profess to be unable to judge poetry. This does not seem to perturb the public, or, indeed, the literary world itself. Again, when a critic claims to "understand" poetry, people do not expect that he "understands" all of literature. Yet when it comes to the drama, a great deal of worthless stuff is produced by critics who seem to feel that because they "understand" the novel they are competent to judge drama as well. That is a logic that I don't "understand."[35]

Kishida suggested further that the work of the critics was made more difficult because of the fact that plays in Japan were usually judged on the basis of their printed form in magazines rather than from stage performances. The critic was thus forced to judge the play on false premises, out of any proper artistic environment.

Eric Bentley has said of the role of a critic that "what he regularly and imperatively does is help to create the climate of opinion in which the playwrights live."[36] Simi-

[35] zenshū, VIII, p. 222.
[36] Eric Bentley, The Theatre of Commitment (New York, 1967), p. 45.

larly, Kishida felt strongly that any critic must bring a sense of measure and proportion to the theatrical scene and provide a progressive learning process for his generation.

On the few occasions when Kishida wrote specific critiques of writers or plays, his opinions were forthright, informed, and effectively stated. He disparaged those critics who did not consistently keep high standards and therefore did not help the writers and acting troupes to improve themselves.

In an essay written in 1934, Kishida discussed the reluctance of young writers of talent to write plays, and ironically suggested a reason for it: "My theory is that any novelist, poet, or even critic can write a play if he decides to! He will have his own motives for doing so, and his natural disposition as a human being will no doubt decide the worth of his work. And he has special privileges. If the play is good, he will be consoled for all his efforts; if it is bad, he need not be ashamed. Because playwriting is only a hobby for a true writer."[37] The reason why plays were not taken seriously, Kishida continued, was that they were not afforded the proper kind of criticism; they were not considered important enough to justify the application of rigorous standards. Since the critics continued to hold these attitudes, the public had no help in learning to refine its own taste.

Let me take the examples furnished by some recent productions at the Tsukijiza.[38] One of them is *Ofukuro* by Tanaka Chikao, another is *Futari no ie* by Kawaguchi Ichirō. *Ofukuro*, of course, was highly praised. Yet no critic pointed out the basis of its effectiveness on the stage. The second was subjected to unjustly bad reviews. Despite the fact that the play demonstrated a real theatrical effectiveness of the sort never seen before on our stage, the critics, almost to a man, missed the fact completely. The lack of artistic principles in the drama critics

[37] *zenshū*, VIII, p. 109.
[38] Not the Tsukiji Little Theatre but another company founded in 1932. See below, pp. 115-117.

these days is intolerable. Worst of all, they create an atmosphere that affects the audience in turn. The right of the public to judge plays in any genuine manner has been snatched away from them.[39]

"To criticize the critic" has always been a pursuit of the creative artist, and Kishida's attitude may reflect the fact that he himself wanted to create an atmosphere in which his plays, or at any rate the kind of plays he esteemed, would flourish. Still, he saw the critic as yet another link in the mutuality of the theatre, a link to help inform and raise the standards of the movement.

In all Kishida's dramatic criticism there is a strong sense of the interdependency of the writer, the actors, the audience, and the critics. The failure of any one of these elements would seriously weaken the fabric of the whole. Such interdependency is typical of any civilization in which the theatre is an active art form: Kishida had certainly seen it in France during his stay there: Copeau's work was written about in all the newspapers and in *La Nouvelle Revue Française* as well, and the public felt such a close identification with the work of the theatre that many members of the audience at Le Vieux Colombier volunteered to appear as bit players.[40]

Throughout his career Kishida struggled to raise standards and to give his audiences a glimpse of the excitement of modern dramatic form. In particular, his critical writing delivered a steady barrage of fact and opinion on the relation between the theatre and literature, on acting styles, on how to write plays, on the shortcomings of ideology in the theatre, and on the work of his contemporaries. Yet although Kishida did not make any compromises in his own critical attitudes, he was forced to compromise when it came to sustained attempts to realize his ideals in the actual theatrical world between 1925 and 1939.

Along with the critical essays Kishida wrote to stimulate

[39] *zenshū*, VIII, p. 110.   [40] See Kurtz, *Copeau*, p. 142.

and encourage others, he engaged in several other important activities in connection with the theatre although some of them were circumscribed by the continual ill health that had plagued him since he had developed a lung ailment in France.[41]

The Teacher

Shortly after Kishida's return from France he was approached by Suzuki Shintarō, his friend and former professor at Tokyo University, who encouraged him to teach French literature on a part-time basis at Hōsei and Chūo Universities. Kishida left no record of his impressions of this particular work, but his continuing translations of French authors, especially Jules Renard, suggest a sustained interest in French literature.

He obtained a more important teaching position in 1932 when his former mentor Yamamoto Yūzō brought him to Meiji University to lecture on the theatre. Yamamoto, the chairman of the literature department, assembled a group of well-known writers to assist him, among them Yokomitsu Riichi, Satomi Ton, Toyoshima Yoshio (Kishida's former fellow-student at Tokyo University), and Iwata Toyoo, among others. When Yamamoto retired in 1938, Kishida took his place as chairman of the department, resigning two years later in 1940.

According to Kon Hidemi, Kishida's lectures on the theatre, although brilliant on the subjects discussed, tended to overlook the traditional Japanese theatre altogether. Kishida showed no enthusiasm whatsoever for *kabuki*, ". . . since he had a strong feeling that *kabuki* had been a great hindrance to the development of the modern theatre in Japan."[42]

[41] Kon Hidemi, an associate of Kishida since 1927, wrote that Kishida wished to carry out the kind of elaborate projects undertaken by Copeau in France, but was prevented from doing so by ill health. See *Bungei*, May 1954, p. 35.

[42] Kon Hidemi, "Moraristo Kishida Kunio," *Bungei*, May 1954, p. 35.

The text of a lecture he gave at Meiji University in 1936 is preserved in his collected works and indicates the broad and sophisticated approach he offered his students. The lecture, entitled *Shibai to seikatsu* (*Plays and Life*), discusses the function of the theatre in the life of an ordinary cultivated person. The major theme of the lecture grew from Kishida's realization that European audiences found "life"—some statement about the meaning of their own lives—in the theatre: this is what drew them to it. In Japan, however, the theatre had failed to achieve this because most plays were not written as literature and the actors were neither cultivated nor thoughtful people themselves. The lecture, full of examples at once amusing, charming, and trenchant, provides a very thoughtful commentary on modern Japanese taste. The lecture gives us only a glimpse of what Kishida was as a teacher, but a very agreeable one.

Director of a Theatre School

The low level of acting among the so-called professionals of the Tsukiji Little Theatre and elsewhere convinced Kishida that Copeau was right in his insistence on training young people who had not yet acquired bad habits.

Early in 1926 Kishida announced his intention to set up a school to train young people for the theatre, if his health would permit it. "The school will not only be for actors but will provide training for candidates in various aspects of theatrical art."[43] The announcement stated further that the students he hoped to attract must be of more than average abilities. As always, Kishida sought out the well-educated and ambitious.

He enlisted the help of Iwata Toyoo and Sekiguchi Jirō, another playwright whose work he admired. The three men formed the faculty of the Shingeki kenkyūshō (New Theatre Research Institute) and began giving lectures on various

[43] See the chapter "Shingeki kenkyūshō," pp. 95-103 in Iwata, *Shingeki to watakushi*.

aspects of the theatre to a small group of students. Among the students were Tanaka Chikao, later to become a leading playwright, and several actors and actresses who eventually achieved considerable distinction.

Iwata, whose account of the project is the most complete, wrote that, after their first enthusiasm waned, all three members of the faculty became aware that their own knowledge was insufficient to enable them to instruct the students properly. Copeau could ask experienced professionals to lecture to his students, but Iwata, Kishida, and Sekiguchi were reduced to using foreign films for their models: an unsatisfactory method, as Iwata pointed out, of evolving a proper national style of acting.

Eventually they grew so discouraged that by 1929 they abandoned the institute, and as a final project, the students presented one public performance of a Pirandello play. Kishida's experiment was not a success. Iwata recorded that Kishida was extremely depressed by the failure of the institute, but that he had been too busy and too impatient to give the school the time it needed. If we can judge from his later comments on acting, from his experiences with the institute Kishida learned the real difficulties involved in establishing a Japanese modern style of acting, and his critical writing and his expectations grew more informed and in many ways more reasonable. The school represented Kishida's first failure and the beginnings of his compromise with Japan as he found it.

THE EDITOR

In 1928, the year after *New Tides of Drama* ceased publication, Kishida decided to sponsor a theatre magazine himself. "My friends ask me why I go to so much trouble," he wrote. "The reason is that I would like to read this kind of magazine, but no such magazine exists, or seems likely to. But I am sure I won't be the only one to appreciate it!"[44]

[44] *zenshū*, IX, p. 199.

The magazine, Kishida indicated, would permit editors and readers to examine together the true nature of the theatre. Rather than providing a record of current events in the theatre, it would analyze different theatrical forms and provide information otherwise not readily available in Japan at that time.

The publication, which Kishida named *Higeki kigeki* (*Tragedy and Comedy*), began to appear in October of the same year. He had several editors to assist him, among them the critic Kon Hidemi and the young Sakanaka Masao, who later gained a considerable reputation as a playwright. Separate issues were devoted to farce, famous world actors, *kabuki*, the art of stage scenery, and similar subjects. Despite its generally excellent reception the magazine suspended publication less than a year later, for financial reasons. Like the institute, such a scholarly magazine was a step too far ahead of the public. More time, more patience, more compromise were necessary. Kishida was extremely disappointed.

His second attempt to edit a magazine came four years later when he organized and assumed general supervision of a new magazine he named *Gekisaku* (*Play Writing*), which continued successfully until 1940 when, like many other specialized periodicals, it was forced by the government to suspend operations.

Play Writing was a somewhat less ambitious magazine than *Tragedy and Comedy* and reflected the lessons Kishida had learned in the nine years since his return to Japan. He finally conceded that contemporary Japanese dramatists were so ill-served by the stage that they would have to acquiesce to the artistic limits set by the printed page.[45] He gathered around him six or seven promising young authors and encouraged them to print their new plays in the magazine. Later he wrote that "in 1932 there were only two or three performing groups of high enough standards to mount

[45] For Kishida's comments on this point, see his 1934 essay "Gikyoku o kaku tanoshimi," in *zenshū*, VIII, pp. 110-112.

these works, unlike the period of the early 1920s, when there was so much enthusiasm."[46] The magazine was a compromise.[47]

Kishida later wrote that his younger colleagues did most of the work of editing. Each paid five yen a month (about $25 at that time) to provide the working capital for the magazine, and the deficit was made up by the playwright Sugawara Takashi, a member of the group. In the opening issue of the magazine, which appeared in March 1932, Kishida wrote:

> I have often expressed the desire that, from now on, magazines dealing with the New Theatre movement should not merely introduce the newest of the European *avant-garde* plays, as they have done in the past, but rather contribute to the development of our own drama through an observation of the current situation in Japan. . . . I hope in particular for this magazine that it may serve as an advocate, through the plays it publishes, for the principles essential to genuine drama, about which so much has been said recently. It is time now for the emergence of playwrights whose work an audience will really "want to go to see."[48]

Kishida's phrase "genuine drama" refers to his opposition to the proletarian drama.

Most of the gifted literary playwrights working in Japan before and shortly after the war contributed to *Play Writing*. Many of them were unknown when they began to have

[46] *zenshū*, IX, p. 148.

[47] Jacques Copeau had also helped young playwrights and was influential in having their plays printed in *La Nouvelle Revue Française* and elsewhere, but his main efforts were directed toward the production of new plays. Kishida was not able to assemble a performing company until 1939, when the major part of his career was finished. See below.

[48] Quoted in Ibaragi Tadashi, *Shōwa no shingeki* (Tokyo, 1956), p. 146.

their work published in the magazine, but at least half a dozen of them had earned considerable reputations by 1940.[49] Kishida's activities with the magazine enabled him to extend his principles of a literary theatre to other writers and to provide them with a forum for their works.[50] *Play Writing* helped these young writers and, indeed, contained a number of excellent plays. Kishida did not publish his own plays in the magazine, although he did contribute some of his most representative drama criticism.

Adviser to Theatre Companies

By the time that the Tsukiji Little Theatre was disbanded after the death of Osanai, only a few smaller companies

[49] Among the writers who participated were the following:

Sakanaka Masao (1901-1958) had helped Kishida earlier with *Tragedy and Comedy*.

Kawaguchi Ichirō (born 1905) began as a student in Kishida's institute and came to be regarded as one of Japan's most prominent dramatists during the early postwar period.

Uchimura Naoya (born 1909) and Koyama Yūshi (born 1906) were also well known during the period.

Perhaps the most brilliant dramatist who published in *Play Writing* was Morimoto Kaoru (1912-1946), considered at the time as the most promising literary playwright in Japan. His early death cut short a splendid career.

Aside from Morimoto and Tanaka, the other writers have not sustained their early reputations. Critics unsympathetic to Kishida's determination to keep politics out of the theatre are of the opinion that these writers showed no great talent. Yamada Hajime, for example, writes that "looking over the work of these men, we see that the plays are very theatrical, but they do not seem related to the contemporary scene." (*Kindai geki*, p. 228.) Even if this judgment is correct, Kishida cannot be criticized for the work of other writers. Many of the playwrights praised by Copeau have also disappeared.

[50] Kishida naturally hoped to have their works produced on the stage. He made efforts to have the Tsukijiza produce the best plays, and he directed a number of these productions himself. When the Literary Theatre was finally organized, he continued to mount good new Japanese works.

went on producing plays that did not promote leftist and Marxist ideologies. Kishida's ideal was always to participate in a company like Copeau's, which would seek out and honor young playwrights, revive the best of the older modern plays, and stage the classics as well. He finally realized this ideal more or less satisfactorily, with the opening of his Bungakuza (Literary Theatre) in 1939, but again he was to learn that time and compromise were necessary before adequate standards could be attained.

Kishida began his work with small theatre companies almost immediately upon his return to Japan from France in 1923. Two in particular produced many of his plays, and he worked closely with them, learning what possibilities existed for improving standards and creating a real ensemble.

The first of these small companies was the Shingeki kyōkai (New Theatre Society), which gave performances from 1919 until 1928. The company was founded by Hatanaka Ryōwa, who had become interested in the theatre while he was a student of acting in New York with Mary Pickford. When he returned to Japan he worked in the new theatre company Shimamura Hōgetsu had formed after leaving the Literary Society of Tsubouchi Shōyō. When Ryōwa formed his own company in 1919, he gave preference to plays by contemporary writers and provided almost the only stage for such dramas. His actors were little more than amateurs and his financial status precarious. Still, by the time he and Kishida met in 1924, Ryōwa had already produced plays by Tanizaki, Kume Masao, Yokomitsu Riichi, Sekiguchi Jirō, and Masamune Hakuchō. At this time the split between the leftist and the literary playwrights was only nascent, and his repertoire also included works by the leftist dramatists Akita Ujaku and Kaneko Yōbun.

Hatanaka had taken an immediate interest in Kishida's work, and his troupe was the first to perform a play of Kishida's on the stage, when *Chiroru no aki* (*Autumn in the Tyrols*) was staged in 1924. Kishida became very interested in the company and sometimes attended rehearsals of the

111

troupe. An account of a rehearsal of a Masamune Hakuchō play he saw in 1925 makes clear Kishida's enthusiasm for the company's potential, if not for their actual level of accomplishment.

The New Theatre Society provides the only opportunity we have to see new Japanese plays on the stage today. At a time when the efforts of the Tsukiji Little Theatre are concentrated on the production of foreign plays, this is the only stage on which we can see new plays written in our own country.

It should not come as any surprise that I am enthusiastic over the work of Hatanaka. He is an acquaintance of mine. I do not know what the future work of the Society will be. But at the least the troupe has two or three dependable actors. Technically its stagecraft is adequate. Its basis for existence has been established. Now, extensive publicity is needed![51]

Hatanaka managed to stage several productions a year with three or four performances of each play, but the group was little-known. An "Opening Announcement" written for Hatanaka around this time by Kishida reveals the extraordinary problems such small groups faced. In it, Kishida assured Hatanaka that he was truly one of the pioneers of the development of the New Theatre; he admired his courage and his talents in struggling against difficult economic and spiritual odds. "And yet on opening night," Kishida wrote, "there were scarcely thirty people in the audience." Of course, Kishida continued, there was not enough publicity. He went on to urge the troupe to greater efforts.[52]

Kishida's enthusiasm for the troupe was shared by the novelist and playwright Kikuchi Kan, whose funds and influence supported the important magazine *Literary Annals* mentioned above. When Osanai ruled out the possibility of

[51] *zenshū*, IX, p. 272.

[52] For a full text of the announcement, see *zenshū*, IX, p. 275.

Japanese plays on the stage of the Tsukiji Little Theatre, Kikuchi decided to put the weight of his magazine behind Hatanaka's troupe, and he underwrote a series of performances of Japanese plays in 1926 and 1927.

Kishida became an artistic adviser to the company, directing plays, sometimes his own, and helping in other ways to improve the work of the company and to publicize its work as much as possible.

The first performances of the troupe under the sponsorship of Kikuchi, in November 1926, included four one-act plays. This production is of interest because of the choice of plays involved. The first two plays (one by Chekhov and the other by Kishida's colleague Sekiguchi Jirō) were unexceptionable, but the third was by Murayama Tomoyoshi and the fourth, directed by Kishida himself, was a play called *Wire-Tapping* by the Marxist playwright Kaneko Yōbun. At this period these young Japanese writers were young and eager to have a chance to see their work staged. But they were seldom if ever to be seen on the same program again once the leftist theatre troupes gained the ascendency in the movement after the death of Osanai. The choice of plays in this and in succeeding productions also spoke well for the catholicity of taste of Kikuchi and his colleagues.

By the time of the third production held under Kikuchi's patronage, the company's prestige had risen enormously. Plays now had a run of ten days instead of three. The third production, which opened in April 1927, also included several short plays: Kishida's *Hazakura* (*The Cherry Tree in Leaf*), which he directed himself; *Tan'ya* (*Short Night*), written and directed by Kubota Mantarō; and a translation by Iwata Toyoo of Jules Romains' *Dr. Knock*, which Iwata also directed. The production provided the first opportunity for Iwata, Kishida, and Kubota to work together, and the mutual respect they developed in the process resulted in their cooperative efforts to found the Literary Theatre a decade later.

113

Iwata has recorded that Osanai himself was curious about the success of the Society.

> On the opening night, before the curtain went up, I went backstage to talk to the actors. Thinking to go out into the auditorium, I opened the door, and there, in the vestibule as yet empty of any people, I saw Osanai stride in. I could not understand why a man like him would have come, a good thirty minutes before curtain time. He was alone and for some reason or other he was wearing high boots. He had a rather disdainful look on his face, as though he were inspecting goods in a shop. When I recognized him, I thought that I would go and greet him. I had sent him a book I had written on stage scenery, for which he had thanked me very kindly. Also, I had been introduced to him once in a Ginza café by a friend, and besides, I knew his picture from the newspapers. I went up to him without any hesitation. He no sooner glanced at me than an unhappy expression came over his face. He turned on his heel and walked out.[53]

Osanai was evidently not pleased by this challenge thrown down to him by Kikuchi's presentation of the Romains play. Within the same year, however, a rift developed between Kikuchi, who wanted to stage only Japanese plays, and Hatanaka, who, encouraged by the success of *Dr. Knock*, wanted to expand his repertoire to include foreign plays. Kikuchi withdrew his support and Hatanaka was forced to struggle on alone. Kishida stayed with him, for he felt that the company would do the theatre the greatest service possible by producing a judicious mixture of translations and Japanese plays. Kishida and Iwata were both sensitive to the fact that Osanai was concentrating on German and Russian plays and slighting the modern French drama.

Later in the same year, Kishida directed a production of *La paix chez soi* (*Peace at Home*) by Georges Courteline.

[53] Iwata, *Shingeki*, pp. 88-89.

Hatanaka hoped that Iwata and Kishida might help him with a production of Vildrac's *Pacqueboat Tenacity* (*Steamship Tenacity*), but deprived of the support and publicity provided by *Literary Annals* the company, despite the good intentions of so many, was forced to disband within the year. Kishida's second attempt to work closely with a theatre company came four years later, in 1932, when he was approached by Tomoda Kyōsuke for permission to stage one of Kishida's plays. Tomoda had begun his career in the early years of the New Theatre Society. Later he met and married Tamura Akiko, one of Osanai's best actresses. The two were discouraged when the company split up after the death of Osanai, and, after working briefly with Aoyama Sugisaku's group, formed their own small troupe, the Shin Tōkyō (New Tokyo) in 1930. Their greatest success was a production of *The Marriage of Figaro* by Beaumarchais.

Tomoda however was interested in producing Japanese plays. He persuaded Kishida, Kubota, and Satomi Ton, the novelist and playwright, to serve as advisers shortly after he reorganized his troupe as the Tsukijiza (Tsukiji Theatre) in February 1932.

Tomoda had chosen a good moment to begin his new troupe. Political pressures were causing certain retrenchments in the activities of the leftist theatre companies,[54] and sufficient public interest in artistic plays seemed assured because of the support shown his earlier ventures with the New Tokyo troupe. During the four years of the existence

---

[54] For details on the reorganization of the various leftist theatre troupes that led to the formation of Shinkyō (The New Cooperative Troupe) in 1934, see Kawatake, *Engekishi*, pp. 406-409. By this time, the kind of cooperation between leftist and artistic playwrights as evidenced in the early productions of the New Theatre Society had ceased. Ibaragi mentions that a few joint performances by competing leftist and artistic troupes were sponsored, and that the troupes knew each other's work, but that there was no exchange of personnel or playwrights. (See Ibaragi, *Shōwa no shingeki*, p. 67). See also an article on the activities of the leftist theatres in this period by Okakura Shirō, "Jūnendai no shingeki," in *Bungaku*, Feb. 1955.

of the Tsukiji Theatre, Tomoda staged a total of twenty-eight productions, mainly plays by Japanese authors. In addition to works by established writers such as Kishida, Kubota, Satō Haruo, Satomi Ton, and Arishima Takeo, he also produced some plays by the younger writers associated with *Play Writing* magazine, often directed by Kishida. In addition to Japanese drama, there were productions of works by European and American playwrights, including Elmer Rice and Sherwood Anderson. (Tomoda had initially chosen O'Neill's *Desire under the Elms* as his opening production, but the play was forbidden by the authorities as immoral.)

Tomoda staged three of Kishida's plays and several of his translations, including two of Courteline. Kishida had high hopes for the group, but Tomoda encountered a variety of difficulties. In 1934, a group of actors left his company to form their own, the Sōsakuza (Theatre for New Plays). Their reasons as stated in their manifesto seem rather vague;[55] perhaps they served to cover certain personal animosities. Tomoda, upset by the event, found the efforts of managing both the financial and artistic aspects of the company more than he could manage, and was forced to disband the Tsukiji Theatre in February 1936.[56]

The Tsukiji Theatre has been generally recognized by historians of the period as having made an invaluable con-

[55] Part of the text of the manifesto of the Sōsakuza can be found in Ibaragi, *Hitobito*, p. 178. The group had a short life, although it managed to produce some good plays by such writers as Mafune Yutaka. Kubota characterized it as active and enthusiastic but found the level of acting inferior. (See Kubota, *zenshū*, XIII, p. 182.)

[56] The specific reasons for the closing seem obscure. Kishida simply recorded that Tomoda and his wife found themselves in business difficulties, the same explanation provided in the standard histories of the modern theatre. Iwata, however, felt that Kishida was to blame, since he was at that time emotionally exhausted and took too pessimistic a view of the future of the company. (See *Shingeki*, pp. 124-126.) Kubota, on the other hand, hinted at personal intrigues and company members weeping on his doorstep. Everyone, it seems, was overwrought. (See Kubota, *zenshū*, XIII, p. 293.)

tribution to the development of the Japanese drama.[57] Only the leftist playwrights of the period refused to acknowledge the accomplishments of the group. Murayama Tomoyoshi wrote that "this company of small scope, limited to a very narrow style, managed to attract a certain number of specialized clientele . . ."[58] yet Murayama's own group did no better.[59]

Kishida had learned a great deal from the experience, however. He had come to find in Tomoda and his wife two excellent stage personalities who were slowly but surely developing the requisite stage technique to deal with contemporary Japanese plays. Second, he had been confirmed in his conviction that the public would respond to Japanese plays of an artistic nature.

All in all, these four years taught Kishida the real possibilities for accomplishment in Japan, even if it was on a lower level than he, Iwata, and Kubota might have hoped for.[60] In 1937, the three of them began talks with Tomoda

[57] See Ibaragi, *Shōwa no shingeki*, p. 144, Fukuda Tsuneari, *Watakushi no engeki hakusho* (Tokyo, 1958), p. 241, and Toita Yasuji, *Engeki no gojūnen* (Tokyo, 1950), pp. 221-226.

[58] Quoted in Ibaragi, *Shōwa no shingeki*, p. 63.

[59] Kubo Sakae also belittles the so-called "*Gekisaku* Playwrights" associated with the Tsukiji Theatre for their limited involvement in larger social questions. See Kubo, *zenshū*, vi, pp. 121-123. The only praise accorded them by any writer or actor connected with the leftist theatre in the 1930s was by Senda Koreya, who remarked that Kishida skillfully showed the troupe the important links between spoken language and human psychology. (See Kawatake Shigetoshi, ed., *Gendai no engeki* [Tokyo, 1966] v, p. 173.)

[60] Kishida also worked briefly with two other small companies during this period. The Shingekiza (New Theatre Stage) began performances in 1921, using *shimpa* actors and occasionally staging serious modern drama. Kishida worked with them during the production of one of his short plays in 1934. The company was disbanded in 1938. The other company, the Teatro Comedie (Comedy Theatre), was, like the Tsukiji Little Theatre, a conscious attempt to combat the influence of the leftist theatre. Founded in 1931, it produced a variety of translated plays, including the Japanese première of Vildrac's *Steamship Tenacity*, although not in Iwata's translation.

117

and his wife, with the aim of establishing a permanent company dedicated to the ideals they held in common. Kishida had hoped to found such a company since his return from France in 1923. In 1925 he had written,

> I have not yet answered those who say ironically, "why don't you start a company yourself?" but in fact I would like nothing better than to do so. How sad that the playwright needs others to help him! Accomplices are necessary; or perhaps the proper word is comrades. Such work cannot be simply delegated to someone. . . . I have been expressing my opinion on every suitable occasion, and I am waiting for the arrival on the scene of an effective colleague.[61]

In fact it had taken Kishida twelve years to find the proper combination of writers (Kubota and Iwata) and actors (Tomoda and Tamura) to enable him to realize his plan. Both Iwata and Kishida knew the methods used by Jacques Copeau, and their interest in promoting a mixture of old and new, domestic and foreign plays paralleled their mentor's.

Both Kubota and Iwata have left long accounts of their efforts to assemble the company.[62] Kishida and his colleagues drafted a statement about the purposes of the Literary Theatre, as they were to call the company, that read in part:

> avoiding makeshifts, pedantry, or subservience to politics, we would like to offer to the intelligent general public through the medium of the stage a glimpse of a genuine "entertainment for the soul." We wish to avoid both the vague "theatrical" atmosphere that has been part of the

---

Kishida was on good terms with the company and had a play produced.

[61] Kishida, *zenshū*, VIII, p. 213.

[62] See Iwata, *Shingeki*, pp. 129-133 and Kubota, *zenshū*, XIII, pp. 202-208.

drama in Japan until now, as well as the various crude aspects of the radical elements in the New Theatre movement. We wish to create a theatre with an intimate connection with the emotional realities of contemporary life.[63]

This joint statement seems to suggest both a positive aspect, in its call for an artistic theatre, and a negative aspect in its rejection of leftist ideologies.[64] Kishida, Kubota, and Iwata chose literature instead of politics when they named the company. As an insignia for the troupe, they combined the letters L (for Literature) and T (for Theatre) into an emblem which has been retained ever since.

They began to assemble their company with their goal an opening in November 1937. The first production was to include two plays, Kubota's Ōdera gakkō (Ōdera School), first staged in 1928 and considered his finest stage work. Kishida was to provide a new play, Sawa-shi no futari musume (Mr. Sawa's Two Daughters), written for Tomoda. Kishida considered it his finest play. Rehearsals were begun and preliminary publicity released. Then came an extraordinary setback. Tomoda was drafted into the army, sent to China, and killed, all in the month of October. Kishida had

---

[63] Quoted in Kubota, zenshū, XIII, p. 208.

[64] Such insistence on expressing openly a strong distaste for the work of the leftist theatre companies may seem unnecessary, but after the closing of the Tsukiji Theatre, only leftist companies gave regular performances in Tokyo. Kubota wrote that "even an editorial writer for a newspaper of the caliber of the Asahi would use the word 'New Theatre' as a synonym for 'leftist theatre' without even noticing it." (See Kubota, zenshū, XIII, p. 267.)

lost his leading man and Japan, from all accounts, the best male actor in the modern theatre.[65] Hard as all three men had tried to create an ensemble, Tomoda was the central figure in the endeavor. Tamura, in mourning for her husband, decided to retire from the stage, at least for a time.

A company was finally assembled, however, and after a preliminary production (rather like a public rehearsal) in which four one-act plays were presented, the official opening of the Literary Theatre took place on March 25, 1938. The repertoire had been changed. Morimoto Kaoru, the young playwright whose first work was produced by the Tsukiji Theatre, contributed *Migoto na onna* (*A Clever Girl*); Kishida directed his translation of Courteline's *Peace at Home*; and Iwata revived his ever-popular translation of Romains' *Dr. Knock*. It was not quite the exciting start they had planned, but the company was performing.

The first real success came later in the season with the production of Kubota's *Tsuribori nite* (*By the Fishing Pond*), a play he had written in 1935. The public began to respond to the kinds of plays being staged, and the attendance was sufficiently large for the three men to continue their experiments. In particular, Iwata mentioned that he was grateful to see a middle-aged audience, as in Europe, rather than one of students coming out of curiosity, as was so typical of the audiences for the earlier New Theatre groups.

Iwata wrote of his feelings when the troupe began to play at Osanai's and Hijikata's old theatre, built originally for the Tsukiji Little Theatre but now rented out to various

[65] Kishida, Iwata, and Kubota were all personally and deeply grieved over Tomoda's death. All published short articles about him, but Kubota, perhaps the most traditionally minded of the three, wrote a *haiku* on Tomoda's death:

shinu mono mo ikinokoru mono mo aki no kaze

This might be rendered as:

What dies and what remains behind as well—
the autumn wind

120

companies. "Never, even in my dreams, did I imagine that we would be presenting plays on the same stage where Osanai, and then the leftist companies, had always stood against us."[66]

Yet even the moderate success of the Literary Theatre was to be thrown into question by the political atmosphere in Japan, now so close to war. By 1939 choices for the repertoire were indeed being circumscribed,[67] and in 1940 the government closed down all the other New Theatre companies. The Literary Theatre was spared because its productions were manifestly unconcerned with politics. The troupe continued to perform throughout the war, despite various difficulties, and emerged as one of the major forces in the postwar Japanese theatrical scene.

With the founding of the Literary Theatre, Kishida made his last and perhaps his only successful attempt to reveal on the stage his vision of a modern theatre for Japan. It had taken him fifteen years, from 1923 to 1938, and his major contributions as a man of the theatre had been made by 1939.[68] In 1940, when the war began, he was fifty years old, ill, and dejected. His wife, to whom he was very attached,

[66] Iwata, *Shingeki*, p. 143.

[67] Iwata gives a trenchant example of the atmosphere at the time. Marcel Pagnol's *Marius* was being prepared for production, but Kishida cautioned Iwata against using the French title, as the foreign lettering on the poster might seem objectionable to the authorities. The play was renamed. (See Iwata, *Shingeki*, pp. 140-141.)

[68] Many historians of the theatre have taken Kishida to task for the fact that he joined a government-sponsored cultural committee in 1940 and made a trip to China as an official observer for the Ministry of Education. Such activities might be seen as another kind of compromise that Kishida made with the world as he found it. Judgments on Kishida's attitudes toward these matters are impossible to make on the basis of the evidence available, and, in any case, remain outside the scope of the present research. The most thoughtful commentary on Kishida's conduct during the war is contained in an article by Nishijima Kenzō, "Kishida Kunio no shōgai," *Bungei*, May 1954.

died in 1942, and he eventually retired to the country to await the end of the war. Kishida was able to participate in several New Theatre productions after 1945, but he was frequently ill and isolated from the central events of the postwar theatre movement.

CHAPTER V

Kishida as a Playwright

KISHIDA'S playwriting remained the part of his work that was always closest to him. He wrote in 1939, "I began as a playwright, and to this day I look on this work as my real profession."[1] His other activities were necessary and stimulating to him, but his basic allegiance was to an attempt to create plays to be judged both as theatre and as literature. Kon Hidemi has written that Kishida was, in fact, never fully comfortable with the world of the theatre because of its various intrigues and complications, but preferred to stand apart and observe, in order to create his own world in his plays.[2]

Scattered through Kishida's critical writings are a number of references to his personal views on the purposes of writing for the theatre. These references are valuable not only for the light they shed on his own artistic choices but for what they tell us about the theatrical and cultural atmosphere of his generation.

THE WESTERNIZATION OF PLAYWRITING

Kishida felt strongly that he and his contemporaries should develop techniques based on western dramaturgy. He first rejected the traditional Japanese theatre after his return from France. Kishida seldom mentioned *nō*, a form he considered too stylized and remote to be of any danger to the New Theatre movement, but he wrote at considerable length about the dangers of mixing any elements of *kabuki* in modern playwriting. From the vantage point of

[1] *zenshū*, IX, p. 316.
[2] See Kon, "Morarisuto Kishida," *Bungei*, May 1954, pp. 34-36.

the 1970s, such fears may seem exaggerated, yet in 1924, when Kishida began his critical writing, *kabuki* actors were playing in many modern plays, and many authors who were attempting to write contemporary drama leaned heavily on melodrama and stylized emotion, both present in *kabuki* and *shimpa.*
Kishida's attitude was not the result of any antipathy to the traditional theatre: he did not find it wanting in spiritual beauty. He touched on this point in his memoir.

Shortly after I returned to Japan, I thought I would like to go to see a *kabuki* play for once, so I prevailed upon Suzuki Shintarō and we went to see Kikugorō, at the Ichimuraza, as I recall. This was my first time to see him act. Of course, I was completely overwhelmed. My heart had pounded in Paris when I saw Rostand; yet now I was so moved that although the play was not a sad one, I found my eyes filling with tears.

When I thought over this experience, I realized very clearly that *kabuki* is a splendid form of theatre. Kikugorō was a great actor. I was certainly captured by the charm of what I had seen and was moved by a genuine artistic experience.[3]

However, as Kishida hastened to point out, the experience was not of significance to a contemporary playwright.

But nothing I saw changed in any way my vision of what a play should be. It can be affirmed that in Japan at that time there were only two possible definitions for a play: that which held to the tradition of the past, and that which held to the tradition of the future. Both traditions could not be pursued at once. In the first case, the past remained tied to the present. In the second, the present was tied to the future, in order to create a new tradition. And indeed, although the play in which Kikugorō appeared seemed flawless in any respect you care to

[3] *zenshū,* IX, p. 189.

name, did it have within it the strength to give birth to anything new? My involuntary tears may give proof of some racial links existing in me as a Japanese, but not of my witnessing the marks of future vitality.[4]

Kishida insisted that the *kabuki* drama, and the emotions it evoked in the spectators of his generation, could not represent the kind of contemporary emotional life on which a playwright must base his work.

The mode of life in Japan at this time disregards to a greater and greater extent the special qualities of the older Japanese traditions. This is not to say that life in Japan will become completely westernized, but we are certainly taking on an international style of life. Soon the special distinctions of individual nations will be discernible with difficulty. This is the kind of world into which we are advancing.

Leaving aside the distant future, if Japan is to have any real contemporary theatre at this time, we must adopt those forms of western theatre that have become the standard for all world culture. From the time of the Greeks, the western theatre has taken and consolidated various contributions from different countries; the form as we know it now is an amalgamation of all the traditions that have emerged before. Such world traditions—and they must be differentiated from those of Japan—must surely provide the basic elements for the development of a modern drama in our country.[5] (1931)

In other words, the use of western traditions would help the contemporary Japanese playwright to find a proper form in which to express the realities of the increasingly international age in which he lived.

Kishida wanted playwrights to study carefully the accomplishments of the western theatre and to immerse themselves in the international style so that they might

[4] *Ibid.*   [5] *zenshū*, VIII, p. 231.

create their own new dramaturgy for Japan. As Kishida often pointed out, Japanese poets and novelists had been able to accomplish this in their own spheres, and there was no reason why dramatists could not do so as well.

THE CONTEMPORARY JAPANESE THEATRE

A playwright must study the western accomplishments in creating a modern psychology on the stage, but he must also keep in mind at all times the fact that his plays are written to be produced and seen in the contemporary Japanese theatre by contemporary Japanese audiences. For the good of the movement, a writer must create works that are scaled to the talents of existing actors and that can be understood by his audiences. A play, unlike a poem, is not written and consumed in private but is involved in a living community of actors and spectators. No matter what the problems, no genuine playwright can afford to overlook this communal aspect of his art.

There is no denying that the drama is one form of literature; yet the drama of literary value is different from the novel or poem with literary value. The playwright works by different rules, and when it comes to judging a play, unless the full creative range of the play is made manifest through a stage production, the play cannot be considered as a fully realized work of art. Indeed the very question of the literary value of the drama is closely bound up in this problem.[6] (1932)

Because a play is written for an audience, the psychology of an audience must also be taken into consideration.

It seems too commonplace even to mention this point: a novel is a work of art read by one person, and a play is one seen by many people. Thus a novel can have as high a tone as its author pleases, while a play, at least to

[6] *Ibid.*, p. 101.

126

some extent, must have something of the ordinary about it. The two forms are difficult to compare in terms of artistic profundity or even of artistic purity. . . .[7]

Yet for what milieu can the playwright compose his plays? Kishida's comments as a theatre critic quoted in the preceding chapter give ample evidence that he felt the current level of accomplishment among actors and directors so low that plays could not be seen to their best advantage. He was wary of the commercial theatres, where plays were staged for mass audiences.

Many complaints can be leveled at the work of the commercial theatres in Japan, but they at least provide a living for those authors who write plays answering to the required standards, and it must be admitted that some plays with a certain artistic merit have emerged from this source and will continue to do so. Yet the conditions imposed on the authors are too many. The works commissioned are not expected to have any relation to the kind of writing that is part of modern literature. The work of these authors is not to depict the thoughts, reactions, psychological responses, or the life style of modern times, and indeed the style in which the plays are acted is redolent of feudalism and a provincialism left over from Tokugawa times.

Thus a writer who decides for the sake of his livelihood to write plays for a theatre of these standards will go on protecting the empty traditions of the stage and will concentrate on introducing new tricks into a stale atmosphere. It is not surprising that no really good results are obtained.[8] (1934)

For different reasons, Kishida found the experimental theatre companies no more promising.

As for the so-called "experimental theatres" and "amateur theatre groups," the best characteristics of the

[7] *Ibid.*, p. 102.   [8] *Ibid.*, p. 110.

New Theatre movement are being lost, the quality of the actors is beneath discussion, and the plays seem merely makeshifts—would anyone go to see these plays unless it were out of mere curiosity, or from a sense of duty? Among those who do there may be a few young people who wish to be playwrights and so, hoping to get something out of the experience, will buy a ticket once. But if these young people have any ability to appreciate beauty, they will realize how little excitement and stimulation they receive from what they see, and they will abandon their interest in the company.[9] (1934)

How different from the situation Kishida had found in Paris.

In Paris, there must be around sixty theatres, large and small. Leaving out the *vaudeville* and theatres only involved in producing ordinary spectacles, there are at least thirty theatres playing works by contemporary authors. Some of these plays are not worthy of artistic consideration, but even leaving out the "society plays" of the bourgeois theatre, a great many plays of real artistic merit are performed. Most of these productions are contemporary plays; on those occasions when a period piece is chosen, it is usually a play of literary value with some links to the problems of contemporary life. The French stage has a clear line from its classics to the freshness of the contemporary scene.[10] (1926)

Kishida's considered opinion was that a playwright must come to terms with his own talents and with the objective situation as he found it; he must do the best work possible under the circumstances. Over the course of time, the plays that he writes will in turn help to improve the theatre in which he works. The view expressed by Kishida below was remarkably close to the course he himself followed in his own creative work.

[9] *Ibid.* [10] *Ibid.*, p. 215.

If we divide into categories the kinds of plays that have appeared [in the New Theatre movement] in Japan, we might find the following:

1. Plays of great artistic purity that, by their very nature seem impossible to perform by contemporary theatre companies.
2. Plays that, although containing artistic elements, are not so forbidding that companies would be afraid to take them on.
3. Plays that merely provide a response to the demands put on the playwright by the companies themselves, or plays created for pure "entertainment value"—whatever that might be!

It seems to me that these three categories more or less cover the possibilities. Unfortunately, it seems that the first and third types of plays maintain their existence, albeit for different reasons, while fewer and fewer authors are willing to try the all-important second category. As no one is attentive to the matter, the demand for such plays is slight; no author can establish his reputation by writing such plays.[11] (1932)

Kishida noted that in France commercial and artistic values were often considered to reinforce each other; writers often tried to make their plays as artistic as possible in order to make them more interesting, more stimulating. "In Japan today, however, the word 'artistic' has come to mean 'difficult,' far worse than uninteresting!"[12] Kishida felt the need for a theatre troupe that could produce plays that were neither sterile experiments nor vulgar entertainment, but plays to appeal to an audience and lift it to a new level of enjoyment in the theatre. In such a view, artistic compromises are required of the writer, as indeed they were for Kishida himself.

[11] *zenshū*, IX, p. 155. [12] *Ibid.*, p. 155.

129

Kishida had strong memories of the achievements of Copeau and Le Vieux Colombier, and he had seen the French example of a theatre company stimulating the creation of first-rate dramatic literature. He wished the Japanese playwrights neither to desert their public nor pander to it. He hoped for cooperation between writer and audience. Yet it was precisely this cooperation, as he continued to acknowledge in one way or other throughout his career, that was hardest of all to achieve.

THE CREATION OF A VIABLE JAPANESE TRADITION OF PLAYWRITING

From the time of his return from France to Japan, Kishida repeatedly wrote that a new tradition of New Theatre playwriting must be created. He intended that such a new tradition, as he called it, would provide a framework to support and extend the talents of an individual playwright. When Kishida began his career there were no common principles accepted by all Japanese New Theatre playwrights, and their styles ranged from sentimental melodrama to bad imitations of German Expressionist experimental plays. He felt that a Japanese tradition must be created; later, perhaps further experiments should and could be made, but, without a base, every writer was reduced to the relative poverty of his own resources.[13]

[13] In this regard it might be pertinent to show the attitude of a playwright of the stature of Berthold Brecht on the burdens of originality. Martin Esslin writes as follows:

Under the influence of the Romantics an even greater value is attached in Germany than elsewhere to the quality of uniqueness, of originality, which is said to be the essence of genius. Brecht thought little of this cult of originality. In one of his Keuner stories, he makes his *alter ego* quote the example of the Chinese philosopher Chuang Tzu, who wrote a book of a hundred thousand words, nine-tenths of which consisted of extracts from other books. "Such books can no longer be written in our country, because we have not enough intelligence. That is why we manu-

In an early essay written in 1926 on the subject of creating a tradition for the modern drama in Japan, Kishida made a sharp distinction between tradition and mere convention. Tradition, he wrote, was of the greatest value because it contained "the essential elements that continue to keep alive the genuine artistic aspects of the theatre and which alone can bring beauty to the life of the stage"; this he contrasted to convention, which he saw as destructive since it was "an element not central to the drama but dependent on it, even though it is often referred to as 'the rules of the stage.' "[14] Convention, he concluded, was useful only in emphasizing the entertainment value of the theatre.

Conventions from the traditional Japanese theatre were of no use in building up a new tradition, he said. And although elements for a new Japanese tradition were to be taken from the modern western theatre, he insisted equally that the western theatre was to be learned from and not merely copied. In this regard he found the influence of Osanai to have been a very destructive one.

"Osanai-ism" has attempted to construct a base for the New Theatre movement by "introducing" modern western drama to Japan. Yet such a method is ostentatious, lacks originality, and perforce leaves far too much to the spectator's imagination. Indeed the performance of a translated play usually gives a sense of incompleteness. What we see is never more than generally correct.[15]

Kishida hoped that the playwrights could learn how to perfect their own craft without facing the constant competition of translated European masterpieces.

---

facture ideas only in our own workshops. Anyone who is unable to put enough of them together feels that he is lazy. That is why there are no ideas worth taking up, and no phrases worth quoting. . . . They build their huts without help and with nothing but the miserable amount of material a single person can build by himself." (See Martin Esslin, *Brecht, the Man and His Work* [New York, 1960], pp. 115-116.)

[14] *zenshū*, VIII, p. 223.   [15] *Ibid.*, p. 243.

What sort of tradition did Kishida hope to create? Clearly he favored a theatre in which literary values predominated; if the dramaturgy he urged was unexceptional by contemporary European standards, it was certainly quite new in this period in Japan.

Kishida, like so many modern European dramatists, felt strongly that the drama was not so much an entertainment to be constructed by rules but rather the reflection of the author himself—his character, his life, and his time. Such a view takes the drama out of the camp of the craftsman and places it squarely in the domain of literature.

In his criticism of Osanai's methods, Kishida wrote that among artists who can appeal to a whole civilization, "there may at best be only one or two a century in the whole world. Such men must first of all possess grandeur of character. Only then can they be called great artists."[16] If the playwright is to be an artist, the basis for his accomplishment must be his ability to observe human nature and to record what he sees, rather than his acquisition of the newest techniques of writing for the stage. It is the human value of the artist which permits him to write a good play.

How can we decide the basic value of a given work of art? Perhaps by examining the manner in which the author is interested in his subject . . . there are many ways in which he may do so. As an educator; as a politician; as a student of society; as a student of religion; as a psychologist; as a student of ethics; as a journalist; as a detective; as a businessman looking to his receipts; as a neighbor; as an acquaintance; as an outside observer; as a parent; as a brother. Yet none of these concerns are the root of any work of art. An artist may feel one or many of these, but they do not represent his main concern. There is still a separate "manner of interest" that is uniquely the artist's. There are as many as there are individual artists. Optimistic, pessimistic, comic, tragic, romantic,

[16] *zenshū*, IX, p. 266.

realistic; however many attitudes there may be, whatever the interest, it must permeate the consciousness of the artist and be filtered through his special susceptibilities and his power of imagination. The result will be the appearance, true and beautiful, of some new aspect of mankind. This "manner of interest" tells us quite clearly the true nature of the artist.[17] (1925)

Artistic techniques are effective only to the extent that they serve an artist's vision. The interests of an author, compounded of his integrity and his sensitivity as a creative person, must always precede the play itself. (Kishida entitled his essay, Gikyoku izen no mono, "What Comes before the Play.")

Kishida realized that such an uncompromising view of the work of the playwright, and of the theatre in general, put him out of step with those of his contemporaries who were looking for easy success, and indeed in his own professional career he met with enough indifference and opposition to provide him with more than sufficient evidence concerning the difficulties involved in creating a genuine art. He wrote in his memoir that in Paris he had become aware for the first time of a possibly necessary distance between the playwright and his own generation.

When I was in Japan, I had picked up a little knowledge of the contemporary French theatre through some things I studied in school, a very few books, and a scattering of newspapers and magazines; yet when I actually went to Paris and saw the situation at first hand, I was faced with the reality. What had been vague for me now became clear. All the values I had stood for and the judgments I had made were now called into question. I then realized two things: first of all, it is not possible to come to any final opinion as to whether or not a play is of the highest quality merely by seeing it acted on the stage. The essential thing is surely to search out the relationship

[17] zenshū, VIII, p. 99.

of a play to the best literature of its time. A drama critic may well miss some aspect of the work that is important. His opinion must be ranged along with those of writers who deal with more general aspects of the arts, so that the full meaning of a dramatic work in relation to its period may be ascertained.[18]

Kishida is not reviving here the perennial argument about plays in the study versus plays on the stage (in fact, he always championed actual productions); rather, he is emphasizing the fact that the meaning of a great work will transcend the immediate circumstances of its production and so must be judged and appreciated on a wider basis of understanding.

For Kishida, a play must undergo the same rigor of critical scrutiny demanded of good literature.

Why is it that many plays which enjoy a great success when first produced soon lose their appeal, while works that are coolly received, or even severely criticized, are given new productions twenty years later and become sensations? . . . Are there limitations on the works any particular age can assimilate? If so, why are some works not assimilated? Isn't the fact that they are not a proof that in many cases, the theatrical conventions of the time are so strong that they blind the eyes of the critics and those with conservative prejudices against any leap forward towards what will become the new tradition?[19]

The playwright will be ahead of his actors, producers, and audience to the extent that they adhere to the theatrical conventions with which they are familiar and within which they know how to work.

Given the fact that Kishida wanted to work toward creating a new tradition, and a literary one, for the New Theatre drama in Japan, what kind of writing technique did he see

---

[18] *zenshū*, IX, p. 186.   [19] *Ibid.*

as essential for the playwright to use in order to manifest his own "interests" in effective literary and theatrical terms?

First of all, he saw the spoken word as the basis of all good drama and so, by implication, he agreed with those in the movement for a modern theatre in the west who insisted that the writer's conceptions were central to a play as performed on the stage, with the director and the actor taking supplementary roles. He was critical of those dramatists whose abilities with language were so limited their plays had no appeal on the stage.

What makes modern Japanese plays so uninteresting? One important fault to be laid to all these plays is the fact that their authors overlook the "value of words." For their "words meant for the ear," even from a literary point of view, have only reached a childish level. As to whether words to be spoken or words to be read have a greater psychological and sensuous effect, [the judgment is rendered all the more difficult because] the writers have been so desultory in their work and the actors so sloppy in their execution of the text. . . . Playwrights will no doubt answer "I'm not concerned about merely writing an interesting play. It must be artistic." Quite reasonable, perhaps, but being "artistic" does not permit the play to be long and boring. In the theatre, to be boring is forbidden.[20] (1925)

Words spoken on the stage were the very basis of the life of the drama for Kishida. Words were the unique element which gave the theatre its stature and its particular appeal. Kishida wrote scornfully of an unnamed Japanese critic who attempted to minimize the role of words in the theatre.

Recently I had an occasion to read something written by a man recently returned from a trip to Europe. It seems that he went expressly for the purpose of making

[20] *zenshū*, VIII, p. 65.

135

a specialized study of the theatre, yet his impressions resulted in a statement something like the following: "Accidentally I went to see a certain play in Paris, and although I don't understand French, I found it quite interesting. Even without grasping the meaning of the dialogue, I was able to a great degree to understand the plot and the emotions of the characters through the skill of the actors. On the whole, I believe that my expectations in going to the theatre were fully satisfied."

What he is really saying is: in the theatre the role of words is an extremely feeble one; as long as the elements appealing to the eye are upheld, the theatre can demonstrate its true appeal.[21] (1934)

It may be that Kishida might have been less hard on the hapless critic had he been in England or Germany, where Kishida himself would have shared the same linguistic disadvantage; still, from an author's point of view, his indignation seems only natural. Elsewhere he remarked that many directors and actors in the New Theatre movement were all too happy to downgrade the value of the text because of deficiencies in their own technique.

Compare the relative attraction of words and movement on the stage. Whatever else can be said about movement, it is surely mechanical and simple. The training to master movement is not difficult. Words, however, are on an altogether higher level. The training necessary to speak well on the stage *is* very difficult. Until one masters the art of delivering lines on the stage, he is not really an actor, and the art of speaking remains the most important of an actor's professional necessities.[22] (1934)

He may have overstressed his point, yet judging from a variety of comments and opinions written about the Modern Theatre movement at this time, problems of voice produc-

21 *Ibid.*, p. 116.   22 *Ibid.*, p. 204.

tion and nuances in stage dialogue remained largely unsolved by New Theatre actors.

It is not surprising that Kishida reacted strongly to a conspiracy designed to unseat the playwright from his position of eminence. His ultimate position was that words and movement do not act in opposition to each other but rather work in harmony, the movements springing from the sense of the words.

To "understand" the dialogue means not only to understand its meaning. Dialogue carries with it its own precise emotional expressiveness. This expressiveness appeals to the ear through the voice and to the eye through the expression on the actor's face. This expressiveness has no independent existence away from the dialogue; indeed, in a broad sense it is included in any definition of "words for the stage."[23] (1934)

The dialogue, the words, and the playwright's conception must always remain at the center of the art of the theatre.

From the beginning, Kishida was aware of the growing importance of motion pictures in the total range of theatrical entertainment. He thought that film had taken over in a very successful way certain functions of the theatre, especially spectacle; now that the theatre must develop a sense of its own unique functions, the importance of the playwright's text would of necessity be reaffirmed.

There is no denying that the progress of the film has narrowed the field available to the theatre. Certainly the aspects of the theatre that appeal to the eye are being preempted by the film, with all the freedom it can bring to its own means of expression. The result is that the important function of words in the theatre has been made all the more secure. The theatre must depend on the words of a play. Surely the theatre will come to demon-

[23] *Ibid.*, p. 116.

strate the essential importance, not of "plays for the eye," but of "plays for the ear." A playwright, more than anything else, must now be a poet.[24] (1927)

A Theatre of Poetic Images

To say that words, as opposed to action or spectacle, must remain at the center of the theatre's appeal, and that the playwright must be a poet, provides a point of departure. Kishida wrote many eloquent pages on the function of words in the theatre. Helped by his knowledge of French, he was able to learn for himself the beauty of language attained by European masters and the relation of the beauty of the texts to the continuing appeal of the plays themselves.

Kishida cautioned that this beauty was not merely a question of the phrases themselves. He found that the great writers displayed a rhythm in their text that could carry an audience to a new emotional level. This rhythm constituted the great function, indeed the justification, of the theatre as a form of art.

We must again re-evaluate from our contemporary point of view these masterpieces, to see what makes them what they are, what gives them their genuine theatrical appeal. For us, this appeal is by no means confined to any theatrical or literary appeal assigned to them by critics in the past. These works hold within them a unique Existence, a life found only in the greatest of plays, an underlying rhythm giving life to the contents of the play and motion to its form.[25] (1934)

Kishida found such qualities in the work of a Chekhov, a Shakespeare, a Molière, an Ibsen, or a Maeterlinck.

What is it that gives this underlying rhythm to the plays? It is the poet's conception, expressed in the words spoken by the characters he creates. "I believe we can say that the

---

[24] *Ibid.*, p. 107.   [25] *Ibid.*, p. 113.

essential nature of the theatre lies in a progressive rhythm of images that gives a heightened sense of life through the medium of the stage."[26] (1935)

How is this heightened sense of life to be conveyed? Not through any direct statement: Kishida wanted no didactic statements, no poster art to sully his poetry. The spectator must learn the meaning of a play through his own responses.

> When we read a play or see it staged, we dislike having the author's intentions bluntly revealed to us. We feel uneasy if the author speaks out to us too directly. For the author, like the reader or spectator, must put himself in a position where he, like them, can observe, laugh, and weep. The readers or the audience, when before a play, forget the existence of the author. They try to form their own judgments concerning the characters before them. Before they know it, they are caught up in the playwright's art, incline themselves unknowingly to his ideas, and so are satisfied with their own judgments, which are in fact, the playwright's own. . . .[27] (1925)

How is this transformation possible? How does the audience fall under the sway of the playwright?

> Human reality can be created in the theatre because the drama, through its artistic methods, is capable of poetic suggestion. The theatre is altogether suggestive, yet altogether direct. These elements are not in contradiction; to understand and make use of each is the secret of composing a fine play. Indeed a scene in which the author makes use of no indirect explanations but says directly all he wishes to would not be accepted as real. For in real life there are no "explanations." Normally the playwright avoids them or mixes them with elements that do not directly contribute to them. The regulation of this process is an outcome of the skill, the genius of the playwright.[28] (1925)

[26] *Ibid.*, p. 125.   [27] *Ibid.*, p. 97.   [28] *Ibid.*

The playwright moves his audience through the total force of the poetic imagery built up as the play proceeds, even though the audience may be unaware of the process.

On their part, the audience may be foolish enough to look only for a "story" on the stage. Their expectations when the curtain goes up are aligned to the idea of "what will happen." Yet the words of the characters and their gestures give rise to a piling up of images resulting in a harmony like that of notes of music. For the lines delivered by the actors are not merely a means to tell the story but are each in themselves a theatrical moment.[29] (1929)

The distinctive idea here, and the one which set Kishida apart from so many of the Marxist playwrights of the period, was his insistence that through this progressive piling up of images, the audience would be made to feel and experience an emotion and not merely to understand it. "[The play of the future] will move from a play 'that taught me something' to a kind of play 'that made me feel something.' For a play, unlike a novel, is basically poetic."[30] (1929)

Kishida's conception of dramaturgy, in its abstract stylistic and philosophical sense, shows ambition, sophistication of means, and sincerity. Kishida often quoted such men as Alain and Valéry, and his general inspiration came from his years in France, in that world of Pitoëff and Copeau, the two men who, as Wallace Fowlie wrote, "helped by the type of play they chose to form literary taste. They were quick to perceive and utilize the influences that were being felt in all domains of literature, the growing awareness, for example, of Freud, Proust, and Pirandello."[31] Much has been written of the "new cosmopolitanism" in Japan during the peaceful years immediately after the First World War, but Kishida, who had seen European productions of European

[29] *Ibid.*, p. 106.
[30] *Ibid.*
[31] Wallace Fowlie, *Dionysus in Paris* (New York, 1960), p. 17.

plays, was in a good position to appreciate how far his compatriots were from a grasp of the new international artistic climate into which he and others felt Japan was moving. Yet in the context of the New Theatre movement, Kishida's ideas can be seen not as mere copies of French ones but rather as a set of independent and cogent observations made by a talented and sensitive Japanese who had undergone certain experiences that he felt would at some point be common to more and more of his countrymen.

CHAPTER VI

The Plays

KISHIDA was an articulate advocate of his style of dramaturgy; yet although he was able to make use of his ideas in developing his own style of playwriting, the compromises and adjustments required of him in his other theatrical activities also restricted him in the composition of his plays, since the very fact that he wished them to be performed and accepted by contemporary audiences led him to make various modifications in his style.

Early in his career, Kishida wrote an essay about the various European antecedents of the modern drama in Japan. He opposed to the Northern or Ibsen style of play another style he called the Southern:

> actually the chief influence for this Southern style is French. There are only a few [Japanese] who follow this style; most of them are young and unknown and lack in their dramas the force of those writers who draw their inspiration from Ibsen and the other Northern writers. These young writers are not inspired by any particular French author; indeed it is not clear if such a movement exists in France itself. As opposed to the Northern play, the Southern is more of a light sketch. Authors writing in this style prefer fragrance more than strength, nuance more than depth. Rather than treating human anguish directly as anguish itself, these authors create comedies through the use of fantasy. Rather than picturing directly the heartlessness of society, they tend to content themselves with merely hinting in a less systematic way at the scorn men feel for themselves when they cannot bear the cruelty of human existence, or at

the laughter and tears of those who rage against it.[1] (1927)

Kishida was no doubt describing himself. All the marks of his style are suggested here, especially his propensity for comedy as a means of social and moral satire. Late in his life he reaffirmed the same conviction.

Through my work as a playwright, I have come to feel very strongly the logic of the necessity for comedy in modern times, and I have continued in my own uncertain efforts to understand the comic spirit and to create its proper forms. While I do not believe that as yet my labors have borne their proper fruit, I do feel that at least I have found a satisfactory means to attack the problem. My methods are not necessarily new ones, but at my age I must use what means I can, with my own angle of vision.

I have always believed that comedy is born of a deep sadness felt over men and over the age in which they live. Yet if sadness only ends with sadness, the result is merely an alliance with despair. I refuse to stay rooted there; I want to push forward. Even knowing the indignation produced by suffering, I still feel a need for laughter pent up inside me. . . .

Surely it is the desire to criticize and comment on mankind that, taking the form of satire, gives birth to what we call comedy. Yet those who comment on mankind suffer from the same defects as the others they criticize. Indeed comedy, more than any other literary form, is a mirror in which the author himself is reflected.[2] (1950)

A juxtaposition of these two quotations, written almost twenty-five years apart, suggests the spiritual development of this gifted author who suffered so many vicissitudes in the course of his career.[3] Both statements, however, affirm

---

[1] *zenshū*, VIII, p. 219.　　[2] *Ibid.*, p. 342.

[3] Some Japanese critics maintain that Kishida's interest in comedy has militated against his acceptance in Japan as a leading literary

the central nature of his personality and his desire to see the folly, and in the folly some kind of beauty, of his own generation. Kishida was an extremely serious artist, and in his own modest way he reaffirmed Ibsen's doctrine of "ex-

---

figure. For example, Fukuda Tsuneari, himself a noted playwright and director and well known as an admirer of Kishida's work, writes as follows:

> There are times in our lives when we face a crisis too grave to be resolved by the tolerance of humor. In the real world of today, the mere strength of our own will or spirit cannot be sufficient to allow us to dominate the obstacles that beset us. Faced with the situation, our independence of spirit crumbles away. To escape from this situation we have our education, our generosity of spirit, and our humor. Yet on the other hand, faced with the social situation, so inflamed by the opposition of one class to another, should not our eyes that have only been turned inward now be opened to the whole of society? . . . if I wished to make any complaint to Kishida, it would be: why have you tried to escape this? (*Gendai Nihon bungaku zenshū*, XXXIII, p. 404.)

The reticence of the Japanese public to accept comedy as a serious form of art is suggested by the following remarks made by the veteran playwright Iizawa Tadasu, quoted in the *New York Times* of June 1, 1970.

> "For a man, one cheek in three years." So runs a Japanese proverb, cautioning that a warrior can afford to wrinkle but one of his cheeks in laughter once in three years. Tadasu Iizawa, Japan's foremost living comic playwright, cited the proverb the other day to explain why comedy is still disdained in this country. "The very word comedy," he said, "came into the Japanese language only in 1891, when Tsubouchi Shōyō published his celebrated translations of Shakespeare. . . ." Mr. Iizawa thinks that educated Japanese still look down on comedy. "It's that old Confucian state ideology," he said, "going all the way back to Tokugawa times when Japan was an isolated feudal society. Of course comedy existed in those days, at the popular level. There were plenty of plays with comic moments, but never a whole play devoted to comedy. I stick to my thesis that under the Tokugawa Shoguns, comedies were not allowed, because the rulers knew only too well that laughter was the most effective and sometimes the only means of protest against authoritarian rule."

Iizawa may overstate his case, but at least the generalization can be

144

periences lived through."[4] For, as Kishida said, he was really writing about himself.

Aside from a few comments in his memoir discussing his early days in the New Theatre movement, Kishida was reticent about explaining the meaning or significance of any particular work. In 1931 he spoke of his plays as providing "a poor and weak record of my life in the theatre,"[5] but he never submitted his own plays to any extended analysis.

Probably the most celebrated statement Kishida made about his purposes as a playwright, and one that drew a great deal of criticism, was an early remark he made concerning the possible themes and significance of his plays.

I don't write a play to "say something."

Rather, I find "something to say" in order to write a play.

There is no reason to become angry with me about this. Don't you theatre critics write your stuff in just the same way? Well, don't you?[6]

---

made that most writers and playwrights of stature in modern Japan prefer serious themes.

[4] Eric Bentley has written a series of remarks on Pirandello and his interest in comedy that may shed some light on Kishida's purposes:

Pirandello's subject is what might be called the Twentieth Century Blues, by which I mean not any particular, localized disillusionment, such as that of the lost generation of the twenties or that of the ex-communists today. I mean the disillusionment that is common to all of these: disillusionment over the failure, not so much of socialism or liberalism, but of humanness itself in our time. In Pirandello's world there is only littleness and passive suffering. Perhaps it was the realization that littleness and passive suffering are untragic that impelled Pirandello to make comedies out of them. As comedies, they are more moving! (*The Playwright as Thinker*, p. 156.)

Kishida's blues were no doubt somewhat more localized: more a well-educated-Japanese-back-in-a-Japan-going-to-pieces-Blues, if I may continue with Mr. Bentley's analogy.

[5] *zenshū*, IX, p. 312.   [6] *Ibid.*, p. 119.

Seen in the context of the whole body of Kishida's work, the statement was probably a playful attack on Japanese playwrights of the Ibsen school who insisted somewhat too heavily for Kishida's sake on the necessity of a serious theme. As Kishida suggested, in the theatre nuance can often be more effective than a sermon.

Within the general framework of comedy, however, Kishida moved through various stages, or rather through a series of compromises, first within the theatrical world and then within his own society, which was at that time headed toward a repression of human values and, eventually, to war. An analysis of these compromises suggests that there were four distinct periods in his work during the years 1925-1939. The texts of the plays themselves show the changes, and some of the comments that Kishida made in the prefaces to the various collected editions of his plays indicate the attitudes governing their composition.[7]

Kishida describes his first playwriting venture, already mentioned above, in a very off-hand fashion.

One day I talked with Pitoëff backstage. He said he was thinking of doing a Japanese play, but what was available? I wasn't able to give him a prompt answer. In the first place, I didn't know enough about the field. I did happen to have the texts of a few modern Japanese plays with me, but—it wasn't that I didn't want to see them performed in France so much as the fact that I thought they would be terrible if they were! I left without answering him, but I suddenly thought I might try some-

[7] Many of Kishida's plays have been collected in anthologies of plays or of modern literature. Editors, however, have tended to choose his earlier short plays as typical of his style and often stress them, rather than the longer, later plays that represent a more solid and sustained accomplishment. The first plays are certainly important historically, since Kishida brought a whole new kind of theatre to Japan. But they do not suggest much about his growth as a person or as a writer.

thing a little underhanded—I would write one myself and give it to him! I had an idea for a modern play; I wrote it out and a week later, with the help of a French friend, I managed to complete a translation into French. I called it *A Wan Smile*. When I showed it to Pitoëff, he told me, "It's really quite interesting." This incident seems like something I made up, but it is quite true.[8]

When Kishida returned to Japan, the text of this play, now retitled *Furui Omocha* (*Old Toys*) was published in *New Currents of Drama* in March of 1924. It was his first published work. There is no record of its ever having been produced.

The play is a tentative work and so atypical of his later work that it can be said to precede the four periods of Kishida's career mentioned above. "Tentative" is the best word to describe the play, not because the situation or the characters seem awkward or incomplete, but because it is full of the kind of direct statements about human feelings that Kishida soon replaced with his much more effective poetic and indirect techniques of composition. A long play in six scenes, it describes the emotional relationship between Shirakawa, a young Japanese artist studying in France, and Louise, a French girl (also presumably an artist) who loves him. They wish to marry but are prevented by the kinds of emotional complications inherent in a conflict of cultures. Another woman in the play, Fusako, the estranged wife of a Japanese diplomat living in Paris, also takes an amatory interest in Shirakawa, but she looks for a rather different emotional response from him than does Louise, educated and independent in a western way. But the play's real concern seems to be over the conflict of cultures: several conversations between Louise and Shirakawa on this subject are notable for both their frankness and their sophistication. There is no evidence that the play is autobiographical;

[8] *zenshū*, IX, p. 185.

Kishida may be Shirakawa, but Louise and Fusako are really France and Japan. The play is a record of his reactions to the two countries.

In scene four, Shirakawa, embarrassed since he feels people stare at him when he is with Louise, indulges in the kind of self-denigration Kishida seems to see as typically Japanese. Louise maintains a European forthrightness.

Shirakawa: . . . I know there is a battle going on in your heart. And I think I know what it is. And while I silently watch it going on, I feel worse than if my own flesh were being consumed. It may seem foolish of me to talk like this, but it is not in your nature, or in mine, to willingly accept the view that most white people take of the yellow race. Yet nothing can be done about the physical defects. With a face like a monkey's, and skin the color of mud. . . . When you see a man from behind with a short neck, square shoulders, narrow hips, and bow legs, you'll say, "That must be a Japanese." Even I, who am not a white man, can feel scorn for the ugliness of any such wretched shape.

Louise: (with a stern look) How you insist on humiliating yourself! You can despise yourself just as much as you please, but please don't forget I am perfectly free to choose my own husband. I have no idea where you picked up these ideas, but if you feel some dissatisfaction over the fact that the two of us plan to marry, then please say so straight out. Even if I were an ordinary unsophisticated girl, I still don't think I would pay any more attention to the body of the man who really loved me than I do now. I realize we have to think carefully about a marriage between two races, but in our case, we both have some comprehension of each other's countries, and there is a genuine feeling of closeness between us. We can easily remove any small obstacles.[9]

The issue as presented is a real one and the emotions felt seem genuinely expressed. But the characters are exchanging emotional *tirades*, permitting Kishida to examine both sides of the question in detail. The small conversations which precede this scene are relatively effective, but the jump from the talk of the weather and dinner to this set of speeches is too great.

Scene five has a fine passage in which Shirakawa's (and Kishida's) dilemmas are most clearly expressed. The couple have been dancing; now they stop to rest for a few moments.

Shirakawa: Sometimes I realize that somehow it is just when you forget yourself that you have a real grasp of your own existence. . . . It seems a paradoxical way to put things. . . .

Louise: You're right, you know.

Shirakawa: There is nothing so harmful to an energetic life than a consciousness of life.

Louise: I'm not so sure. You have an acutely developed sense of life in Japan, but I do not think it would withstand the kind of pressures that are woven into the very fabric of life in Europe.

Shirakawa: But even though most Japanese haven't completely given up those feelings you speak of, I'm not satisfied with that particular pastime any more.

Louise: What you mean is you've given up your old toys and are looking for a new set, but when it comes time to play with the new ones, the conditions are different and it's no fun. Isn't that right? But I know how to have fun with

[9] *zenshū*, I, pp. 34-35.

149

all of them. (The orchestra stops playing and applause and laughter can be clearly heard.)

Shirakawa: In Japan, you know, we talk about a compromise between east and west.

Louise: But to say "compromise" doesn't necessarily mean to be at cross-purposes. Now don't get angry. You may speak slightingly about compromise, but your *own* life is not being led at cross-purposes. You are affirming the quality of western life, and you set your thoughts at odds with your own feelings as a Japanese, feelings as refined as any in the world. Why set them back to back like that?[10]

The argument continues in a similar fashion: Louise wants to go to Japan to see what life there is really like, but Shirakawa cannot bear the idea of returning to a Japan that "from any point of view is a society terrible to live in, full of contradictions, bankrupt." She ends by finding him altogether too "difficult," and goes off to the Orient to see for herself, leaving Shirakawa behind to fall ill and be looked after by the less intellectually rigorous Fusako. Kishida's treatment of the relationship between Louise and Shirakawa is effective because he is sensitive enough to see the emotional nuances in the situation he has created for his characters, but strong-minded enough to avoid an easy solution, or a purely emotional one, to the complexities he presents. The only difficulty was that his sense of theatre was not yet strong enough to transmute a philosophical conversation into a drama.

Even so, the basic skills necessary to compose a fine play are in evidence. Louise's speech about "old toys" and "new toys" (which presumably gave Kishida the idea for his revised title) suggests the technique by which Kishida later used images to heighten poetically an ordinary conversation and extend its emotional range and meaning. The example

[10] *Ibid.,* pp. 27-28.

seems all the more vivid because it stands out as something of a contrast to the rest of the play, but in his play, *Chiroru no aki* (*Autumn in the Tyrols*), also probably written in France, the technique of the poetic image is already perfected.

Autumn in the Tyrols, the second of Kishida's plays to be published, appeared in the September 1924 issue of *New Currents of Drama*; it was the first of his plays to be staged in Japan, that same year by the New Theatre Society. Like *Old Toys*, it attempts to deal with problems of east and west, but the arguments have been transmuted into personal visions of life shared by a Japanese man named Amano and a European woman named Stella, both of whom are staying in a small hotel in the Tyrols. Human emotions treated as national characteristics in the earlier play are now seen to be personal, yet nevertheless involved in the whole ambiguity of human existence.

Amano: Actually, I still don't really know where you are from.

Stella: Just look at the hotel register.

Amano: A hotel register is only a hotel register. I don't think you are an American. . . . (He gazes at her.)

Stella: Oh? (She takes her last sip of coffee.)

Amano: Actually I don't think so much about the fact that I'm Japanese. The bare fact of where someone is from is not very interesting to me. The disparity between our lives is really not so great.

Stella: That's true. (She gets up from her chair and sits down near him on the settee.) Yes, that's really quite true.[11]

Although the two are more or less strangers, Amano suggests that they find some way to share their feelings on this quiet fall evening.

[11] *Ibid.*, p. 46.

Amano: . . . there hasn't been an opportunity like this before. As soon as a meal is finished, you always avoid the others and lose yourself in reading or meditating. I've never been near you, except in this dining room. This is our last night here, you know.

Stella: The last night . . . that too is playing with daydreams, isn't it?

Amano: Of course. . . . Yet isn't there any way to make the game more interesting . . . since there are two of us? That is, if you would permit it. . . . Tomorrow, when you travel away over that mountain peak, I will be the one who simply fades forever from your dreams.

Stella: Do you really mean what you say?

Amano: Yes. Yes, I think so. Travellers can be bound together by a kind of friendship not restrained by any promises. . . . Are we involved with others or not? In my hand, that I can stretch out to you, lies all the strength, the freedom and the strength, of a traveller. . . . Don't you think so?

In the deep mountains, here in the Tyrols, two people can talk about themselves . . . on the basis of the fact that they swear they will never meet again. . . . They can pass a night like two lovers who part for a long time. . . .

How interesting that would be. Would you like to try?

You look at your dreams. You will see another . . . that is all. . . .[12]

The two decide to talk aloud of their dreams and proceed to do so. They assume various roles in relation to each other, as lyrical effusions alternate with humorous and sporting rejoinders.

[12] *Ibid.*, p. 50.

Stella: If it's just a play . . . really just a play. . . .

Amano: (taking her hands) It's no good to be afraid. . . .

Stella: (brushing his hand aside) No . . . no. . . . That won't do at all . . . you can't enter into my dreams. That is the first thing that I . . . you see, someone like you, spoiling my dreams. . . .

Amano: I am the man who begs things of you. I am the man who cleaned your shoes by the side of the road. I am the man who gave you his seat on the train. I am the man who picked up your handkerchief for you in the theatre.

Stella: (with emotion) You really don't know anything about a woman's feelings, do you?

Amano: (taking her hand) I know no way to read the heart of a woman who is indifferent.

Stella: (As if thinking better of him, grasps his hand.) You're right . . . yes, let's play the play together.[13]

The two continue to toy with each other's emotions, never completely sure of each other. Stella tells Amano that her mother was born in Nagasaki, but he (and the audience) never learn her nationality, nor, for that matter, why either of the two is travelling. The play is a mood piece, a lyrical treatment of the conflict between illusion and reality. But there are no open encounters such as were found in *Old Toys*. Both Amano and Shirakawa are learning how to handle themselves in a vast and real world, but Kishida, in moving from polemics to poetry, began to create in *Autumn in the Tyrols* his own art in terms of the theatre.

Both plays had a considerable success when printed, and Kishida was soon considered a brilliant addition to the Japanese theatre and to the Japanese world of letters generally. Yet he met with difficulties almost at once; Osanai Kaoru, on the board of editors of *New Currents of Drama*,

[13] *Ibid.*, p. 52.

153

was not at all impressed by his work. Kishida noted wryly that Osanai turned down *Autumn in the Tyrols* for possible production at the Tsukiji Little Theatre because "it seemed to be looking at human nature from inside the theatre."[14] Kishida knew as well as anyone that he was a beginner in a difficult field and that he would have to extend his range of vision and his writing techniques. In fact, the problems of conflict between cultures underlying both his early plays were not of general interest to the Japanese theatregoing public; although the spectators might have felt the "cross-purposes" of life in modern Japan, they lacked the sophistication necessary fully to appreciate the special world evoked in these two plays.

Kishida now began to write a variety of plays dealing directly with that Japan "so full of contradictions" in which he found himself. These early plays were written between 1925 and 1930 and mark the first division in the progression of his work.

The period 1925-1930 was a time of experimentation for Kishida. He wrote an extraordinary number of plays, often several a year, and always of high quality. He chose a variety of themes, used different writing techniques, and created works not only for the small New Theatre troupes, but for *shimpa* and *shinkokugeki* troupes as well. It was the time when he tried to search out the range of his artistic possibilities.

Kishida began by writing many short one-act plays, in a variety of moods, dealing with contemporary life on the psychological and spiritual level, for he never relied on scenery and spectacle. *Buranko* (*The Swing*), first published in *New Currents of Drama* in April 1925, is usually considered one of his best short plays, although there is no record of its having been performed. Like *Autumn in the Tyrols*, it is a two-character play in which Kishida attempts to establish a poetic mood. Rather than confrontation, he is

[14] *zenshū*, IX, p. 317.

interested in intermingling the moods of the two people involved, in this case a husband and wife. The play shows the love the two characters feel for each other; they begin emotionally far apart and are drawn close together. The plot, if it can even be called such, is very simple: the husband recounts a dream to his wife. At the beginning of the play, the two seem to be living in different mental worlds, and the contrast is quickly and humorously made.

Husband: (appearing) Say, you know, I had the most fabulous dream last night.

Wife: (paying no attention to him) The toothpaste tube has split open, so be careful.

Husband: (coming into the kitchen) No rats in the kitchen last night? . . .

You know, I've had lots of dreams before, but never one so surprising as this one.

It was really wonderful.

Wife: Was there a towel in the bathroom?

Husband: Yes there was.

Just because I said it was a dream is no reason to make a fool of me.

When I tell you something like this, you always come back at me by saying that I give too much importance to my dreams. But just because I dream I'm a millionaire doesn't necessarily mean I'm going to be one. I'm not so foolish as to take *that* seriously.

I mean, good heavens, a dream is always a dream. No question about it.

But you know, a real dream is different from a daydream. A dream has something to do with what really happened once in real life. That's why dreams just appear like that when we sleep.

Wife: I think the green leeks have boiled too long for the soup, you know. . . .

155

Husband: Leeks . . . are we having leek soup for breakfast?[15]

The wife insists on being practical, reminds him of the
time, and tries to organize her enthusiastic husband for the
day. Dreams are what give beauty to life, he insists, and he
finally succeeds in telling her his dream: lost in a forest, he
came on a lovely girl and they swung together. Naturally
the wife is not very taken by this story and tries to make
her husband stop talking, telling him to finish when he comes
home that night. He asks her if she knows who the girl on
the swing was; offended, she says she does not care to know
anything about it. He continues to press the point.

Husband: This girl, this girl who looks like someone.
Who is it?
Don't you think it is strange?
How old were you when I first met you?
Nineteen?
Or twenty?
It must have been. . . .
What did you look like when you were twelve
or thirteen?
There is no way that I could know, is there?
Wife: I suppose you've seen a photograph. . . .
Husband: Perhaps. . . .
I see,
You're just as cool as a cucumber, aren't you?
Quite merciless.
But you've not had any doubts about me up
until now. . . .
And you'd like to believe I'm very happy,
wouldn't you?
Wife: I'm . . . I'm happy too.
Husband: Good, good, that's a good answer.
(a pause)
Shall I go on?

[15] *Ibid.*, I, pp. 77-78.

156

That girl, in some way, looked just like you.
No, more than that, she was an exact image of
    you.
But here is the interesting point of the dream.
When I first noticed this, I wasn't surprised or
    flustered at all.
I was sixteen,
You were twelve, and I was holding you
Calmly, quietly,
And on the swing
We passed the whole night through.

Wife: Oh, for ever and ever. . . .

Husband: The swing,
    even though we did little to move it,
Glided happily.
(a pause)
Each time you bent over,
Your locks of hair
Tangled in my face.
You said it was delightful
And brought your face close to mine.

Wife: (laughing) My goodness . . . !

Husband: The swing,
Of its own accord,
Seemed to be swaying.[16]

The two are reunited, and their dream of love becomes
more and more extravagant until the mood is suddenly rup-
tured by the arrival of a friend with whom the husband
rides the train to work every day. He has important news
of his own to relate, but the husband also wants to tell his
friend about his dream, and as they go off together, "there
begins from somewhere or other the sound of whistling,
quite out of tune with their voices; for an instant we hear
the sounds mingled together."[17]

Kishida does not name his characters, possibly because

[16] *Ibid.*, pp. 82-83.   [17] *Ibid.*, p. 86.

they are merely manifestations of the mood he wants to create. *The Swing* is surely a young man's play, full of lyric optimism. The dialogue is based on a close observation of human reactions, and the characters now react with each other, so that there is more movement, more theatrical tension, than can be found in *Autumn in the Tyrols.*

It was about this time that Kishida made the statement that " 'I find something to say' in order to write a play."

The Swing was merely the first of such "sketch plays." The next of them, *Kamifūsen* (*Paper Balloon*) is sometimes cited as his single most effective piece for the theatre. The play first appeared in the May 1925 issue of *Literary Annals* and was staged a year later by a small New Theatre company, the Aoidori (Blue Bird) troupe. It was subsequently produced on several occasions by the Literary Theatre and other groups. Like *The Swing*, *Paper Balloon* has two characters without names, again a husband and wife. It is still another variant on the theme of dreams, but this time the couple dreams together. It is a lyrical examination of the emotions of two young people who are trying to learn how to live and love together. The opening of the play, which includes a good deal of banter about the proper independence for a modern wife, is quite charming. The wife tells her husband that she ought to have the right to go off by herself on a Sunday, to assert her own independence. They make up a conversation in which they pretend that she is going out.

Husband: . . . well then, I suppose that is all right with me. But if you're not here, what will I do about lunch?

Wife: I've made a few simple preparations for you.

Husband: And in the evening?

Wife: When I go out, I'll stop by the corner restaurant and have them deliver some eggs and rice to you.

Husband: Again? And I suppose you'll be late coming home.

Wife: That's a good question. I really don't know, but if it gets past ten o'clock, go ahead and fix your bed and go to sleep.

Husband: Do you have any money?

Wife: Not a penny.

Husband: Well let me give you this. Here's ten yen.

Wife: Thanks.

Husband: The night wind is cold now, so don't forget to take a muffler.

Wife: Sure.

Husband: Well now, I guess I'll just curl up and read a book. Just heat the water up for a bath before you go. If any guests drop by, we have some old biscuits left. I don't think I'll shave today. Ah, what a nice, peaceful Sunday this is. . . .

Wife: (Silent, she stares at the floor.)

Husband: Now what?

Wife: You're impossible!

Husband: Impossible? In what way?

Wife: In every way![18]

In fact, the couple has no money to do anything at all. The central section of the play involves an imaginary trip to the seaside resort of Kamakura, in which they pretend to have a great deal of money, take the best seats on the train, go to an expensive seaside hotel, and then go walking on the beach. As they act out their private fantasy together, they draw closer and closer together, until the husband carries the joke a bit too far.

Husband: . . . let's go walking then. . . .
Where's my walking stick?

Wife: You didn't forget it in the train?

Husband: No, I gave it to the bellboy at the hotel. Ah yes, that's it.

[18] *Ibid.*, p. 88.

159

Wife: Which way shall we go?

Husband: That's the island of Enoshima you can see over there. . . .

Wife: Such a lovely spot.

Husband: Be careful, or you'll tumble over. Let's take hands.

Wife: But people will see us.

Husband: So much the worse for them. Are you tired? Let's rest here a moment. If you like, you can go swimming in the sea.

Wife: I think I will.

Husband: Go ahead. When you take your clothes off, you really have a lovely figure. Don't go too far in the water now. . . .

Wife: I'm all right.

Husband: Stop, stop, let me have a look at you. Shall I take a picture of you? Fine. Ah, that's just marvellous! (He becomes more and more excited.) I've never seen you look so lovely as you look now. How do you manage? What splendid coloring. I didn't realize your hair was that long. That your bosom was so plump. Ah, you're laughing! Turn this way now. Are those your eyes? And that mouth! (He cries out as if he had forgotten himself.)

Wife: (Lifting her head, as if to reprove him.) Now really.
(A long silence)

Husband: Come here and let me look at you.
(She laughs)

Husband: (extending both hands) Come and look.

Wife: Certainly not.

Husband: Come on now.

Wife: (Rising, she takes both his hands and moves them back and forth.) You just don't know when to stop, do you?

Husband: What do you mean? (He tries to pull her to him.)

Wife: Don't do that.

Husband: (still holding her hands) You aren't really angry with me, are you? You seem to be acting that way, but. . . .

Wife: What do you think?

Husband: I was just having more and more fun playing this game with you. That's the truth.[19]

The dream fades and the banter begins again; she doesn't want him to stay home on her account, and she remarks that after all, "Sunday is a frightening day." A paper balloon floats in from next door, and as the curtain falls she goes off to chase it with her husband and the children from the neighboring house. The balloon seems a charming symbol for the emotional currents of fantasy and humor that dart through the play. The emotional arc of the author's conception is created with great skill and delicacy.

The technique of an imaginary journey without scenery seems to have been original with Kishida, although the same effect was also created by Thornton Wilder in his 1931 play *The Happy Journey from Trenton to Camden*. Kishida indicated in one of his essays that, unlike Jacques Copeau, he was not opposed in principle to the use of scenery, but he created here a remarkable opportunity for actors to create their own atmosphere, a chance which, at the time when the play was first presented, may well have required too much of them.

Paper Balloon received very high praise from Kishida's contemporaries. Kubota Mantarō wrote that "this play became Kishida's most effective piece, for with his creation of this two-character play, without a definite plot and loosely constructed, he gave a sense of freshness. Kishida showed in it his ability to create his peerless dialogue, so rich in poetic

[19] *Ibid.*, pp. 92-93.

spirit. His star rose and he far surpassed the other established playwrights. With this play he took his unwavering position at the head of his field."[20] Iwata Toyoo was of the same mind. "Surely this is his most beautifully worked-out play. It is very short, but so beautifully written. From the beginning he was best at writing in short forms. . . ."[21] The particular kind of poetic world Kishida created in this play was so effective and so special that *Paper Balloon* remains even today the hallmark of the Kishida style.[22] Yet it must

[20] Quoted on p. 410, *Gendai Nihon bungaku zenshū*, XXXIII.

[21] *Ibid.*, p. 411.

[22] Definitions of Kishida's style based on this play misrepresent the general thrust of his work. Writers and critics sympathetic to the aims and ideals of the leftist theatre in the 1930s refused to admit the artistic value of the plays by Kishida and his literary colleagues. Shimomura Masao remarks that "even if such plays . . . never escape the limitations of portraying the emotions of lower middle-class city people, the label given by the writers of the proletarian theatre to such plays as 'mere comedies of manners . . .' was surely a mistake." (*Shingeki*, p. 79.)

This attitude, however, continues to exist. Odagiri Hideo writes in his history of modern Japanese literature that "although *Old Toys* deals with the confrontations between Japanese and western culture, Kishida never again chose a special environment about which to write, and, as in a play like *Paper Balloon*, he chose to deal with the environment of lower middle-class city people." (See *Kōza Nihon kindai bungakushi*, III, p. 170.) The same view was expressed by Ueda Makoto in English when he wrote that "the characters [Kishida] was fond of depicting were lower middle-class people as they modestly lived their family life. . . ." (See his article, "Japanese Literature Since World War II," *The Literary Review*, August 1962, p. 8.)

To this reader at least, the implications of Kishida's poetic style are quite different. Unlike the Marxist writers, he found his motivating force in human character, not in economic forces. Most of his later plays deal with families so well educated or wealthy that they were altogether atypical of Japan at the time, but, again, critical opinion remains centered on these early plays. Yet even in the case of *Paper Balloon* Kishida scrupulously avoided any description of social detail. We know only that the couple is married, the husband works, and the two do not have enough money to do everything that they wish

be noted that the play was written only two years after his return to Japan. It was the last of his short dream plays and he never wrote in the style again. Because of the extraordinary range of plays that followed, it seems unlikely that Kishida did not repeat his success because he could not, but rather that he was interested in other treatments of other themes. Still, after the freshness of *Paper Balloon*, none of the later plays would seem quite so unexpected.

Nineteen hundred and twenty-six saw the publication of several more short plays, among them two that served to broaden his style, *Hazakura* (*The Cherry Tree in Leaf*) and *Shūu* (*Sudden Shower*). *The Cherry Tree in Leaf* was published in the April 1926 issue of *Woman* and was produced on the stage the following year by the New Theatre Society. The play represents a new departure from the dream plays; although punctuated with humorous scenes, it is a gripping, almost bitter treatment of love and marriage. Again the play has only two characters, a mother and a daughter. The mother tries to sound out her daughter about her feelings toward a young man who has been courting her in a very desultory fashion. As the discussion proceeds, it becomes clear that the girl has no real idea of what marriage entails. The boy does not seem especially interested in her, and the mother is horrified to see her daughter slipping into marriage and committing her life away for no good purpose.

Mother: . . . but if you don't make up your own mind, it is very difficult for me. (Pause.) Just to say you'll marry him . . . you make me feel uncomfortable. He hasn't even definitely said that he'll marry you. The whole situation is somehow too uncertain.

Girl: I think he's just left it up to his mother.

---

to do. The characters here, and in the other early plays as well, are surely too well educated and well spoken to be "lower middle class."

The repetition among literary critics of these same misstatements about Kishida's work is most disheartening.

Mother: And he has no qualms about that?

Girl: Well, I don't know exactly how he feels, but. . . .

Mother: And I suppose you're taking the attitude that it doesn't matter much either way.

Girl: You know I'll do whatever you say, don't you?

Mother: No, it's different for you. (Pause.) That's why I want you to ask him, "When you say you want me, is it you saying it, or your mother?"

Girl: Oh no, I'd be embarrassed to ask anything like that.

(Silence.)

Mother: Listen, you are a woman now yourself. I think you are old enough to understand something I, as your mother, want to tell you. (Pause.) I don't want to put you in a situation where you will spend your whole life flattering a man. Excuse me for saying this. But every woman, once in her life, is bound to meet a man who will really show affection for her. And if this man doesn't love you for yourself. . . .[23]

The mother decides to tell her daughter how badly treated she was by her own husband, whom she married as a result of a formal arrangement. The daughter is shocked, as she always loved and respected her father.

Mother: As far as you were concerned, he was a perfectly splendid father. That's why, even now, I don't think of him as all that bad. But it is just that I don't want you to suffer through all I went through. That's all. (Pause.) His attitude might be common to most men. . . . I don't know.

Girl: But you are talking about something that happened a long time ago. Nowadays men aren't like that. You know, I've seen the movies.[24]

[23] *zenshū*, I, p. 120.   [24] *Ibid.*

Portrait of Kishida

Hamlet

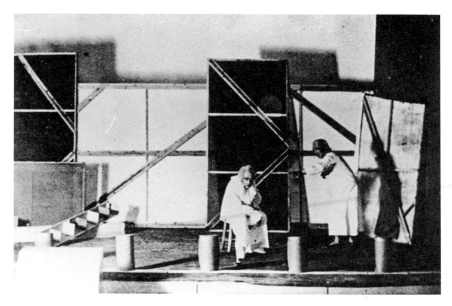

The Holiday

Wolves

Autumn in the Tyrols

Paper Balloon

A Space of Time

The mother questions her daughter closely and decides that she must marry the boy. She thinks of the possible honeymoon trips the couple might make and says that they should go to Europe; then in a fury of pent-up emotion, she tells her daughter that she intends to accompany them on their honeymoon, since she has a right to some excitement in her life as well. She looks at her daughter, who is powdering her face and admiring herself in the mirror, apparently not listening. The mother turns on her.

Mother: What is that white powder on your neck?
Why do you put it on that way?
Girl: But I haven't spread it too far.
Mother: In the first place, it's too thick.
Girl: It's not. No it's not. (While speaking, she straightens up.)
Mother: How old are you . . . nineteen? You've got to take yourself in hand. . . . (Silence.) From now on you . . . and your mother too, from now on. . . . (She heaves a sigh.)
(The daughter says nothing.)
Mother: (lonely) You say that everything will be fine. When is that going to be?
Girl: Do you mean . . . fine for me?
Mother: (without strength) Yes, yes I do. (Pause.) The whole thing is all wrong . . . all wrong. There's no way to know how things will turn out, but you. . . .
The daughter quietly rises and stands behind her mother, who, feeling her presence, turns obliquely and glances in that direction. A silence. Suddenly the daughter, as if realizing the situation for the first time, covers her face with her sleeve. Then suddenly she breaks down crying beside her mother. Curtain.[25]

The Cherry Tree in Leaf is a fairly realistic play, but even here, Kishida uses a poetic image, that of cherries just past

[25] *Ibid.*, p. 126.

their bloom, to heighten the effect of the situation; just as the branches of the cherry trees, their blossoms faded with the green leaves now showing, can be seen outside the window, so the girl's relationship with the young man is pictured as somewhat past its first enthusiasm; the girl herself describes to her mother how they walked down a lane of cherry trees in bloom, "the petals falling, the branches forming a tunnel." The emotional situation presented in the play, however, has moved beyond this lovely lyrical moment.

The second play, *Sudden Shower*, published in the September 1926 issue of *Literary Annals*, was also produced on the stage, in 1930, by a *shimpa* troupe. Like *The Cherry Tree in Leaf* it deals with disappointments in marriage and might almost represent a picturing in theatrical terms of the sufferings of the mother with her husband in the earlier play. Both plays treat their subject matter with considerable detachment and no trace of sentimentality; indeed, often an element of humor is interjected.

Sudden Shower involves a young bride who, disgusted with her husband's rude behavior to her on their honeymoon trip, leaves him to return to Tokyo, resolved to seek a divorce. The play is mainly taken up by her recounting to her sister and her husband the various problems she had had with him. The happily married couple attempts to calm her and persuade her to keep trying to find some means by which she can come to respect and love her husband. The story line, it is true, veers close to sentimentality, but Kishida maintains a certain dry tone throughout. It is obvious that he feels the seriousness of the problem of human isolation, but he also creates in the character of the new wife a certain element of naïveté that permits her to reveal herself in a variety of amusing ways, as when the married sister Akeko asks her sister Tsuneko what went wrong. Incidentally, this is one of the first plays in which Kishida gave names to his characters.

Akeko: So I suppose you had a fight.

Tsuneko: No, it wasn't that. . . . (Pause) Well, it just didn't work out.

Akeko: What do you mean it didn't work out? You mean that from the beginning. . . .

Tsuneko: No, nothing like that . . . but I did tell you he had bad manners, didn't I?

Akeko: Is that what all the fuss is about?

Tsuneko: No, that's not all. Well I mean, yes, it's true, but it's not just that. Really, I'm altogether disgusted with him.

Akeko: Oh, men are all that way, you know.

Tsuneko: Don't you remember the time he came and yawned in front of mother? . . . and she looked angry afterwards? He's always doing things like that. Of course, if he yawns or something in front of me, I don't really mind, but when other people are around he does some things without thinking that just make me tremble.

Akeko: What sort of things?

Tsuneko: I can't tell you what they are one by one. I mean there are so many of them. . . . For example, when we got on the train, he suddenly sat crosslegged on the seat and started snoring away. That was on the very day we left.

Akeko: And he didn't talk to you?

Tsuneko: Talk to me! I really don't even know why we bothered to go on a honeymoon! Everyone looked at us so strangely. He didn't even cover his face with a handkerchief but slept with his mouth wide open![26]

Like the girl who had "seen it in the movies," Tsuneko was not prepared for reality. This bantering tone fades as

[26] *Ibid.*, pp. 143-144.

167

the play progresses; Akeko sides with her sister and begins to argue with her husband in an increasingly acrimonious atmosphere. Akeko's husband agrees that men can be selfish and unfeeling but urges his sister-in-law to try to bring her husband to the point where he will feel some affection for her. "Anyway," he tells Tsuneko, "go back home today and stay with your husband. Look as though you didn't notice anything. Put on an act." Just as Tsuneko is about to go, there is a terrible downpour of rain. The three stand, watching as the curtain falls.

In these two plays Kishida shows himself able to compose strong dramatic scenes with considerable bite and shading while still maintaining elements of his light and fluent style. The plays may not be masterpieces, but they suggest that he was extending the range of his means of artistic expression in order to handle longer and more difficult themes. By now he had seen several of his short plays produced on the stage, usually by small companies. He left no specific comments on these early productions, but his general comments on the level of performance during the period indicate that he must have been dissatisfied. Kon Hidemi wrote that "the *shimpa* troupes performed some of Kishida's plays, but he was always dissatisfied and disappointed with the results."[27] Yet if his plays proved too difficult for the actors, they nevertheless earned him a place of honor on the literary scene. Six were first published in a collection in 1925, and similar volumes followed every few years.

Only after the experience of writing a variety of short plays did Kishida attempt his first important full-length work, *Mura de ichi ban kuri no ki* (*The Tallest Chestnut in the Village*), first published in the October 1926 issue of *Woman*. The play was not produced until 1954, when it was staged by the Kurumiza, the best New Theatre troupe in the Kyoto-Osaka area. (*Old Toys*, his first play, was a full-length work, but, as was pointed out above, the circumstances of its composition were somewhat special.) Kishida's

27 See Kon, "Morarisuto Kishida," p. 35.

earlier plays were sustained by mood rather than by plot. What means would he choose to sustain and unify a more complex conception? Hints of the method could be found in *The Cherry Tree in Leaf*, built around an image of spring blossoms and the passage of time. Now Kishida chose another symbol, a huge chestnut tree, to tie his play together.

The play concerns the early married life of a young couple. Ryōtarō, the husband, is the elder son of a wealthy country family living in the mountains behind Karuizawa; he has received a good education and now lives in Tokyo, where he has met and married his wife Ayako. The plot revolves around Ryōtarō's taking his wife to the country to meet his family. The play has only two speaking characters whose relationship evolves toward one of love and understanding. But the list might almost be increased to three, since the chestnut tree is talked about incessantly. The play goes through a considerable variety of moods, perhaps too many, but the general emotional thrust is clearly worked out.

In the first scene the couple waits in a little railway station in the mountains for the local train that will take them to a still smaller station within two hours' drive of the home of Ryōtarō's parents. The scene is full of amusing banter; Ryōtarō tells his wife that "Both of you will be surprised. I have some idea of how you picture my father, and what kind of woman he imagines you to be. And both of you are equally off the mark."[28] He tells her about his family, especially his younger brother, who, although quite brilliant, never came to the city for an education. Ryōtarō adds that his brother has become quite eccentric.

In talking of the country, he asks his wife if she knows the kinds of trees, birch and laurel, that grow high in the mountains, and then he describes his favorite chestnut tree.

Ryōtarō: I wonder, did I ever talk to you about the chestnut tree?

[28] *zenshū*, I, p. 162.

Ayako: What?

Ryōtarō: The chestnut tree. The huge tree we have on
our property.

Ayako: Oh yes. . . .

Ryōtarō: What did I say about it?

Ayako: You said it was the biggest tree in the whole
village.

Ryōtarō: It is really worth seeing. The trunk is huge, twice
as big around as my arms can go. There aren't
many like it. When the chestnuts fall, every
morning the little girls in the neighborhood come
to pick them up. But there are so many they
can't finish in a morning.

(Ayako remains silent.)

Ryōtarō: This fall we ought to have some of the chestnuts
sent down to us in Tokyo. Before, I never would
have enjoyed boiling and eating them just by
myself. (Pause) You mustn't be upset if the
house is terribly old and dusty. Country families
are proud because their houses are so old. . . .[29]

In the second scene, the tree itself is shown on the stage.
We learn that Ayako does not yet feel herself a part of the
family. She has realized, however, that the other members
of the family, especially the younger brother, are resentful
because Ryōtarō went off to the city for an education and
now lives there, without any regard for his family responsibilities. It also becomes fairly clear in the course of the scene
that Ryōtarō has a complex emotional relationship with his
brother and that the brother finds Ayako attractive.

Ryōtarō defines his relationship with his brother, again using the tree as a point of reference.

Ryōtarō: . . . there is something quite unforgiving about
him. And I haven't told you everything. Somehow
I even feel a bit afraid of him.

[29] *Ibid.*, p. 161.

Ayako: That's only a prejudice on your part.

Ryōtarō: What makes you say that? I don't mean that he conspires against me or anything. It's something I can't explain, some strange fateful connection we seem to have between us. (Pause.) That wasn't true before, when we were children. Actually as brothers we got along quite well. (He looks up at the sky.) We used to play so often here, under this tree. One day we said we would play school, and I was the teacher. I thought that this was perfectly right, because I was the older. But suddenly he said, "If you're the teacher, then I'll be the principal."[30]

In the third scene, Ryōtarō senses that his brother may be having an influence over his wife; Ryōtarō now reveals to her why he has brought her to the village and deliberately exposed her to all the spiritual dangers he feels she must face.

Ryōtarō: Why did I bring you to this house? Certainly not just to show you this broken-down place, and not really to show off how much respect I have for my parents. How you feel about it I don't know. Just as I told you before, my father is getting older, and my younger brother has an interest in, and the hope of, getting the family property for himself. I thought that before my father dies, I ought to come home for once and live here a bit. But when we arrived, I realized it was already too late. A lot of the mountain land that used to belong to us was already turned over to other people now. When you learned that, didn't you feel a little disappointed yourself? (Ayako remains silent.)

[30] *Ibid.*, p. 170.

Ryōtarō: And that chestnut tree too, before long somebody will come and cut it down, for all I know. I feel that day is coming.[31]

Ryōtarō feels that his family is in a state of decline. Ayako shows affection for her father-in-law, but she realizes that she had been a disruptive force; in fact, her father-in-law has told her that ever since she came the boys in the village have started dressing up. Ryōtarō, suspicious, tells her, "Did he say that? Or did you make it up because you think so yourself?"[32]

In scene four, the younger brother has a terrible scene with his family which we do not witness, but learn of through a running commentary provided by Ayako and Ryōtarō, who add their own bitterness and confusion to the situation.

Scene five, the last of the play, shows the couple returning to Tokyo. Ryōtarō is terribly agitated. He has realized for the first time what his childhood environment means to him.

Ryōtarō: The countryside has come to seem so completely gloomy to me. Melancholy. The mountains. The forests. The valleys. Houses, trees, grass, animals, people, all of them are gloomy. And not only that. They seem to be charged with a poison . . . am I the only one who feels that?

Ayako: Yes, you are. And you've somehow transferred your feelings to me.[33]

With this comes a consciousness of the childish view he had taken of the world.

Ryōtarō: From the beginning, in the village we always gossiped about things being the biggest or the best there, always comparing things in those terms. Somebody or other was the richest man in the village, somebody or other was the oldest man

[31] *Ibid.*, p. 175.   [32] *Ibid.*, p. 176.   [33] *Ibid.*, p. 181.

in the village. Even the children, hearing such talk, would remember it. I remember something quite ridiculous: when I was a little fellow, I sneaked into the garden of the house where Oshō-san lived, the girl they called "the prettiest girl in the village." To see if it was true. Of course, I didn't go alone. (Pause) But now this kind of thing doesn't seem to have any significance any more. The world has become so much larger. (Pause) To talk about the biggest chestnut tree in the village was, for me at that time, the seed of my own pride. (Pause.) When you actually saw my home, you were disappointed, weren't you?[34]

What Ryōtarō has come to realize is that the possibility of real love between him and his wife is the reality, above all the others, on which he can build his life.

Ryōtarō: . . . love from your own flesh and blood is not enough to bring up a real human being, you know. . . .

Ayako: . . . and the love between husband and wife?

Ryōtarō: That is something you must not dare to speak of.

Ayako: Why . . . what do you mean?

Ryōtarō: Because it is too precious. (He looks at his watch.) It will soon be time to buy our tickets.[35]

More secure now in their relationship, the two prepare themselves for a final leave-taking from his past.

Ryōtarō: Don't you ever want to come back here again?

Ayako: No I don't.

Ryōtarō: No matter what happens?

Ayako: No, no matter what happens.

Ryōtarō: And so you will never leave me?

Ayako: I will never leave you.

[34] *Ibid.*, p. 182.   [35] *Ibid.*, p. 184.

Ryōtarō: No matter what happens?
  (Ayako nods.)
Ryōtarō: Let's go. (He rises.)
  (Ayako, turning her head away, wipes away a
  tear with her finger.)
Ryōtarō: This year too, the tallest chestnut in the village
  has borne a great harvest![36]
  Curtain

The structure of the play is arranged in terms of the progressive changes in Ryōtarō's emotional attitudes. Ayako's attitudes are thus less simple to discover; she seems to be more a foil for her husband than a character in her own right. The chestnut tree does not hang quite so heavily over the text as these few extracts would indicate; still, it is perhaps too obtrusive a symbol, and Kishida need not have explained its various meanings so often. Nevertheless, as a unifying force the tree serves very well, and through this symbol Kishida was able to extend a mood and show a developing human relationship in a more complex set of circumstances than he had done in any previous play. In every way, *The Tallest Chestnut in the Village* marked a real advance in his work.

In recent years the play has received favorable critical attention. Yamamoto Shūji, for example, has admired the use of the symbol of the tree as an image, "not of the real tree itself, but of the deepest feelings in Ryōtarō himself . . . it is a phantom tree of which he speaks."[37] Yet, despite the fact that the play required only two actors, Kishida never succeeded in having it staged, a fact that must have added to his growing list of frustrations. His plays were getting better, but the actors and the audiences were not yet ready for them.

[36] *Ibid.*, p. 185.
[37] See Yamamoto Shūji, "Gekibungaku ni okeru kindaiteki shujusō," Part II, *Gekibungaku*, edited by Tanaka Chikao, p. 257.

174

Kishida's next two important plays show a further broadening of his interests. The first of them, a one-act play called *Okujōteien* (*Roof Garden*), is the only one of Kishida's plays that can be said to involve "lower middle-class people," although the fact of their socio-economic status is not the real point of the play. The second, however, *Ochiba nikki* (*Diary of Fallen Leaves*), is set in a wealthy, aristocratic milieu. Along with a more precise social setting, in these two plays Kishida changes his theme from love and marriage to loneliness—the loneliness of poverty, and the loneliness of old age.

Roof Garden was first published in the November 1926 issue of *New Currents of Drama* and was performed the following year by the *shinkokugeki* troupe. It is a rather slight piece, though doubtless effective on the stage; it recalls the manner of Somerset Maugham, who achieved limited objectives with a certain grace and skill.

Two couples happen to meet in the roof garden of a Tokyo department store. The husbands, Miwa and Namiki, were classmates in school; Miwa has been a success and is well on the way to wealth, but Namiki, who had had high hopes of becoming a writer, has as yet had no success and is very poor. The two men introduce their wives and, while the ladies go off to shop, the men discuss their past and future prospects. Namiki, knowing that his wife wants an *obi* for her *kimono*, finally blurts out that he wants to borrow some money from Miwa, who, although rather startled, gladly lends it. Namiki is soon embarrassed by what he has done and tries to return the money to Miwa, who eventually takes it back. The scene is well sketched and both figures are portrayed in sufficient detail to sustain interest.

Miwa now invites Namiki and his wife to dinner, but Namiki declines. After Miwa and his wife leave, Namiki explains the situation to his wife.

Namiki: Should I borrow some money from him and buy you an *obi*?

Wife: Could you do a thing like that?

Namiki: I could . . . if I wanted to.

Wife: I'm sure that's not true.

Namiki: What do you mean? Why couldn't I?

Wife: I wouldn't want you to do anything like that, no matter how little is involved.

Namiki: (with a serious look) I would do it. If it was for your sake.

Wife: (with feeling) Just to hear you say so is more than enough for me. (Abruptly changing her tone.) But please, please don't do anything unreasonable. I am very worried about the whole thing.

(Namiki remains silent.)

Wife: I can hardly stay calm when I think that for something so trivial as this you would forget your self-respect, especially with such a friend.

Namiki: Well of course I wouldn't bring it up with him myself. But you see, he was the one who. . . .

Wife: That's what I thought. So then please refuse his loan flatly . . . but not so as to offend him. (Pause) From now on, even if I want something, I certainly won't say anything about it.

Namiki: You're talking about two different things. If circumstances permit, we can borrow, can't we?

Wife: No we can't, and that's why I always want you to maintain a clean and straightforward relationship with your friends. No matter what happens, you mustn't lower yourself in their eyes.

Namiki: You don't have to worry about a thing like that.

Wife: I certainly do worry about it. Up until now, I've never noticed . . . but something like this. . . .

Namiki: What do you mean, something like this . . . ?

Wife: From now on you must stop hanging around at loose ends and get to work. If ever we can manage to save a little money, there will be no talk about buying things like an *obi*. Even if it's just a little bit, we'll save what we can.

Namiki: How sweet of you to suddenly come out with something like that!

Wife: (Her eyes wet with tears) But there's a good reason why I said it . . . you see . . . you are losing all your friends. . . . (Suddenly she buries her face, weeping, on her husband's chest.)

Curtain[38]

Not a profound moment, perhaps, but a touching one, and in the context of the play, not oversentimentalized.

Kishida recorded his dissatisfaction with the staging of this play. He mentioned the fact that when the *shinkokugeki* troupe asked for permission to perform the play, he was concerned over the possible quality of the actors but finally consented to go ahead with the production. He had two expectations, "first, to show that a New Theatre play need not be boring . . . and second, that it might provide an additional occasion for the public to become better acquainted with the New Theatre by means of a production staged by an existing troupe that has not been involved heretofore in the movement."[39]

For Kishida, the secret of a successful production lay in the ability of the actors to grasp the inner meaning of the play. He was most disappointed in what he saw. Kishida found that the actors felt unsure of themselves and evidently made the audience uncomfortable as well. In addition, he thought that the spirit of the play had been altered. Had the change been to achieve some particular artistic purpose of the director he might not have objected, but the changes brought no good results. The spirit of a work is always hard

[38] *zenshū*, I, pp. 194-195.   [39] *zenshū*, IX, p. 310.

177

to capture, he wrote, but there is a great virtue in the production of a play by a modest director who merely tries to relay the spirit of the play without distorting it. Kishida found the director "not necessarily insensitive to the play, but certainly nonchalant in his attitude."[40] The part of the audience that was bored, he concluded, would now be lost for future productions.

An author's complaints are as old as the history of the theatre, and the modern American theatre offers its own celebrated examples, from Tennessee Williams to William Gibson,[41] of writers who thought that they had been misrepresented by their director and actors. But Kishida's use of the word "nonchalant" suggests that he was correct in his apprehension over the fact that the troupe did not attempt to preserve the spirit of his writing or, in fact, any particular spirit at all. This was the only play he ever authorized the *shinkokugeki* troupe to perform, and although he did allow *shimpa* troupes to perform several of his lesser plays, these experiences taught him that the chances of seeing his plays satisfactorily performed were slimmer than he had at first supposed.

Kishida's next major play, *Diary of Fallen Leaves*, was published in the April 1927 issue of *The Central Review* but did not receive its first performance until 1965, when it was staged in Kyoto by the Kurumiza troupe. It is one of Kishida's very finest. He took a continuing interest in the themes and characters in the play; when it became evident that he could not manage to have it performed on the stage, he expanded the story of the play into a full-length novel that he published in 1936.

Diary of Fallen Leaves is the first play since *Autumn in the Tyrols* in which Kishida makes more than a passing reference to France and to his European experience. The play records the last year in the life of an aristocratic, rather

---

[40] *zenshū*, IX, p. 311.

[41] His book on the problem of writers and directors, *The Seesaw Log*, is more stimulating than any of his plays.

strong-minded, but altogether charming old Japanese lady. Her son (now presumably in his late forties) had had a French wife who died many years before. Saddened by her death, he has left his daughter Henriette to be brought up by her grandmother in Japan while he remains in Europe to continue his work as an archaeologist. The old lady (she is never named) feels that he has treated his daughter badly, but she seems to understand her son's pain and sorrow as well.

The excellence of the play makes it difficult to summarize, since its effectiveness lies in the shifting moods of each scene, rather than in any particularly evocative bit of dialogue.

In the first act, the old lady is sitting on the terrace of her house in the suburbs of Tokyo to enjoy the beautiful fall day. She talks with her cousin Osamu, who is very fond of his niece Henriette, then about sixteen. Osamu is a rather pensive and nervous boy of fifteen or so, and the old lady, who has been teaching him French, chides him and urges him to be more energetic and optimistic. He tries to explain to the old lady how much Henriette means to him and how he wishes she would return his affection; she replies, quite correctly, that Henriette is only a child, much too young to consider loving, or marrying anyone. Henriette enters with Hiroshi, a boy with whom she often plays tennis. The two had intended to pick some chestnuts from a tall tree nearby, but Hiroshi, already late in going home, says he will have to wait for another day. Osamu, anxious to show his affection for Henriette, rushes off to pick them for her instead.

Next follows a remarkable scene. The old lady, although anxious to watch over the children and make sure that no harm comes to them, nevertheless becomes absorbed in reading a book by Anatole France, murmuring phrases to herself, half in a daydream over her own past. Henriette calls out to her repeatedly that Osamu is being reckless in climbing the tall tree and urges the old lady to make him

179

stop. She hears the girl but, slowed by age and by the intensity of her own dreaming, she does not react quickly enough. She realizes too late what is happening: Osamu falls and is killed.

The scene is beautifully constructed. The characters, especially that of the old lady, are quickly sketched; by the time she sits in her chair to read, she has been established as a kindly but sophisticated woman, with a streak of wit, whose life is comfortable but melancholy. There is a sense of incipient fatigue suggested in many of her lines, and it is her fatigue, and melancholy, that develop swiftly during the rest of the play.

Act Two, which takes place in the following spring, shows Henriette passing from the borders of childhood into womanhood. She has developed a great fondness, although unspoken, for Hiroshi, and the old lady supposes that he returns it. The act opens as the old lady and Henriette receive a letter from Henriette's father in which he says that he will return to Japan soon to take charge of his daughter's education. The old lady reflects again over her terrible feelings of remorse over her carelessness with Osamu. Osamu's mother comes to call. She still suffers greatly from the death of her son, and the old lady finds it hard to find anything to say to lessen her grief. She tells Osamu's mother that she has had the chestnut tree cut down and thinks to plant in its place a kind of wild rose Osamu liked. "I feel as if I have quickly grown very old since last fall,"[42] she adds. They talk of Osamu, Henriette, and her father. The old lady, forgetting herself, begins reminiscing over a variety of woes with her visitor, who is prompted to ask why all of this should be on the old lady's mind at this moment. Suddenly Henriette bursts in, crying, to tell her grandmother (and in front of Osamu's mother) that Hiroshi will be sent by his father to take a job in Osaka. Hiroshi enters; the old lady quietly asks Henriette to leave the room and questions the boy, who says that his father

[42] *zenshū*, I, p. 297.

180

has chosen a bride for him in Osaka, without his consent, and that he will be sent to marry and work in one of his father's companies. The old lady gently wishes him a happy future. The scene is nicely shaded, for the old lady's conflicting emotions are discreetly suggested: her own feelings of inadequacy, her disappointment that her son is not there to take a more active part in his daughter's future just when it would be so important for her, and the shock of realizing that, since last fall, Henriette has become a woman. Henriette comes back briefly and then goes sobbing to her room. The old lady goes out to comfort her, then returns to her guest.

Osamu's Mother: Is everything all right?

The Old Lady: What do you mean? Henriette? (to herself, without answering) Well, it just didn't work out.

Osamu's Mother: But you know . . . that is just the way things are sometimes.

The Old Lady: (taking a deep breath) I thought to myself, "not again."

Osamu's Mother: Not again? What do you mean?

The Old Lady: The feeling you want to cry. Sometimes it is good to cry as much as you want. A woman . . . a young woman can wash away her sadness with her tears.[43]

The third act, which takes place in the fall of the same year, shows her succumbing to time, age, and her own failing sense of life. The old lady has been making frantic preparations for the return of her son; now, on the day of his arrival, she and Henriette plan to go to the Tokyo station to meet him. An hour before they are to leave, she has a sudden physical collapse and must remain at home. She shows Henriette an old photograph so that she may recognize her father; angry with herself and her failing

[43] *Ibid.*, p. 303.

181

physical resources, she says to herself, "when you get old, you begin to lose all your self respect."[44] Henriette and the maid have sent for the family physician, who arrives, examines her, and insists that she rest quietly. She finally sends Henriette off with a warning not to tell her father that she is so ill.

Alone with the doctor, she begins to tell him about the spiritual aspects of her illness, and how she has been affected by the death of Osamu. "I knew he was climbing the tree. He was doing a dangerous thing and I should have stopped him. . . . I knew it, but in the end I couldn't stop him because my attention was absorbed by my reading."[45] She presses further in explaining her feelings; the doctor, kindly but detached, insists she remain quiet and rest. The scene contrasts her restlessness with the gentleness of the stolid doctor, who shows his considerable concern by sending the maid for medicine and stimulants.

In a last burst of frenzy, she pours out her thoughts and fears.

The Old Lady: I have already lost a son. I have lost a daughter-in-law, and the boy. My other son has abandoned me for ten years, always travelling, never wanting to come home. And here, in my house, I have always treated my other grandchild, the girl you saw just now, as my one unique treasure in the world . . . but today a complete stranger to me will steal her from me. This stranger will not really be my son, home from such a long trip. No, he will have become someone else, appearing unexpectedly from somewhere or other, bragging about himself, calling himself my son.

(The doctor is silent.)

[44] *Ibid.*, p. 304.　　　　　　　[45] *Ibid.*, p. 308.

The Old Lady:	"My own daughter." That's what he'll say, and he will try to take Henriette away from me. If he were truly my son, he would not do that. Isn't that so? (The doctor takes a thermometer to check her temperature. He bends his head down and looks quite uneasy.)
The Old Lady:	Because of Henriette, I have really . . . yes, really killed a man. And this man was a boy I loved so much. That melancholy boy, who had lost his father and who felt his whole life to be somehow clouded over. It is I, I who killed Osamu. (She takes a deep breath.)
The Doctor:	Please, my dear. . . .
The Old Lady:	Yes . . . yes . . . from the top of the tree . . . Henriette's heart . . . red . . . is hanging.[46]

With this electrifying phrase, in the midst of the silence, she slips into a kind of final delirium, asking Osamu's mother to forgive her her crimes; then, sinking, she begins quoting the French verse she had been reciting in the first scene, ". . . O Thébains! Jusqu'au jour qui termine la vie. . . ."

The doctor quickly sends the maid to telephone any relatives; she soon returns to say that everyone has gone to the station to meet the returning son. The old lady, dying completely alone, has a final vision of reconciliation.

The Old Lady:	(rather calmly) Ah, so you've come back . . . if you had been a little later, your mother would not have seen your face. Well then, come this way. I hope that the sea was not too rough? I'm so glad you came home. It took you so long . . . I was worried that you might have forgotten

[46] *Ibid.*, pp. 311-312.

the way and were lost . . . my goodness,
where did all that dust come from?

(A long silence)

Why are you all lined up like that? Osa-
mu, what happened? Osamu? (a pause)
Ah, someone, hurry. . . . (pause) Forgive
me . . . oh please forgive me. . . . You see,
I have just lived . . . a little . . . too long.
That's all . . . a little . . . too long.

(The sun sets, and the stage becomes dark.)

Curtain.[47]

The play is an extremely demanding one for the leading
actress, but, well-acted, it can make a rich and poetic
effect. The well-to-do but rather lonely atmosphere of the
house and of the life lived by the old lady is skillfully
created, of course, but, more than this, Kishida extended the
range of his dramatic technique by making direct use in his
play of his growing powers of observation of human character. The early one-act plays are very poetic and the
characters are perforce only sketched in a general fashion:
they strike us as true and human, in a general way, but they
deserve their non-names. In a play like *Paper Balloon*, Kishida showed his ability to create natural responses to human
situations (quarreling, reconciliation, teasing, etc.) but he
used them only in terms of the rather quickly-sketched
characters who inhabit his plays. Now, in *Diary of Fallen
Leaves*, he attempted a full portrait of a specific woman in a
variety of situations, and he was able to weave a credible
and rich emotional tissue of reactions and responses unlike
any he had created before. Second, for the first time since
his return from Europe four years before, he made use of
his French experience in order to set apart and contrast two
different sets of values and two ways of life. Such was to be
the ultimate use of his understanding of European culture,
and it formed a part of this and two others among his best
plays: *Ushiyama Hotel* and *Mr. Sawa's Two Daughters*.

[47] *Ibid.*, p. 313.

Ushiyama Hotel, his next important play, was published in the January 1929 issue of *The Central Review* and was produced in 1932 by the Tsukijiza and later, in 1954, by the Bungakuza. *Ushiyama Hotel* was the last of Kishida's experiments, the last and perhaps most demanding test that he set himself. The play resembles *Diary of Fallen Leaves* in that Kishida was interested in specific character portrayal to create a mood: but instead of one central character, he here attempted half-a-dozen. In addition, he used his French experience in an unusual way: drawing on his visit to French Indochina, when he was travelling to Paris, Kishida decided to compose a play about the life among the Japanese living there in order to illustrate, on a spiritual level, something about the breakdown of the human spirit. Kishida himself wrote of the play:

> I wrote *Ushiyama Hotel* in the fall of 1928. Thinking to write a very straightforward play, I made use of a plot, which I had scrupulously avoided until then, and using my own observations and experience, I tried to pursue an objective method in treating my subject. I had of course visited French Indochina, and the name "Ushiyama Hotel" is close to the name of a real hotel there. Many of the characters are not based closely on any particular models, but I tried to create them to resemble the kind of persons typical of this colonial atmosphere.[48]
> (1946)

In addition, Kishida set himself the often difficult task of writing in dialect; if the play was to be objective, then the characters would have to speak naturally. Most of the dialect is confined to conversations of a group of girls of doubtful reputation who live in the hotel. They use Kyūshū speech.

It is this countrified speech of the girls which gives this little Japanese colony within a colony its peculiar flavor, and for this reason I was very reluctant to give up the idea of using dialect. With the help of a friend, I was able

[48] *Ibid.*, IX, p. 319.

to write down the dialogue sufficiently well enough to escape that censure of being "impossible to read." When the play was printed in *The Central Review*, I was criticized for its use, but when the play was later staged by the Tsukijiza, and the speeches were "fleshed-out," as it were, by real performers, such criticism ceased.[49]

Kishida's description of the play as "straightforward" is accurate only insofar as *Ushiyama Hotel* involves a plot and a variety of well-defined characters. The play was actually Kishida's most complex effort up to this point, weaving various sentiments, atmospheres, and personalities into his own commentary on the human condition. It is difficult to translate (and sometimes difficult to understand) because of the dialect, but at least the general outlines can be given here.

The setting, a small boarding hotel in Haiphong where Japanese residents and visitors live, provides a pretext for Kishida to introduce a wide variety of characters, many of them in various states of physical and moral decay.

The proprietress, Yoné, is kind to everyone and seems appreciated by all.

Yoné: Yes, I've seen a lot. Not only Japanese people either, if you want to talk about the people I've gotten to know up until now.... First there were those French. For the longest time, all I saw, all I heard were French people. But good human feelings, they're the same all over. As for the Vietnam people, I'm in charge and they're working for me. Now they've got their own ways among 'em, and when there's some trouble, there's always a lot of confusion. You know anyone who's a big shot in this place is bound to have a lot of worries. You see, I never went to school properly. Probably because I'm as old as I am, the young girls here call me, "ma," "mother" . . . and they always bring me in for advice.[50]

[49] *Ibid.*   [50] *Ibid.*, II, pp. 34-35.

Among the guests and hangers-on are Tomi, Yoné's step-daughter; Makabe, a trader who was formerly married to a white Russian named Lola; Sato, his mistress, whom he wishes to marry; Lola herself; and some interesting minor characters, among them Oka, a photographer who is also interested in Sato; Mr. Mitani, a newly arrived company employee from Japan, and his wife; and several others.

In Act One, Lola appears after an absence of several years, to find her husband Makabe. Lola tells Yoné that she does not live with her husband but bears him no grudge. She is now completely penniless and needs money to take her back to Europe. Yoné, feeling sorry for her, gives her some money and promises to talk to Makabe. Lola thanks her, crying.

In Act Two, Makabe and Sato discuss their future when they wake up the next morning. Sato is especially depressed: she feels constrained and embarrassed over her relations with Makabe because of the newcomer, the very proper Mrs. Mitani, who, Sato feels, must be looking down on her. Makabe, for his part, explains to Sato how he first met Lola and how they found that they were not suited to each other. Sato reveals that she intends to go back to Japan with the money she has earned over the years and give it to her father, so that he can open a saké shop; Makabe is touched by her strong feelings of loyalty, but he cautions her that her father is apt simply to drink up her savings. Makabe himself had intended to regularize his relations with Sato but has recently lost his money in a business misfortune. Now the two think it may be necessary to separate. Sato goes to order some breakfast brought to them, and they drink a "goodbye toast" to each other. Sato still is not able to decide if she really has the courage to leave for Japan the next day.

Act Three includes a party attended by a mixture of all sorts of people, ranging from the nicely dressed Mitani couple through some riffraff from a bar a few doors down. As the curtain goes up, the after-dinner speeches are be-

ginning, and one old man, Shimetomo, goes into a long
harangue about how his bringing families from Japan to the
area to develop it had earned him a commendation from
the French government. "We've heard it all before," they
say, shouting him down. Mitani tells Makabe that he finds
the people here not really Japanese any more; Makabe in
return explains to him something of the real atmosphere of
the place.

Mitani: I was just saying to my wife that although it
      seems like Japan here, I feel there is something
      a little changed about it.

Makabe: It wouldn't be that way if you had come alone.
      Except for you two, we are all here alone. All
      of us are little by little becoming less Japanese.

Shimetomo: There's a lot in what you say. For those who
      really soak themselves in the slovenly life of
      these colonies . . . but there are only one or
      two people like that. For the most part, every-
      one is still Japanese. In any case, I intend to
      consider myself so, to the bitter end.

Makabe: Actually that's not what I meant. Because
      even you—excuse me for saying it—show all
      the marks of an international vagabond your-
      self. As far as I'm concerned, I think and feel
      as an individual and as a cosmopolitan. From
      Mitani's point of view, I would probably fit
      perfectly his definition of the word "adven-
      turer," but perhaps Shimetomo disapproves of
      that word being applied to him.[51]

Various people at the table take exception to the term "ad-
venturer," and Makabe explains himself.

Makabe: There are all kinds of adventurers. The ones
      full of spirit and ambition have a fine time for
      themselves. There was a man who came here

[51] *zenshū*, II, p. 25.

at some point, the one who had been a dentist in Bangkok without a license or something. He had swindled some fancy medical fees out of a millionaire in Siam. By the time his patient thought something funny was happening, he had pulled up stakes and disappeared. You know, when he turned up in Hong Kong he was using a calling card that said he was the representative for some fancy transportation company. He victimized his hotel out of a month's bill and then turned up here. Now I would never get mixed up in a thing like that.[52]

The party continues, to end in bickerings and disagreements. Later a group of girls, talking among themselves, wonder at Sato's desire to return to Japan; in her place, some would "go to Shanghai and have a little fun" instead. Yoné defends Sato's decision and reminds them that there is still time for her to change her mind. Later Sato appears and, crying, tells Yoné she just doesn't know what she wants to do. Just then a woman's voice calling "liar! liar!" comes down the stairs. It is accompanied by the sounds of a pistol shot. The atmosphere of the scene is most carefully constructed, and the nihilistic atmosphere in which Kishida's characters live, outside the context of any real society, remains the dominant motive throughout.

The fourth act again shows us Makabe's bedroom, where he is bandaged and resting. Lola has shot him while in a nervous state, he explains to Yoné, and he tells everyone quite coolly that they should not worry about him. Mrs. Mitani is dumbfounded because of the disparity between reality and the picture of Indochina she had in her mind before she came; she finds lizards instead of peacocks, in every sense of the word. Makabe asks Mrs. Mitani to think well of Sato and not to despise her. He is worried over

[52] Ibid.

Sato's future, and he reminds Mrs. Mitani, who is rather shocked by his disclosures, that life is hard for girls who begin badly.

Makabe: Mrs. Mitani, I don't want you to take too high a view of me. That girl might have been . . . well, I don't know what. Thinking over my own life, I certainly have no desire to pass any judgment on her. And I haven't got the strength to really think out her future for her. When I see her, before my very eyes, trying to decide what to do with herself, I start thinking about everything and I get very worried. The more I think about it, the more frightened I am that my existence as a human being is going to influence her destiny. I might as well confess to you this is a feeling I've never had before.

Mrs. Mitani: Men are relatively indifferent about this kind of thing.[53]

He asks Mrs. Mitani's help, and the help of the other girls, in looking out for Sato's future. Mrs. Mitani wonders why Makabe doesn't marry her.

Makabe: (after thinking a long time) I think it would be fine to marry her. And yet if I did, it would be very unfair to her. For, if in less than half a year, I . . . it's too stuffy in here tonight. Are the stars out? . . . the stars? . . . could you open the window, Mrs. Mitani?[54]

Too fatigued by his accident to think and plan, Makabe refrains from taking any action.

In Act Five, Sato is making her last secretive goodbyes. The hotel habitués talk of the excitement caused by Lola's

[53] *Ibid.*, p. 36.   [54] *Ibid.*, p. 38.

shooting Makabe. Yoné insists that Sato say goodbye to Makabe and forces her up the stairs. She tells the others that Sato has been up all night tending him but will not now say goodbye. Yet since the two are not having a quarrel, she cannot understand what Sato is feeling and doing. Eventually Sato comes downstairs and says that she could not manage to wake him up. She leaves. A moment later, Mrs. Mitani comes down and asks if Sato has gone, then retires again upstairs.

Finally Makabe manages to make his way downstairs, obviously wanting to find out what has happened. When he realizes that Sato has left, he painfully and slowly makes his way upstairs.

In this brief summary, the play (even more difficult to excerpt than the others) may seem diffuse and banal. Yet in actuality the atmosphere of the play is beautifully maintained, not through the use of any local color but by the continual piling up of the slightly odd and weary reactions of the characters to each other: the world created by Kishida in this play exists in more detail than any other so far, and with no loss of poetic nuance. He has added the skill of *reportage* (in a special, limited, theatrical sense) to his gifts of language, poetry, and humor.

As Kawamori Yoshiro remarks, the play is not merely a recreation of the Indochina Kishida saw. "What was the writer trying to picture in this play? Of course he wanted to show a sad quality to the life lived by these Japanese in Indochina and to sketch a group of them in detail. But more important, Kishida had a deep interest in the nihilistic way of life expressed by that gentleman villain, Makabe."[55] Kawamori thinks that Kishida himself, like Makabe, was a man of high ambition and sensibility who nevertheless failed to achieve his goals; Makabe is thus a self-portrait. A foreign reader of the play has difficulty commenting on such judg-

---

[55] See Kawamori, "kaishaku," *Gendai Nihon bungaku zenshū*, XXXIII, p. 411.

ments and can confirm them only to the extent of saying that the portrait of Makabe is scrupulously created.

At the end of this first period of experimentation, Kishida had attempted with considerable success to write in a variety of styles, and had mastered the sketch and the long play as well. He was now a well-known figure on the literary scene and was published in the best magazines. His plays had been collected in anthologies. Yet for him there could be only dissatisfactions. Some of the plays went unproduced. Neither of his best efforts, *Diary of Fallen Leaves* nor *Ushiyama Hotel*, had achieved a production; those that had been staged were poorly acted.

His next step was one of compromise. He stopped writing for himself, and changed his style of writing, lowered it, simplified it, to suit the possibilities he saw for production. Kishida was not the only creative artist to have made this same decision, but, as he was to learn, there would be many difficulties involved in such a step.

A successful work of art can mirror reality, or it can create a new reality. The satisfaction of the first comes from the feeling that all our perceptions about life have been confirmed in the work of art; the second can lead us to places we can never go by ourselves. Both realities are difficult to create, but perhaps only the true poet can summon up the image of the second. In many ways, the early works of Kishida live, or at least flirt, with this second world. There is a poetry in the plays that creates a kind of open emotional atmosphere all the more exhilarating for being slightly unreal. Kishida often accomplished this mood through his generalized views of character and a kind of overview of the situation with which the action is concerned; he and the spectator are not concerned with the minutiae of the dramatic situations but with a metaphor of life whose specific situations are only a point of comparison.

Now everything changed. After *Ushiyama Hotel*, Kishida's work veered sharply back toward a representation of the first world, the creation of specific social situations, treated with dry wit and a cold moralist's eye. All these qualities were visible in the work of his first period, of course, but the proportion of his interests now became drastically reversed.

The first of Kishida's new experiments in this second period was *Mama sensei to sono otto* (*Professor Mama and her Husband*). Kishida later wrote of the play that "although I am certainly not satisfied with it, it does serve to some extent to indicate the new direction in which I wished to go."[56] A description of the play will serve to indicate the directions and perhaps the reasons for Kishida's change of style.

It was first published in the October 1930 issue of *Reconstruction* and was one of the first of Kishida's long plays to reach the stage when it was produced two years later by the Tsukijiza troupe. *Professor Mama* tells a disagreeable story: The four major characters are all, in varying degrees, quite unpleasant. The world of *Paper Balloon* has shrunk and withered. Insofar as Kishida's treatment of his material is lively and humorous, however, the play itself is not unpleasant.

"Mama" is the nickname given by her students to Okui Machiko, who manages a secondary school in a newly settled area outside Tokyo. Ostensibly the school is to provide a good and healthful education for children and keep them out of the grime and confusion of city life; actually it is understaffed and underfinanced, has very poor medical facilities, and is only a money-making device by which Mama and her husband Sakurao support themselves by looking after a high proportion of unintelligent sons and daughters of wealthy patrons who evidently cannot manage to place their children in more orthodox establishments. Mama is assisted by Miss Akita, "an inconspicuous woman of twenty-four or twenty-five."

56 *zenshū*, IX, p. 315.

The play opens with Mama lecturing the children, and the nature of her strong and subtly offensive personality soon becomes apparent. Her husband, a weak and venal man, tries to express his dissatisfaction with her, but she pushes right past his every attempt to manifest his feelings. The doctor has warned the couple that the school is unsafe for the children, because when the dirt road becomes impassable he cannot come to handle any sudden illness.

Sakurao: I agree completely with what that doctor said. We can't manage the children, and if we took them off for a picnic or something, a child might die. Even though I wouldn't have to take the responsibility, I would feel terrible about it. You always delight in saying that you chose this work because of my poor health, but clear air is certainly not the only thing I need.

Mama: I'm perfectly aware of all that. That's why you have nothing to worry about.

Sakurao: . . . . .

Mama: If it is too noisy here for you, I'll borrow a cottage close by for you to use during the day.

Sakurao: In this case there is certainly no reason for you to go to such trouble. You are always deciding things in this one-sided way, and it's just no good. I'm slowly losing my self-respect.

Mama: But if I discuss things with you, then things just drag on forever. When all is said and done, I'm the one in charge here, you know.

Sakurao: . . . . .

Mama: And you make a terrible face. You think your pride has been hurt. But there's nothing to be done about it. This is a big problem between us, and the start of many other things as well.[57]

[57] *Ibid.*, II, p. 119.

Mama does understand her husband: in his case, most of the "many other things" are summed up in his pathetic attempts to philander; on her side, she is always jealous and imagines that he is having affairs even when he is perfectly innocent. With Mama in charge of the school, the natural roles of husband and wife are reversed, and as a result both are miserable. Sakurao tries desperately to justify his contribution to their marriage.

Mama: . . . if you feel I'm becoming a nuisance to you, I don't mind if we split up for awhile. I think it would be quite reasonable.

Sakurao: Don't try to get around me like that. When did I ever say you were a nuisance? Don't you know that I couldn't even eat if you weren't around? Nowadays no one can live contentedly unless he manages to screen off some part of his conscience. As far as that goes, I can't even look you in the face.

Mama: Say anything you feel you want to.

Sakurao: You think of yourself as a realist, but you are really living on dreams. I don't have the strength to carry things out, but I do have the habit of being able to see things precisely as they are. What kind of relationship do we have? The more I understand it, the less you do.[58]

The school is visited by Mrs. Hanamaki, a young and attractive widow whose child, a former student in the school, has recently died. She has taken to visiting the school to sustain her memories of her son. The school handyman presents her with some clothing her son had left behind, and, as the other children come to talk with her, Mrs. Hanamaki breaks down into sobbing.

The second act is a series of disagreeable revelations.

[58] *Ibid.*, p. 120.

Mama, curious as to why the widow continues to visit the school, decides on the basis of some observations made by the handyman and his wife that the widow is using her visits to the school as a means to have a series of *rendezvous* with a man. Mama suspects her husband as the man in question, but later learns that the lover is the man who always drives Mrs. Hanamaki to the school, whom the widow calls her "cousin." Mama decides to obtain a forced contribution to the school from her, as a kind of hush money. The widow arrives, and the two women go off to discuss the affair. While they are gone, Sakurao and the "cousin," Togashi, have a conversation in which Togashi admits his affection for Mrs. Hanamaki but says that so far she has not taken him very seriously. He goes on to ask whether Sakurao might help plead his case. Sakurao replies that Togashi has mistaken the extent of his abilities; he is not a strongly moral person and could be of no help in such a situation. ("I thought you were a Christian!" Togashi tells him.)

The two ladies return; Mama tells of the generous contribution made by Mrs. Hanamaki and leaves to see her guest off, leaving Sakurao alone. Miss Akita suddenly enters and Sakurao tries to embrace her; at first she is bewildered by his actions, then finally manages to push him off just as the handyman enters. When Mama returns again, Sakurao asks what she intends to do with the money. She replies cynically,

Mama: I'll use it to send you on a trip. You can go any place you like.

Sakurao: Now wouldn't that be nice!

Mama: My only condition is that you come back in a month. Three hundred yen ought to do it.

Sakurao: It would do, I suppose. But it's really not enough.

Mama: Well then, four hundred. . . .

Sakurao: Give me five. I'll send you a postcard every other day.

Mama:	I don't care about the postcards one way or the other. . . . Just come back and say, "It was fun."
Sakurao:	Five hundred yen? You really must have gotten a lot out of her.[59]

Sakurao is finally forced to admit that he not only finds Mrs. Hanamaki quite attractive but feels quite sorry for her. "I think I can save her from ruin," he tells Mama. An unpleasant conversation follows.

Mama:	By what means will you save her?
Sakurao:	I'll have to think about that. The trip will give me time to work out a plan. I'll leave immediately, so hand over the money quickly.
Mama:	. . . . .
Sakurao:	Please hurry up.
Mama:	I'm not giving any money for such a trip.
Sakurao:	But you just said you would, didn't you?
Mama:	That was before. Now is now.
Sakurao:	You won't give it then?
Mama:	No.
Sakurao:	Then I'm getting out.
Mama:	Where will you go?
Sakurao:	Where will I go? That's entirely up to me.
Mama:	But you don't have any money, do you?
Sakurao:	I'll go and get some from her.
Mama:	Could you do a thing like that?
Sakurao:	If you won't give it to me, what else can I do?
Mama:	(in a point-blank manner) Here, take it then. (She hands him the envelope.) Take it all. Go wherever you like. Spend it any way you like.
Sakurao:	I don't need it all, you know.

59 *Ibid.*, p. 131.

Mama:	It's all right, take it. And remember, if you're up to something, I'll know just how long you can last.
Sakurao:	(silently taking the envelope) Very well. I accept. Is it all right to come back in a month?
Mama:	Yes. Fine.[60]

Sakurao is testing Mama in a new way. Although his conduct is reprehensible, there is a note of desperation in his attempt to assert himself against this strong-willed woman.

The final act rounds out the portraits in this rogues' gallery. Sakurao is still away. Mama and Miss Akita have been exchanging confidences. Mama reveals that Togashi has informed her of Mrs. Hanamaki's disappearance, presumably with Sakurao. Miss Akita consoles Mama, then finally tells her that she has something to confess. Miss Akita shows Mama a letter she has received from Sakurao written since he left for his trip, in which he tells Miss Akita that he could not understand her rebuffing him and asks her to join him immediately. Miss Akita, just as weak as Sakurao, is in love with him; she wants to go. Sakurao wrote in the letter that if she would do so "it would be rather a shame for Professor Mama. But she has her work and believes in her own strength." Miss Akita now asks Mama's permission to join him. Mama replies ironically, "I guess it is 'rather a shame' for me, but since I supposedly have 'my work' and 'believe in my own strength,' I guess I don't mind. Go ahead."

At this point, Sakurao unexpectedly returns from his trip. Mama, angry, leaves him alone in the room with Miss Akita, who asks if he really loves her and tells him that Mama has given permission.

Sakurao:	It's too late.
Miss Akita:	What do you mean?
Sakurao:	Why didn't you come at once?

[60] *Ibid.*, pp. 132-133.

Miss Akita: But . . . but the whole thing was so sudden. . . .

Sakurao: One day to think it over would have been quite enough. I waited for you a week. The result of my waiting was that I got tired and came home. There was nowhere else for me to go.

Miss Akita: You wanted to come back to be near Mama.

Sakurao: I suppose you're right. You believe in her strength even more than I do.[61]

He then bursts forth in a terrible confession of spiritual weakness.

Sakurao: . . . for me, whatever it is, it has to be decided by itself, naturally. That's how I do things. I haven't the strength to select. If I ever actually choose something myself, I always regret it afterwards. Whether or not I hold back my feelings, the amount of fights and suffering is still the same. So-called evil and so-called good —they both hold an equal fascination for me, and the same terror. Whichever I choose, the same doubts arise because it takes the same quantity of courage to respond to either one of them.[62]

Mama takes matters into her own hands. In a chilling scene, she calls in the children and has them sing a little goodbye song to Sakurao and Miss Akita. She tells the children that the pair will be leaving, and, as the curtain falls, she informs them, "The car is here, to take you away." She has won. And lost.

At first the play strikes the reader as a lesser work of the author's imagination, since it lacks any of the poetic expansiveness of the early plays. Yet Kishida's powers of observation remain acute in still another social milieu, and

[61] *Ibid.*, pp. 137-138.   [62] *Ibid.*, p. 139.

his ability to write dialogue with nuances and feeling keeps the scenes moving in *Mama* as well as in any of the earlier plays.

The reason for Kishida's shift in style and subject matter is best suggested in the comments he made concerning the production of the play by the Tsukijiza in 1932. This was the first production of one of his plays in which he had been directly involved and the first in which his favorite actor Tomoda played an important part, that of Sakurao. Kishida frankly admitted that most of the actors were too young to play their parts correctly. Miss Akita's role in particular, he wrote, needed more experience than the actress who played it could bring to it. He also met some surprises: for example, he had imagined Mama as a strong and physically ample woman, but Tomoda's wife Tamura Akiko created the character as a somewhat frail and nervous person.

Kishida told the cast, "do not count on your own powers of imagination. I want you to choose various living people and actually make a study of them." He added, "the one thing I feared most was that the actors would play the characters in the play as types."[63]

Kishida had arrived at a new view. In order to see his plays performed and to encourage the performance of Japanese plays by the New Theatre movements, Kishida tried to limit himself to creating situations and characters that the actors and directors could manage. *Mama* was the first such "experiment," and he concluded hopefully that "through the efforts of these actors, a new and significant phase has been opened for the New Theatre."[64] By giving his actors specific and precise roles to play and by keeping the dialogue much closer to ordinary speech than it had been in the earlier, poetic plays, Kishida provided a challenge for the Tsukijiza that he felt they had successfully met, in their own way.

[63] *Ibid.*, IX, p. 314.   [64] *Ibid.*, p. 318.

But what of the play itself? Kishida later wrote that he was surprised during rehearsals to discover what a "disagreeable" play he had written. He commented that "there were few elements in it that could warm the spectator's heart. It left behind it a very cold impression," stronger than he intended. A careful reading of the play reveals that Kishida was now beginning to develop a variety of new interests and techniques that would sustain him in the writing of later, more carefully constructed plays.

In a sense, *Mama* may be viewed, as Kawamori Yoshirō suggests, as an artistic manifestation of Kishida's emergence "into the world of social criticism—in this case, of a working woman."[65] Evidence of an awareness of social problems on an individual level can be found earlier in *Ushiyama Hotel*, and, in a generalized and not very effective way, in *Roof Garden*. In keeping with Kishida's resolve to use comedy as a means to mirror the "sadness felt over men and the age they live in," *Mama* represents a step forward. The clearly defined nature of his characters permitted Kishida a precision of dialogue that was biting and real, for all the loss of poetry.

Mama is no doubt the central figure of the play, but, examined from the vantage point of the later plays, Sakurao emerges as the more important creation of the two. In his weakness and vacillation (Tomoda played him in too expansive a manner, Kishida observed), Sakurao represents the modern man who, however educated, intelligent, or perceptive, has suffered a terrible loss of strength that leaves him a prey to his own emotions, to other people, or to the forces of society. The creation by Kishida of a nihilistic, self-pitying hero refused even the comforts of self-deception may begin with Makabe in *Ushiyama Hotel*, although he is a rather special case. Sakurao is the first fully developed example of the type, and Sawa, in what is perhaps Kishida's finest play, *The Two Daughters of Mr. Sawa*, is the quintes-

---

65 Kawamori, "kaishaku," p. 410.

sence of all these characters, representing not only himself but a loss of authority in one whole segment of Japanese society during the decade of the 1930s.

As a play, *Mama* has certain defects, however, that make it a significant experiment rather than a complete success. Although the play is about a "working woman," it is only superficially so; essentially it records a contest of wills between husband and wife. The children of the school are used at the beginning and the end of the play, to good effect, but otherwise the atmosphere of the school is never utilized; the whole setting, indeed, seems contrived. Regardless of Mama's profession, she would dominate her husband. Thus the end of the play, so effective on first reading, is something of a theatrical trick, since the school as such has served no function in sustaining the plot or theme.

There is also an arbitrary quality about the minor characters. Mrs. Hanamaki's weeping at the end of the first act seems touching but hardly prepares us for her behavior in the second, and Miss Akita, whom Kishida described as "maneuvering in a naive way," seems confused in her motivations. In addition, the play seems somewhat artificial in the arrangement of its plot in comparison with such a skillful work as *Ushiyama Hotel*. But the problems Kishida set himself in *Mama* were somewhat different. *Ushiyama Hotel* indeed contains many characters, but the familiar theatrical device of a hotel as the setting permits Kishida to evolve the relationships among his characters without much difficulty. *Mama*, however, is Kishida's first play to involve precision in plotting. He manages to motivate successfully the major scenes of his two chief characters, but only at the expense of the credibility of the minor ones. By the time he wrote *Mr. Sawa*, he had learned how to conceal the mechanics of his plot in an admirable fashion, in particular by the device of spreading out the action over the space of several years. In the later play we are given only the confrontations. *Mama* is the first step in this direction.

Kishida continued to modify his playwriting techniques

to meet the standards of the contemporary Japanese theatre. His next, and worst, play, *Asamayama* (*Mount Asama*) was first published in the July 1931 issue of *Reconstruction* and has never been produced. The Tsukijiza troupe, which presumably might have staged it, chose instead to mount, along with *Mama*, several of his earlier plays, including *Ushiyama Hotel*.

Mount Asama is rife with melodrama and has an ending worthy of the silent films. It is a study of the final crisis in the relationships among three people; Niwa, an impoverished mining inspector living in the mountains, his daughter Futaba by a former wife, and his common-law wife Toné. Kawamori has suggested that the idea for the play may have occurred to Kishida after he built a small villa in the mountains near Karuizawa.[66] The characters are from a much lower social milieu than those of most of Kishida's other plays, and his treatment of them is rather sentimental. He made every attempt to appeal to popular tastes with the play. "I wrote *Mount Asama* in response to the wishes of a theatre troupe looking for a play designed with the current level of professional actors in mind,"[67] he wrote. He did not identify the troupe nor did he discuss why the play was never presented on the stage. Since the Tsukijiza troupe was not organized until the year after the play was published, it seems unlikely that Tomoda asked him for the play; perhaps the request came from a *shimpa* company. In any case, Kishida's efforts to work on the "current professional level" compromised his talents completely. Because of his skill as a writer the play is not without some effective scenes, but the general tenor of the text is melodramatic and even mawkish.

In the first act, Niwa, who lives in the mountains behind Karuizawa with Toné, is waiting for the visit of Futaba, now a grown woman who has received a good education in Tokyo. Her father has high hopes for her. Niwa, never a

[66] *Ibid.*, p. 411.   [67] *zenshū*, IX, p. 314.

203

success in life, is now heartened by the discovery of hot spring water on some mountain land he owns; if he can develop the land and sell it for building lots for summer houses, he will be a rich man. He wants success for the sake of his daughter.

Niwa: I have tried my hand at so many things, but I've never gotten anywhere. The more excited I get, the bigger the chances of failure and setbacks. I've been chasing after money all my life, it seems. Now, if I can feel some security over my daughter's future, I can fuss with flowers like all the other old men, and that will be fine with me.[68]

Toné is worried as to how Niwa should introduce her to Futaba, who knows nothing about her, and is concerned for the future relations of all three of them.

Toné: (to Niwa) You are a very difficult man. Please think and tell me what I'm supposed to do at a time like this. Haven't I been asking you about it since last night? I'll do whatever you think is right, but I don't know myself what I ought to do. How should I act in front of Futaba? I'm not her mother. Well, should I pretend to be the maid? If that's what you want, I wouldn't mind. I'll do whatever you think best.

Niwa: Let's just let the truth stand as it is. Wouldn't that be best?

Toné: Do you think so? Isn't that just what you are worried about the most? It won't do any good to hide me, you know. Somehow in the past two or three days your whole attitude toward me has changed completely. I suppose you can explain it by saying that you've been thinking about your daughter, but I want to try to understand your real feelings.[69]

[68] Ibid., II, p. 179.   [69] Ibid., p. 182.

She wishes to have the girl accept her on whatever basis Niwa feels is appropriate. He tells her how fond he is of his daughter, how his wife left him for no apparent reason after Futaba was born, and how much suffering the girl has gone through. Now she has an education, which she has mostly paid for by herself. Toné feels pride in the girl too. They both wait for her anxiously.

The second act shows the growth of a friendly relationship between Toné and Futaba. On her arrival the spirited and happy Futaba brings the news that she is engaged to marry Aoki, a young man of good family. Niwa chides her for not consulting him first but says that if she is pleased with the choice, he is content. Futaba asks him about Toné. He admits that their relationship is irregular but says he will marry if Futaba wishes. She does not answer him directly, to avoid embarrassing him. The following scene, in which Toné and Futaba become friends, is probably the best in the play.

Futaba: In a place like this, what do you do about buying food when the snow piles up?

Toné: All the transportation stops. There's nothing you can do about it. So you just do without certain things. This past winter it seemed the rice might run out, and we were really worried.

Futaba: What would you do if that happened?

Toné: A cart might pass. Otherwise, death by starvation. But before that happens, someone will do something to help you out.

Futaba: You don't worry about anything, do you?

Toné: It's at a time like that when a man is pretty helpful to have around.

Futaba: Yes that's true, isn't it? . . . You're such an interesting person . . . I really like you.
(*Toné* looks at her sharply.)

Futaba: Oh, please excuse me for saying that, I'm sorry.

205

Toné: Excuse you? Why it makes me happy to hear you say a thing like that. Even a woman like me, you know, was young once. I could say right out that I liked the things I liked and hated the things I hated. Now, no matter what I say, people don't take me at face value. But I have the feeling that you, you alone, would like to know about things the way they really are.

Futaba: This is getting very serious! Actually I don't think I'm really so good at understanding things. But I don't think I'm afraid of people. If people think I'm too frank, well let them think it. And in return, I don't give any false praise.[70]

The two talk of Tokyo and of their various individual experiences. Finally Futaba asks Toné about her relationship with her father.

Futaba: I do have something I would like to ask you about. Are you busy now?

Toné: I came out to empty the kettle, but never mind. What is it?

Futaba: You . . . you don't think you might like to be my father's wife . . . ?

Toné: Why, what are you thinking of? . . . That is all I've ever wanted. But there's nothing I can do to help the situation along.

Futaba: If that's really how you feel about it, then I'll do everything I can to help.[71]

Toné tells Futaba of her own bad experiences.

Toné: Before now I've been involved with two men. Every time the arrangement became a formal one, surprisingly enough something very bad happened.

[70] *Ibid.*, II, p. 189.   [71] *Ibid.*, p. 190.

Futaba: Something very bad . . . ?

Toné: The first time, the man died of a sudden illness. The second time, the man ran off and left me just like that, for another woman.

Futaba: . . . . .

Toné: So somehow it seems almost better to leave things this way.

Futaba: . . . . .

Toné: Now you must think badly of me. I am very aware of how kind you are being to me.[72]

Futaba wants to make certain that, whatever the relationship, her father and Toné are happy.

Futaba: Do you think you are happy when you are together?

Toné: (looking blank) Happy? Now what do you mean by that?

Futaba: Well!

Toné: I understand what the word means. But if you ask me what real happiness is, I'm hard put to give you a good answer. Something that makes me feel happy is usually the beginning of something bad. Yes, always. It has always been that way . . . when I was young, it was different. Once, twice . . . I was really filled with happiness . . . but now, being around a man . . . it's like leaning on a door made of paper.

Futaba: Then I feel sorry for my father.

Toné: Yes, of course you should. This is a side of your father that you don't understand. It should be that way.

Futaba: What kind of thing is it, the side I don't understand? . . . Please tell me.

[72] *Ibid.*

Toné: It can't be summed up that simply, you know. But perhaps I can say there is something cold about him.

Futaba: I wonder about that. . . .

Toné: . . . . .

Futaba: Then . . . then you are the unlucky one.[73]

The scene subtly reveals both Toné's emotional weariness and her natural dignity.

Unfortunately, the play quickly degenerates. In the third act, Futaba receives a letter from her fiancé Aoki that, although she permits no one to read it, seems to indicate that the engagement is soon to be broken off. Even Toné cannot seem to comfort her, and says that she is a failure in her new role as a mother. Futaba's father is too happy to notice any change, since his own plans seem to be going so well. Suddenly Aoki himself appears, having made the long trip to talk with Futaba personally. They retire to the back room. Toné, eavesdropping on their conversation, indicates to Niwa that they seem to be breaking off. The workmen now appear, demanding that Niwa pay them for all their work. He cannot do so, and violence seems ready to break out until Futaba enters and gives her bankbook to the workmen. "I have three hundred yen in my account. You don't trust my father, so take it and go and get your money." Niwa permits his daughter to give her money away, and she tells him that Aoki cannot marry her.

Act Four is divided into two scenes. In the first, Toné tells Niwa's assistant about the disappearance of father and daughter. She seems resigned to the likelihood that they will commit suicide during the night. Even if Niwa comes back, she says, she is unwilling to live with a suicidal man. She belongs to no one now. Toné is afraid and forces the assistant to remain with her.

In the second, the setting is the top of Mount Asama. Niwa has indeed brought Futaba with him, intending that

[73] *Ibid.*, pp. 190-191.

208

they both should die. He tries to force her to tell him what happened between her and Aoki, but she eludes him. "I never can speak frankly to those closest to me," she tells him. When Niwa asks her to die with him, she refuses. He finally agrees that she must go away to let him die alone, but warns her not to go near Toné, who has, for him, "the beauty found in impurity." Futaba, growing increasingly overwrought, declares that if life is really so difficult she will join her father. They go to the edge of the cliff, and, before Futaba can come to her senses, they both tumble into the crater. Here is the discouraging stage direction that concludes the play:

> Early morning light sifts down on the volcano.
> Futaba appears. She has brought herself up out of the volcano by the sheer will to live. She seems in a trance and quite exhausted. She leans on the rocks. Finally, she slowly opens her eyes. In the far distance, a group of mountain climbers making its way to the summit bursts into song.[74]

In the midst of such claptrap, Kishida's sense of words never altogether failed him. Even in the absurdity of the final scene, the dialogue between father and daughter manages to convey the emotional situation with appropriate force; still, it is hard to imagine how the author could write such nonsense. The subject of suicide is certainly a possible one for a play, and indeed the character of Niwa in many ways resembles the other disappointed and sometimes worn-out heroes in the later plays. But in *Mount Asama* Kishida sacrificed his strongest point as a dramatist, his ability to create an emotional and even poetic atmosphere in which his characters can move. *Mama*, his first experiment, sacrificed atmosphere for a conventional plot; *Mount Asama* sacrificed a conventional plot for melodrama. The results were disastrous.

Kishida knew that the play was a failure. When *Mount Asama* was first published, in 1931, he wrote an essay con-

[74] *Ibid.,* p. 213.

209

cerning his purposes in composing it. He stated that there were several possibilities for playwrights in Japan at the time—to write plays meant to be read, plays meant for "ideal" actors who in fact were unavailable in Japan, or plays that would suit the existing inadequate style of acting. There was still another category, plays that "the actors today could probably play but which would have a certain novelty: plays that can be produced." This was his compromise.

This last category seems not to have been chosen by the young writers today. Yet I am not alone in hoping that they will appear. If I may say so, I too hope to extend my own efforts in this direction, and although I do not know if I have succeeded in this instance, I have certainly tried to write this play with today's actors in mind. It is quite a different sort of play from the kind I have written up to now. . . .[75]

A year later, Kishida was better able to see his mistakes.

The play was conceived not only to give the actors some specific characters to create, but also to limit myself to selecting the kind of form and content to which an audience today would be able to respond. Specifically, I tried to consider carefully the performing traditions of the actors in order to avoid any undue difficulties for them in the psychology and attitudes of the characters and in the style of language in which the dialogue was written.[76]

He realized that the compromise had failed.

Yet in the end, there was little novelty in my script itself; it savored far too much of stage tradition mixed, moreover, with an immature "literary style" designed to cover over this fact. It goes without saying that the fault was in my lack of skill, the fault of trying to write out of

[75] *zenshū*, VIII, p. 230. [76] *Ibid.*, IX, p. 314.

my proper sphere. Yet this experience was not without meaning for me. It forced me to realize that I must not try such a project again.[77]

In effect, he had come close to assuming the traditional role of the playwright in Japan, where the writer served as the craftsman who constructed scenes to show off the established talents of a troupe. The results of his experiments with *Mama* and *Mount Asama* convinced him that as a creative writer he must retain his integrity of vision; if he sacrificed that, he realized, he sacrificed everything.

The period of the early 1930s appears to have been one of great stress for Kishida. The public was unable to accept the kind of plays he was best qualified to write. His attempts to write what he thought they wanted ended in disaster. It seemed for a time that he might even leave the theatre: he began writing and publishing novels and stories. Even though he still considered himself to be a playwright, he was prepared to compromise in still another way.

But in 1932 a fortunate set of circumstances produced the establishment of the Tsujikiza, and after the first production of *Mama* Kishida realized that in Tomoda and Tamura he had at least one actor and one actress capable of performing successfully in plays of literary and theatrical value. Kishida wrote for their talents, and during this third phase of his prewar career, he composed perhaps his two finest plays, *Saigetsu* (*A Space of Time*) and *Mr. Sawa's Two Daughters*. It was during this third phase of his work that he truly was able to write, as he put it, "in the pride of my profession."[78]

This third period of Kishida's work was marked by a maturity in his observations of the quality of life in Japan during the period coupled with a similar maturity in writing technique, plus the happy occasion of writing with specific

[77] *Ibid.*   [78] *Ibid.*, p. 319.

211

and talented players in mind. This period of professional felicity was to be a short one, however, for the Tsukijiza was dissolved in 1936.

Kishida's refreshed and enthusiastic attitude aroused by the possibility of accomplishing work of quality can be seen in the charming short play *Shokugyō* (*Vocation*), written as a kind of practice play for the actors at the Tsukijiza. The play was first published in the August 1935 issue of *The Central Review* and was performed by the troupe in the same year.

Vocation is a light-hearted illustration of the methods through which Kishida wished his actors to develop their imaginations. The stage is bare and young actors and actresses are preparing for a rehearsal class. They chat about their personal affairs, the sad state of the New Theatre movement, and so forth, until interrupted by the Chief Actor, who tells them that in today's rehearsal they are to improvise in a new way. Up until now in their improvisations, they have been given a plot, but today he wishes them to choose a character and, as these characters intermingle a few at a time on the stage, they are to create a consistent plot by themselves. "Don't lose the context of the scene, and keep your wits about you," he tells them.

The little play created by the actors turns out to be slight but quite amusing. Actor A, waiting for his friend in the park, meets Actress D, who is pushing her baby in a cart and who turns out to be the wife of the long-lost friend. Eventually Actor B, the friend, turns up. He supposes that Actor A is flirting with his wife and flies into a jealous rage. Actress C enters and seems to know Actor B, whom she soon abandons for Actor C, a painter. Actress B now enters, as the sister of Actress C, and tries to convince the painter to marry her sister. At this point, Actor D rushes in with a sword.

"Let's stop at this point," says the Chief Actor. "As I always tell you, your imaginations are too limited, and we must work out a way to expand them." He reminds them

212

that it is through flexibility and spontaneity that actors can bring real appeal to their performances. As a "punishment," he sends two of them to try again. This time, their imaginations take them a bit too far; they find themselves in an enchanted forest (where "natural ice-water" flows out of a spring) while they discuss the fact that the Lady (who is closely associated with a Princess) wants the Actor to manage her accounts. The pair finally grinds to a halt.

Chief Actor: It was pretty difficult, wasn't it? Now let's look together at what we've accomplished today. But before we do that, let me remind you that there is one thing we actors must think of before anything else. The actor must never be the slave of his script. This is obvious, of course, but even though we acknowledge it, we still go on depending too much on what the author has written, and the play may not make its point because we don't really help him out. I'm leaving writers like Chekhov and Ibsen out of the conversation for the moment. Within our own sphere, how many real playwrights with literary ability do we have? This is important! What we can create ourselves, all the seeds from which we must bring forth fruit in our own garden, depends on just those very writers.

We actors ourselves have not yet grasped the meaning of a man's appearance, or of the psychology of an ordinary person. Nor have we made even the slightest observation on the times in which we live. Nor have we grasped the significance of the devices available to us in terms of the stage, this narrow stage itself.

If we wrote plays like the stuff you made up today, the theatre in Japan couldn't possibly interest anybody![79]

[79] *Ibid.*, II, p. 382.

A genial challenge for mutual cooperation between actors and writers, the play seems to suggest that Kishida regained a real hope that the actors could respond to him, quite the opposite attitude he revealed only a few years earlier at the time he wrote *Mount Asama*.

As his part of the bargain, Kishida labored for two years to write the two long plays on which a good deal of his later reputation rests. The first of them, *Mr. Sawa's Two Daughters*, was published in the January 1935 issue of *The Central Review*. Kishida originally intended the leading part of Mr. Sawa to be acted by Tomoda himself, but when the Tsukijiza troupe dissolved in 1936, Kishida withdrew the play for a later production. He hoped to give the play to the Literary Theatre troupe, but with Tomoda's death in the China war in 1937, he was forced to change his plans again. The play was not produced until 1951, when it was staged by the Kurumiza in Kyoto.

The play deals with the family relations of Sawa Kazu-hisa, a former Foreign Office employee, who now leads a somewhat irregular life as an employee in a hospital of rather dubious standards. Although his wife had died many years before, he, like the son in *Diary of Fallen Leaves*, continued to refuse the responsibility of rearing his three children, two girls and a boy; he remained in Europe and they grew up without any guidance from him. Hatsuo, his son, has run away to sea and died several months before the play begins, and Sawa now lives with his housekeeper and two daughters. The play is a satire of manners but, more important, it is a study of irresponsibility and the decay of family values.

In Act One, Sawa is visited by an old acquaintance in the Japanese Foreign Office, Mr. Kamitani, who informs him that a French acquaintance of his has fallen in love with Sawa's younger daughter Aiko. Aiko, the most independent-minded member of the family, is working for a recording company, but she has won the privilege of doing so only through the lassitude and weakness of her father, who does not especially approve. Etsuko, the older daughter, is quiet and reserved; she works in a school for underprivileged children. Sawa next receives a letter from a friend of his dead son, Tadokoro, who urgently requests an appointment. When Sawa shows the letter to his daughters, they react strongly though in a fashion difficult to interpret; they tell their father only that the man had been introduced to them by their brother at a picnic.

Later in Act One Etsuko, thinking over the meaning of her brother's death, asks her father if there is no way for them to share their inner lives more fully.

Etsuko: (going to her father) Papa, don't you think that between parents and children it is a bad thing if there are any secrets? To say "secrets" is an exaggeration I suppose, but if someone is suffering in silence over something, don't you think . . . ?

Sawa: What makes you say such a thing?

Etsuko: Nothing special. Still, talking about my brother again makes me wonder if something mightn't exist between human beings closer than what this family has found. There is too much we never tell each other. No one ever talks over anything. Why?[80]

The play is organized around the principle of secrets. In each act, a member of the family reveals a secret, and the reactions of the other family members to each revelation push their relationships toward a final estrangement from each other. The first revelation occurs at the end of the first act, when Sawa informs his daughters that Raku, his housekeeper, is in effect his common-law wife. He blurts out the truth after Aiko is rude to her.

Sawa: (irritated by the tone of his daughter's words, he shuts his eyes in distaste) Now listen, Aiko. And Etsuko too. I have something I want to say to both

[80] *Ibid.*, pp. 392-393.

215

of you. (A long pause) Raku is not to be treated any longer as just an employee here.

(At this sudden declaration, the three women, each surprised in her own way, seem to withdraw in consternation; they then exchange looks of subtle recognition.)

Sawa: I don't care whether or not you choose to call her "mother." I am sure you will both have your opinions on the subject. But there is nothing to keep secret from you now, I realize. The two of you have nothing to worry about. Go ahead and keep leading your lives in the same happy-go-lucky way that you have been. This woman has been unfortunate for many years. I too have been weak. This is the way life is. Please overlook the past, for my sake.

(Raku and Etsuko look away, as though they had previously reached some kind of understanding. Aiko alone gazes disdainfully at her father.)

Curtain[81]

In Act Two, Tadokoro comes to see Sawa and asks him for Aiko's hand in marriage. He is overly assertive but seems basically a naïve and likeable young man. He is upset when Aiko refuses to see him, a fact that suggests to Sawa the possibility there is something between the two that he does not know about. Tadokoro leaves angrily; when Aiko then appears, Sawa expresses his regret that she has not taken her father into her confidence. But in fact, as Sawa told Tadokoro early in the act, he has relinquished any real responsibility over his children.

Sawa: (To Tadokoro) I see. You want me to give you Aiko. Now you might as well know that she never asks me about anything. You can try to use me as an intermediary if you want, but look at the situation from a parent's point of view. There's a lot of responsibility involved. Aiko always insists she can take

---

[81] *Ibid.*, pp. 395-396.

care of things by herself. If she thinks she's that clever, then it seems to me I just have to trust her. So I have adopted a policy of non-interference. Considering the way the world is, parents have to look out for their own good. Anyway, how should I know what's best for my daughter?

If she wanted to talk to me about such a question, that would be a different story. There's nothing wrong with giving a little bit of harmless advice. But those daughters of mine. Especially Aiko . . . she really has too much self-confidence. Why if I even tried to suggest a husband for her, she'd be sure to turn me down flat.[82]

Aiko is finally goaded into giving a description of what really happened at Hatsuo's picnic, and she eventually admits her secret: she was seduced, and she believes by Tadokoro, that night in the dark of her bedroom. Etsuko and Sawa try to comfort her, but her own determined independence of spirit makes her abhor their words of appeasement, and she cries out her contempt for everyone, including her father.

Aiko: (suddenly, with intensity) Even if I did know for sure that it was him, what good would it do? Was it my responsibility? (harshly) Disgusting. Disgusting. It is just the same as if nothing had happened. No woman anywhere would willingly permit such a thing. What did he prove by treating me that way? What advantage can a man gain from such an action? I suppose he can flatter himself, selfishly. If there was any promise between us, what sort of promise could it have been? Proofs of love are given in other ways. You probably ask why I didn't refuse him. . . . Oh God, a woman is a creature you cannot understand. . . . (She puts her head down on the table)[83]

[82] *Ibid.*, p. 397.   [83] *Ibid.*, p. 406.

Aiko too is weak, but she has surrounded her weakness with a hard and self-protecting shell. Later in the play she is accused by her sister of being an opportunist, but her seeming self-centeredness is a reaction from her childhood, when she went unloved. Aiko rejects her sister and father, and announces to them her intention to going away to live by herself, away from the rest of the family. She departs, leaving the others behind, stunned.

In Act Three, it is Etsuko's turn to have her secret uncovered; when this happens, the family dissolves. The action in this act takes place two years later. Sawa is living alone in a dirty apartment. Raku comes to do his laundry and asks in return for a bit of money for her daughter's schooling. Sawa is now apparently living on the charity of his daughters, who come to visit him once a month. Aiko is now married to the Frenchman mentioned in the first act. After the sisters arrive, Etsuko says that she is now eager to resolve her differences with Aiko and save the family. She confesses to Aiko and her father that she is in love with a teacher in her school and that, to avoid a scandal, the principal will transfer her to another school. As Etsuko reveals the somewhat sordid details of the affair, Aiko laughs derisively, to her sister's dismay and annoyance. Like her father, Etsuko is blind to her own weaknesses and cannot bear to have them exposed. Etsuko sees herself as a self-sacrificing and noble figure, as she told Tadokoro in Act Two.

Tadokoro: Are you as interested as ever in teaching?

Etsuko: I suppose there are other kinds of work that might suit me better. But when I'm at the school, I seem to lose all interest in luxury. That is the most important thing. To live every day without giving rise to any desire in yourself. Why, to live in any other way would be unthinkable to me. It wouldn't be the same at all if I went around to the homes of those poor children with a proud heart. I'm not the kind to be charitable so as to really avoid thinking about the problems. I give my all to it, I exhaust myself completely. I use all the money I can get my hands on to help those poor starving ones. Without any fancy theories. It gives me something to live for.

Tadokoro: You sound just a bit pastel-colored.

Etsuko: No. Absolutely transparent. I detest work in the name of society or of religion. I have no intention of flying any flag for "humanity" because of what I do.

Tadokoro: A question of natural disposition then.

Etsuko: Do you mean I am sentimental? If you think so, then leave it at that. Because I certainly am weak-spirited. I think I was formed by something very dark in my childhood. I suppose I can never forget the terrible food I had to carry to school when I was a child. I just can't.[84]

As her confession proceeds, it is clear that Etsuko, despite her repeated pleas for family solidarity, has enjoyed keeping her own secrets the longest of the three.

Aiko: Dear Etsuko. Have you forgotten what happened before? When I told you and father about that terrible incident in my own life? Even though you soothed me then with your sweet words, you felt superior. You were laughing at me, weren't you? You thought I was a fool. You thought I had besmirched myself, and you were delighted, weren't you? That is the only kind of sympathy we can have for each other. You want the others to feel grateful to you, don't you? Well I am not grateful to you. I don't treat other people that way myself. And please do not think badly of me for it.

[84] *Ibid.*, p. 402

Etsuko: I don't like to hear you respond this way. I felt sorry for you from the bottom of my heart.

Aiko: What was the meaning of your feeling sorry for me? Even if human unhappiness is born from some stupid mistake, it is human nature to laugh. I know the way you laughed at me. I am laughing now, in the same way. But without concealing it. I laugh out in the open. I don't mind. Do you understand?[85]

Now it is Etsuko who feels forced to leave the family.

Etsuko: (to Aiko) Well then, we have balanced our accounts. We will be complete strangers from now on. I thought I had a sister. I worried to think I might somehow lose you. Now, I doubt that we will meet again. (She gets up.) Goodbye, Father. I'll be in touch with you soon.[86]

Aiko and her father are left alone. Aiko, the kindest and most responsible member of the family, urges her father to be kind to Etsuko. When she tries to give her father some money he refuses, and she leaves. The concluding stage direction brings to the fore the nihilistic and nervous tensions that have created the rhythm of the whole play.

Sawa is left completely alone. He takes a crust of bread out of the cupboard, takes a piece of cheese in his fingers, and, as he paces around and around, he keeps bringing the food to his lips. The gay music from a radio playing somewhere can be heard, in an ironic contrast to the scene on the stage. The curtain falls.[87]

The play is a rich and ironic comedy of manners, but the real subject of Kishida's concern is loneliness. All the characters are estranged from each other; in this Sawa himself is the central figure. He is the best-developed of Kishida's male characters. Kishida, having seen Tomoda play

[85] *Ibid.*, p. 417.   [86] *Ibid.*   [87] *Ibid.*, p. 418.

Sakurao in *Mama* and Makabe in *Ushiyama Hotel*, felt himself quite justified in creating such a long and complex part for him.

Sawa has cut himself off from Japan, from his family, and even from his own emotions. He is well-educated, but suffers from the terrible ineffectuality that bedevils so many of Kishida's male characters, and is that familiar figure in twentieth-century European and American literature, an anti-hero. He is a pathetic manifestation of the slogan "Western manners, Japanese heart" that had been so strongly advocated during the earlier Meiji period: he has all the accouterments of a western gentleman but only succeeds in living in a half-world between the two civilizations.

Like Sakurao, Makabe, and Niwa in *Mount Asama*, Sawa is a failure; like them also, his failure can be blamed, at least in part, on the state of contemporary society. His weak and, it must be admitted, in some ways idealistic turn of character prevent him from achieving success.

Sawa: (to Etsuko) People who can push their way through life will succeed. Look at Kamitani, just look at him. His wife suffered and got sick. Not him. If there is anything he wants to do, he just goes right ahead. As he pleases. No wavering. No hesitating. I'm one of the people he has made use of. To hell with it.[88]

In Act Three, Sawa has finally realized what real loneliness can mean. In a long speech he warns Etsuko she must maintain her good relations with Aiko, but he is really warning himself.

Sawa: (to Etsuko) As a matter of fact, relations between you and Aiko have not been so bad as all that. They could be far worse.

I might have told you about this before, but when I first entered the Foreign Office, I was sent to study French at Deauville. In the lodging house where I

[88] *Ibid.*, p. 411.

221

stayed, there were two old ladies, oh, about fifty years old or so. One was named Madame Depaze, and the other Mademoiselle Poirer. They were both older sisters of the owner of the house. They lived together, but each took care of her own expenses. They looked at each other every morning and every night for I don't know how long, those two sisters. Except maybe for the two years when Madame Depaze had been married and away.

Do you know that for more than ten years, those two had never spoken? That's what I heard. Isn't that extraordinary? They had disagreed about something or other, and they never spoke. Of course in front of other people they maintained a perfectly normal appearance. I used to watch one following the other as the pair of them would sweep, right up to the gate. It was quite charming, in fact.

As I said, they never spoke, for ten years. I suppose there were some things that had to be discussed between them though. . . . I can remember sitting in the dining room, looking at the two of them, countless times. One would occupy one side of the table, and the other would sit across on the other side and glare at her. Sometimes it made me nervous, but sometimes it struck me as really quite amusing, you know. When things really got bad, they would have a terrible quarrel.

You see, it wasn't just the fact that something had happened between them that made them angry. They *disliked* each other so much. You would think one of them would just go away. But they didn't. How interesting that foreigners seem to react in this way. For them, to go away would mean to lose.[89]

Just as the two old ladies could not be reconciled to each other, neither can Sawa nor his two daughters accept what

[89] *Ibid.*, pp. 412-413.

it is necessary to accept in order to maintain the family; unlike "the foreigners," they all go away.

Mr. Sawa's Two Daughters is Kishida's most thoughtful and best-constructed play. He himself stated that he wrote both this play and *A Space of Time* "in complete absorption, in a kind of freedom and composure . . . that permitted me to compose them smoothly."[90] All the necessary conditions came together for Kishida to produce mature work, and he felt that in these plays he had displayed his real abilities.

> Both plays can be said to represent a new stage in the development of my thought, and they remain works with a deep emotional meaning for me. Both are confessions, records of a mutiny against feudalistic attitudes and of a yearning for freedom, a yearning that is unstoppable, even if the nature of the freedom wished for is imperfectly understood. If the plays have a somewhat nihilistic flavor about them, then I must admit I meant them as caricatures, even if rather solemn ones, of contemporary Japan.[91]

Tanaka Chikao, himself a distinguished critic and playwright, has expressed quite well the essential quality of the play in his essay on *Mr. Sawa's Two Daughters*. He finds in Sawa a reflection of the underside of Japan's modernization; Sawa is completely a free man, but the contradictions of his wanting to be part of a family in the Japanese tradition are "both funny and painful." The cruel humor in the play at the expense of Sawa is also self-scorn on the part of the author, "a fate with which both of them must struggle."[92] Tanaka is surely correct in his analysis; indeed, the strength of the play seems to be that the loneliness Kishida creates is as much international and universal as it is Japanese: a change of values, no matter what they might be, produces

---

[90] *Ibid.*, IX, p. 319.   [91] *Ibid.*, p. 320.
[92] Tanaka, *Gekibungaku*, p. 172.

dislocations and anxieties common to modern man everywhere.

Yoshida Seiichi also finds a singular strength in the character of Aiko, who with her openness and honesty represents for him a kind of Japanese Nora, breaking down the doll's house of pretense that had existed in the family until she left it.[93]

Through his careful construction of the scenes, Kishida is able to keep the ever-darkening tone of the play moving in a consistent and believable way. The exterior incidents of the plot (Etsuko's involvement with the teacher, the seduction of Aiko and her marriage) are not shown, as they are in *Mama*, where too much time is spent in manipulating the superficial events of plot. Instead we are shown a sequence of crucial scenes, all dealing with the major concerns of the playwright. If the mood of the play is pessimistic, it is not without a consistent and somber poetry.

Poetry is an important element in the second of the two important plays Kishida wrote during this phase of his work. *A Space of Time* was published in the April 1935 issue of *Reconstruction*. Like *Mr. Sawa's Two Daughters*, it was not produced until after the war, when it had its first production at the Literary Theatre in 1947. The play is dominated by the image of time, which permeates every scene and governs and shapes the whole meaning of the events that pass through a sequence of almost two decades.

This play, which is Kishida's most carefully wrought study in feminine psychology, follows the changing attitudes toward life of the heroine Yasuko, the daughter of a distinguished government official. The play also has a hero, or, more properly speaking, a Kishida anti-hero; although he does not appear on the stage, we form an opinion concerning his weak and vacillating character through the rest of the family's reactions to him. *A Space of Time* might be described as a woman's view of the kind of male irresponsi-

[93] Yoshida Seiichi, "Kishida kaishaku," *Nihon gendai gikyoku shū*, edited by Iwata Toyoo, p. 231.

bility pictured in *Mr. Sawa's Two Daughters*, and is no less interesting for the fact that we never see the man. Some critics have commented on Kishida's "skill" in composing a play in which he never shows his hero, but the trick is common enough in commercial Broadway fare in New York. The opinion might rather be ventured that Kishida leaves him off the stage because he does not wish to dilute the focus of his, or our, interest in Yasuko and her family. The members of the family are close and loving, and their reactions to the various events befalling Yasuko provide the emotional undercurrent that pushes the play along.

Each of the three acts presents a different glimpse into Yasuko's life and her relationship with Saiki Kazumasa. Act One plunges us into the central situation of the play. Yasuko, twenty-three, has fallen deeply in love with the young man and is going to bear his child. We soon learn that she has just contemplated committing suicide but has lacked the courage to do so. The play opens as her two older brothers, Keiichi and Shinji, learning of her attempt, express their horror and debate how to inform their parents. They try to force Yasuko to reveal precisely what has happened.

Yasuko: Don't ask me his name. That is the one thing I will not tell anyone.

Keiichi: You don't have to. But tell me what kind of person he is. How old is he?

Yasuko: . . . . .

Keiichi: What kind of work does he do?

Yasuko: . . . . .

Keiichi: You don't have to tell me every last detail, but. . . .

Yasuko: He's still a student. . . .

Keiichi: Is his family wealthy? Is he poor?

Yasuko: About average. . . .

Keiichi: From Tokyo? From the country?

Yasuko: From the country . . . but he's staying with relatives in Tokyo.

225

Keiichi: How did you come to know him?

Yasuko: At a friend's house.

Keiichi: Well, I think I've got the general idea.

Yasuko: You couldn't possibly.

Keiichi: I mean the circumstances. You've had a fast one pulled on you. You've gotten mixed up with some delinquent.

Yasuko: Don't be absurd. He's not a delinquent. He's an excellent student, and what's more, there's nothing objectionable about him. My friends respect him very much. He's a good friend to everyone.

Keiichi: That doesn't prove a thing. I meant the word delinquent as a joke, but it seems to me he cannot possibly be sincerely in love with you.

Yasuko: If he has any fault, it's that he's so unassertive. He's too pure, too genuine a person. We were attracted to each other from the start.[94]

Keiichi accuses Yasuko of living in an illusion, and he adds, "I can't say that the fault is entirely on his side. No girl your age should be living in a dream." He asks if they have ever discussed marriage, but she answers merely that they cannot marry until he finishes school: their only choice is to go on trusting each other. Yasuko tries to explain the young man's point of view to her brother. He is desperately eager to succeed in life. If he discloses to his family his desire to marry, they will surely stop giving financial help and thereby frustrate his plans. Yasuko believes in him, of course, but Keiichi, incredulous, demands to know the boy's name.

Keiichi: I know that you don't want to, but you must tell me his name. You know that, as your brother, I will do anything I can to help you. I've told you that so often. And what helps you will no doubt help him too. His life is important, but a woman's life is equally so. And no one, absolutely no one, has the right to put the child's life in jeopardy.

Yasuko: I cannot go through with killing myself. But I will endure any other hardship for him. If there is anything I can do, I will do it. His child and I will wait for him to achieve his grand success.[95]

Yasuko believes in her lover and is willing to wait all her life for him to succeed, even if she can never marry him. Her brother finds her decision a poor one and upbraids her for what he considers her willful naïveté. Yasuko's sister-in-law Yoshiko arrives. She informs the family that the boy's name is Saiki Kazumasa and that Yasuko met him at a friend's house. Armed with this information, Keiichi decides that he will confront Saiki in order to see what responsibility the boy is willing to shoulder. The arrival of the parents stifles the discussion. The curtain falls as Keiichi worries over his sister and her future. The dialogue in the first act is effective; although the dramatic situation seems banal, Kishida uses the rest of the play to explore the human truth underlying these over-familiar elements of plot.

The second act takes place seven years later. Yasuko and her child, named Midori, are still living with her family. This interval has been a difficult one for Yasuko, and she appears now in a moment of acute despair.

Yasuko: (to Keiichi) I tell you, I can't stand it any more.

Keiichi: Can't stand what?

Yasuko: Living like this, day after day....

Keiichi: Naturally. But what can be done about it?

Yasuko: Please help in some way. As quickly as you can.

Keiichi: What can I possibly do?

Yasuko: I want to take him out of my mind. We are a couple in name only . . . in the end it's no good

[95] *Ibid.*, p. 14.

227

for either one of us. When I go to see him now, I can't seem to communicate with him at all. I haven't the strength of will to try to find a way to share our lives in any real fashion. . . .

Keiichi: . . . . .

Yasuko: I realize it was wrong of me to have forced him to register our names together, so that there would be a legal tie between us, even though we don't live together.

Keiichi: I believe he told Father about it. I'm the one in the family who never hears about such things.

Yasuko: I must say you have changed a good deal. You never used to be so cold-hearted.

Keiichi: Actually, I'm just learning to know my limitations.[96]

The strains in Yasuko's own life are beginning to tear at the fabric of the family. She is losing her trust in Saiki, and she tells Keiichi that although Saiki has finished school, he now wants to defer their living together until he can afford a home for them. She would be willing to give up her pleasant life with her family and go with him, she says, but she no longer believes that he is being truthful. She fears that he is trying to avoid all contact with her and the child. Yasuko senses that "some kind of obstacle is growing between us, and there is nothing we can do about it. I can't say what it is . . . some kind of gloom in the atmosphere." She finally confesses that her real desire is to make her life by herself, without him. "So you don't want to die any more?" Keiichi asks her. "I don't want to live either," she tells him.[97]

At this juncture, Saiki himself comes to call. Yasuko leaves to talk with him and soon returns to say that she and Saiki have decided to sever their relations. She insists that they are in agreement on the point. Saiki had asked to see Yasuko's father, but her brother Shinji goes to speak with

---

[96] *Ibid.*, p. 22.   [97] *Ibid.*, p. 23.

him in her father's place. When he returns, Keiichi upbraids him for his lack of tact, since Shinji's strident voice could be heard all through the house. Shinji admits he vented all his pent-up anger at Saiki, who only told him in return that he and Yasuko had indeed loved each other, but in different ways. Shinji, however, remains unconvinced of Saiki's sincerity.

Yasuko: Shinji, don't be too hasty in thinking badly of people.

Shinji: Yasuko, you have still not understood the true nature of this man. When he consented to marry you legally, he no longer had any real desire to do so. Today, I think you finally understood at least this. Yet before, you were willing to die for him, weren't you? I am going to ask you again about what happened seven years ago. Did he really ask you to wait until the proper time came to get married? Didn't he really tell you that he wanted to leave you? It was then you lost the will to live. Isn't that right? Because that is what he just told me now. Very clearly.[98]

Yasuko, startled, decides to tell the family for the first time what really happened.

Yasuko: I'll try to remember exactly the words he used with me . . . yes, I remember. I was sobbing, and he said, "No matter what I do, I will be in trouble if I tell my family about this. I can only promise to marry you if the right time comes. Until then, you will just have to wait for me. And what can we do about the child? What would your own family say about it?"[99]

It is clear from what follows that Saiki's real concern was always for himself.

[98] *Ibid.*, p. 30.   [99] *Ibid.*

229

Yasuko: (continuing) More than anything else, I want to try to do something really worthwhile with my life. Until I accomplish this, I have to keep going. And to do that, people must be able to put their trust in me. I don't think you would be able to get by without telling people whose child it is. In a case like that I'd be ruined. If you really love me, then somehow, somehow, when I'm not around . . . (her voice becomes thick with emotion) somewhere, quite far from Tokyo . . . you must dare . . . must dare. . . . (she bursts into tears)

Shinji: To kill yourself for him.[100]

The family is shocked. They revile Saiki, and Shinji demands to know how Yasuko could have listened to this and said nothing.

Yasuko: I'm not to be made a fool of. I know what he asked . . . yes, I know. But none of you, none, knows the way in which he said this to me. No, he is not a bad man. He . . . he . . . was only expressing to me directly the anguish he was suffering . . . I don't hate him for that . . . I can't hold anything against him . . . I thought I really ought to do it for him. I was happy to do that for a man like him. . . .

Shinji: And what do you think about it now?

Yasuko: Now? Now . . . now . . . when all is said and done, I really love the man. Even with the situation as it is, if I can just keep on living and can see him accomplish what he wants to . . . if only I can see that, then I . . . (her voice becomes choked with tears, and she falls to the floor in agony)

Curtain[101]

100 *Ibid.*, p. 31.   101 *Ibid.*

Out of context the scene may seem overwrought, but Yasuko's last speech forms the natural climax to the act, which maintains an ever-increasing level of emotional tension. To a western reader, the willingness of a woman to sacrifice herself completely for the man she loves no doubt strikes a false note; it did not seem so to Kishida, and he created the scene to reveal in some detail the depth and complexity of her womanly feelings, for which he felt an obvious sympathy.

More of the truth has now been understood, but as the full meaning of any situation only reveals itself in time, so the real nature of Yasuko's love for Saiki is not revealed until the third act, which takes place yet ten years later. This final act takes place on the day of a Buddhist memorial service for Yasuko's father, who has died seven years before. As the scene opens, Midori, now grown to be a young lady, is playing the piano for her aunt Yoshiko. The family reminisces about the father and his death. A visitor is announced; again it is Saiki. Yasuko informs Midori that he is her father; she wonders if she herself should see the man after so many years, and on such an inappropriate day as well.

She decides to see him; after she leaves the room, her brothers discuss Saiki's possible motives for a visit. Shinji is suspicious and wonders if Saiki might not have heard of Midori's inheritance from her grandfather. Eventually Yasuko returns, having sent Saiki away.

Yasuko: He said he wanted me to go with him.
Shinji: That's what I guessed.
Yasuko: Is that what you really thought, Shinji?
Shinji: Yes, I was convinced of it. What did you tell him?
Yasuko: I didn't answer him. I only listened to him, without saying a word. . . .[102]

Yasuko tries to explain her feelings.

[102] *Ibid.*, p. 40.

231

Yasuko: I couldn't have appeared more composed. But in fact, that was just the way I felt naturally. It seemed somehow that what I had been expecting was merely coming to pass naturally . . . you see . . . I saw his depth of emotion, but it didn't really touch me deeply. How can I best explain it? For some reason I just didn't think the man in front of me now was the same person in whom I had been trusting all these past years. I can't really say that anything had changed in him. But he was not the man I had been waiting for. It seemed to me he was someone else. I was happy to hear everything he said, but I wondered what I should answer. . . . I could not recognize the real person.[103]

Yasuko describes again how much she loves Saiki.

Yasuko: I have never said a word against him. And I have never even thought badly of him. My brothers may think I am saying this to console myself and to flatter my pride, but there has never been any question as to whether or not I would forgive him. If only he were the same man I dreamt about. When I met him today, I realized he had aged a little, but more than that, he just wasn't himself anymore. . . . Had he really changed? I truly don't understand myself. . . .[104]

She asks her brothers to try to comprehend her own logic and not merely to judge the situation on the basis of their own prejudices.

Yasuko: The man I was waiting for was not the one I met today, I think it was another. I believe Yoshiko will understand what I mean . . . you see, I am not really disappointed.

[103] *Ibid.*   [104] *Ibid.*

Keiichi: The moment in time that was coming has come. But the one who came with it was not the one you were waiting for.[105]

Next Yasuko tries to explain the situation to her daughter.

Yasuko: You see, my dear, someday your real father will come to get us. We'll have to wait for him, won't we? As long as we have to. It's no use to keep wishing he would hurry![106]

The curtain falls to the sound of Midori playing the piano.

To this reader, the play is far less appealing than *Mr. Sawa's Two Daughters*. Still, there is no doubt that Yasuko's emotional growth and her final, quiet victory over her own emotions are skillfully manifested. The plotting of the play, like that of *Mr. Sawa's Two Daughters*, also shows considerable skill. We are not shown the moments of high emotion but only reflective ones in which the family observes the passing of time and the inevitable changes it brings to their lives. In the second act, Keiichi tells Yasuko that every member of the family has changed in the passage of time; nothing, no emotional attitude, remains fixed. "You are changing too," he tells her. "Everything is moving, slowly; for me it is a process more fascinating to watch than reading any history I know. I wish that I could remain all my life, quiet in one place, and watch things, as they go by."[107] There is under the surface of the play a peaceful, lyrical conception suggesting dignified withdrawal that gives the play a much softer ambience than *Mr. Sawa's Two Daughters*. The atmosphere here recalls that of *Diary of Fallen Leaves*, which also deals with human responsibility and the passage of time.

A Space of Time may have been Kishida's perfect compromise. The poetic and elegiac atmosphere of the early plays has been retained, although assigned perhaps to a lower level of importance, but the human situations have

[105] *Ibid.*, p. 41.   [106] *Ibid.*   [107] *Ibid.*, p. 23.

been made easily intelligible for the sake of both audience and actors. The play bears the stamp of a highly skilled craftsman. Yet something has been lost: grandeur has been sacrificed to smoothness and workability in terms of the contemporary stage.

Evidence of Kishida's success in creating a workable play is provided by the high reputation *A Space of Time* has enjoyed with most Japanese critics. The editors of the *Engeki hyakka jiten* have chosen it as Kishida's most accomplished play, an opinion seconded by Odagiri Hideo[108] and Kawamori Yoshirō, who wrote that Yasuko's final speeches constitute a song of victory over herself. "In this later work," he adds, "Kishida has written an elegant and dignified play in which he has concealed something of the lyric genius manifest in his early work."[109] Yamamoto Seiichi also wrote of his admiration for Kishida's skill in creating the changing images that Yasuko (and the audience) has of Saiki, as well as for the way that image changes during the course of the drama.[110]

A Space of Time represents what Kishida thought he could realistically accomplish. But the balance he achieved in this play proved to be precarious. Looking back on *A Space of Time*, he described it in 1939 as "a play based on hints derived from a very ordinary incident and written very quickly." He called it the last of his "what shall I write about?" plays and said that there was little room for dramas of such tranquility at that point in history. "I am weary of wondering 'what shall I write a play about?' I have come to the point of adopting the idea, 'what can I say by means of a play?' "[111]

The worsening of the political climate and (in Kishida's opinion) of human values caused him, in his last period of

---

[108] See his comments in *Kōza Nihon kindai bungaku shi*, IV, p. 170.
[109] See Kawamori, "kaishaku," p. 411.
[110] See Tanaka, ed., *Gekibungaku*, p. 260.
[111] *zenshū*, IX, p. 319.

playwriting, to modify his style by still another set of compromises, in order to try to accomplish a different aim.

The world of the Japanese theatre, inevitably influenced by currents in the political and economic situation, now found itself facing increasingly difficult conditions. The government began to regulate the New Theatre movement with greater severity, and the proletarian theatrical companies were greatly limited in their activities. Among the nonpolitical theatres, the Tsukijiza was closed in 1936, as was noted above, for financial and possibly personal reasons. Kishida directed their last production, a new play by Uchimura Naoya. Teatro Comedie, another troupe that produced several works by Kishida, also ceased its activities about the same time.

The political climate in Tokyo had become very tense. In February 1936 a celebrated *coup d'état* was staged by dissident young army officers, and many prominent public figures were assassinated. A mild but fairly general popular revulsion against the army followed, but the public was powerless to resist or to interfere in the steadily worsening situation. The general decay in society soon produced an increased military adventurism, a further spread of the war in China and, eventually, the attack on the United States.

In the circumscribed conditions of authors at this time, what role could Kishida play as a commentator on society? *A Space of Time*, he said, represented his last play on purely personal themes. The decay of social values, he thought, required a different kind of technique; he turned from reflective romantic drama to satire in order to accomplish this purpose. The result was the play *Fūzoku jihyō* (*A Commentary on Manners*), first published in the March 1936 issue of *The Central Review*. It has never been produced. Before a discussion of the circumstances surrounding the writing and publishing of the play, it may be useful to give a brief summary of its contents.

The play is in one act divided into a number of short scenes, rather like a European or American stage revue, and chronicles the progress of a strange disease that sweeps through Japan. The disease remains undefined, but Kishida uses it to create a social fable criticizing his period. The pace and pressure of the play builds as one after another person is struck by the strange malady.

The first scene is set in a doctor's office. A patient has come to complain of a mysterious pain that neither he nor the doctor can identify. As there are no special symptoms, the doctor concludes that it must be "nerves." But when another patient turns up with the same complaint, the doctor begins to wonder if some new virus isn't going around. The second scene takes place in a police station. A man (apparently a politician) comes in to report that he was assaulted while riding on a public bus. The Police Chief asks him if he was dozing at the time.

Man: On the contrary. I had to get to town by 10:30. I was already late for a speaking engagement. I was trying to make good use of what time I had, so I was reading aloud the manuscript of my speech.

Chief: Were there any people you knew on the bus?

Man: Except for two or three they were all perfect strangers. A bunch of nobodies from somewhere or other! Ouch! It hurts![112]

The Police Chief is surprised at the man's sudden pain. The man demands that everyone on the bus be arrested. A policeman goes to investigate and hurries back to report that there are unruly crowds in the streets, complaining that they are in pain. The man hurries off to find a doctor; the office of the Police Chief is deluged with telephone calls.

The third scene takes place in a primary school. The teachers have also been struck with sudden pains, and they express concern for themselves and for the children.

[112] *Ibid.*, III, p. 48.

Principal: If the situation goes on like this, there is no point continuing classes for the day. Let's send the children home. Now let me be sure that I understand the situation correctly. In the First Grade there was just one who screamed "It hurts!"

Teacher A: Yes, that's right. Once during the reading hour and once during the chorus singing. But I myself have been suffering the most terrible pains since morning. I've broken out in a sweat.

Principal: You're not the only one. Mr. Takagaki has been writhing on the ground for more than an hour. And among the students there are six cases in second year, and in third. . . .

Teacher B: Eleven. My ethics class was hardest hit of all. . . .

Principal: Above the fourth grade we can't even keep count.[113]

The nature of the malady gradually becomes more apparent from the reference to the ethics class, where pupils were taught morality and discipline prior to 1945. Kishida seems to suggest that there is a connection between the "terrible pain" and the doctrines taught in the class, and each victim experiences a different kind of pain.

Teacher B: It feels now like a kind of prickling sensation. Yet a moment ago, my ears were tingling.

Principal: It's strange that the pain seems to be different in each case. Physiologically speaking, that seems to be its weak point![114]

Although the Principal had at first intended to send the children home, he has had a change of heart and decides to give them a formal address instead. He arranges for report-

---

[113] *Ibid.*, p. 49.   [114] *Ibid.*, p. 50.

ers and press photographers to be present. "For the sake of our town," he declares, "indeed for the sake of all Imperial Japan, in the name of the students and teachers of this school, I have called a Prayer Meeting for Pestilence Dispersal." His long, pompous, and self-serving speech concludes as follows:

Principal: Well then, my friends, what can we, the students and teachers of our school, do when our entire nation is faced with this crisis? You need not raise your hands. Your teacher will tell you. We must pray. We must pray to the gods. That is all. Everyone of us, a silent prayer.

                    What shall I say? In this time of natural calamity . . . this unprecedented misfortune has struck, but how far will it spread? In any event, all of us, with the greatest compassion, must . . . oh! I feel a pain! Ouch! Ouch! It's in my feet . . . my ankles . . . I'm done for. . . . Where's that photographer? Never mind helping me, just take my picture. . . . It's nothing. . . . Oh! It hurts!

Photographer: If you would kindly stop moving. . . .

Principal: Umm . . . of course. Like this—is that all right? It hurts, it really hurts! Hurry and take your picture! . . . once again, I pay my deepest respects. . . .

                    Don't worry about me! . . . send all the children home safely. . . . Hachiman Bosatsu! Inari Daimyōjin! Great Powers of Kompira! The Seven Gods of Luck! Nine-armed Kwannon! The five hundred rakan![115]

---

[115] *Ibid.*, p. 52. The various gods mentioned are popular Shinto and Buddhist dieties. The Principal evidently seeks safety in numbers.

The fourth scene takes place in a barber shop. The barber and his customers discuss the strange malady and wonder about its cause. A young customer says that people of his generation are especially baffled and depressed by the spread of the disease. This gives the barber the opportunity to expound his theory about young people: he insists that they have no energy, no spiritual strength.

Young Man: I agree with you completely. We haven't got any drive. But the thing is, we haven't got any hope either. Look at the way we sing group patriotic songs together. We all ask ourselves why we do anything so silly. But still, when the time comes, we all say "let's sing!" All of us.

Barber: Young people don't drink as much saké as they used to.

Young Man: The ones who want to, drink—in private. They get drunk, then they stumble around in the dark.

Barber: What a gloomy idea!

Young Man: The real loneliness of young people nowadays arises because there is no longer anyone who really tries to see them, understand them as they are.[116]

The barber has to agree that older people tend to judge on the basis of appearances.

Young Man: That's because people can no longer see properly. When people look at each other, they no longer trust what they see in each other's eyes. Then they don't trust what they see reflected in their own. Everything has been corrupted. You cheat other people, and you get cheated yourself. Even this comes to be

[116] *zenshū*, III, p. 54.

accepted as perfectly normal. The only hope when someone cheats you is to be taken in as little as possible. And you try to get as much as you can when you go out after someone else. It's a psychological reaction to living in a world filled with propaganda.[117]

The young man goes on to tell the barber that if a man like the French author Beaumarchais were alive in Japan now, he would find subject matter for some fine satirical plays. The barber urges him to go ahead and write a satire of his own, but the young man is not very sanguine about his chances of success.

Young Man: If I did write something, it would mean the end of my job. And then what would happen if I couldn't sell my writings? It's no good trying to do or say anything different from other people. The world isn't made for those who want to blurt out their true feelings. All you can do is look down at the ground and keep quiet. Oh! Ouch! It hurts.[118]

The fifth scene takes place in an ordinary household.

Father: Is that a newspaper extra?

Son: Yes. This thing seems to have hit all over the country. It doesn't seem to have affected China or America, though. A telephone report from Shanghai indicates that the Japanese there are affected too. And even in San Francisco, the ordinary Japanese emigrants who work for the consulate there are complaining of terrible pains, it says.

Father: Every last Japanese, no matter where . . . ?[119]

The son complains to his father that he is losing his interest in life and his ambition. Young people are not permitted to

---

[117] *Ibid.*   [118] *Ibid.*, pp. 54-55.   [119] *Ibid.*, p. 56.

dream any more, he feels, and their natural ambitions are thwarted by regimentation.

Father: Are you saying you are sorry you were born in Japan?

Son: No, I'm not making any such pointless complaint. I have no quarrel with being a Japanese. What else would I rather be? No, my only concern is that I want some satisfaction in *being* Japanese. Why is Japan the way it is? I don't know anything about how it used to be. I'm talking about now.[120]

The son, cataloguing what is wrong with Japan, wonders how his country can claim to be an enlightened nation. In other countries, human beings can recognize themselves as human, but in Japan, none of the progressive movements has succeeded in bringing about any recognition of the true worth of the individual. His father replies that genius can surmount obstacles; the son insists that genius flourishes only in a healthy society.

His father explains that western cultures also underwent transformations when they had to assimilate new influences, and that the son must wait patiently for the day when Japan will have been equally successful. At the present stage, the father continues, it is small wonder that the conservatives are so determined to cling to the past.

Son: But you didn't really answer my original question, did you?

Father: No. I suppose not.

Son: Then, what do you expect people like me to do?

Father: Follow the Golden Mean.

Son: But there isn't any left for us to follow. It would certainly help if there were.[121]

He tells his father how touched he had been when he saw from a bus window a barber shop called "Medium-grade

[120] *Ibid.*, p. 57. [121] *Ibid.*, p. 59.

Barber Shop," since it was more honest than if the proprie-tor had named his shop "High-class Barber Shop," in the usual fashion. The son wishes he could meet the barber.

Father: Some kind of revolutionary, I suppose.

Son: The Golden Mean must be the real revolution of our time. Oh . . . ouch![122]

Scene Six takes place in a hotel. A kindly middle-aged couple debates whether or not to go through with their plans for making a trip, in view of the sickness spreading everywhere. The husband is an ordinary doctor, with no special training, but he has been taking notes on the disease and wishes that he could find a way to cure at least a few who have been stricken by it. In the course of the discussion between him and his wife on proper leaders for Japan, he ventures the opinion that third-raters, indeed fifth-raters, are running the country.

Husband: You can't count on the general public to have any common sense either. They can be broken down into three groups. The first are the fools without intelligence. Second are those who pre-tend to be intelligent. I mean those who have a college education. Finally there is a small seg-ment that takes their responsibilities seriously as intelligent people. Those are the cultured people who can be counted on.

Wife: But is there anyone not belonging to the general public?

Husband: Sure! the government officials and the poli-ticians![123]

This long conversation unfortunately becomes a catalogue of a whole series of Kishida's complaints about Japanese families and social relations, far too many to mention here. Toward the end of the scene, however, there is a passage on national pride.

[122] *Ibid.* [123] *Ibid.*, p. 61.

Husband: People are so proud of Mt. Fuji and the cherry blossoms, but what good are they for boosting national prestige? They aren't anything we made ourselves. At this point, Japan has no business putting on some kind of vain display in front of the rest of the world merely in order to boast that we have this or that aspect to our culture the others don't. What we have to do is to tell the rest of the world that we really want to contribute to the establishment of the happiness and the progress of mankind. That we believe in their ideals even more than they do. But somehow, I don't believe the time has come when a simple doctor like myself can presume to speak for the whole Japanese people.

Wife: Don't talk that way. You should have some confidence in yourself. . . .

Husband: Fine. Let's see if I can get some.[124]

The seventh scene returns to the police station. The Chief is delighted that, so far, none of his men seems to have been affected by the disease. A policeman on duty reports that a lady and some children have brought some money to donate to an indigent mother who, according to a newspaper account, has been thrown out of her own house by her son. In fact, however, the mother has been squandering her son's money. Under the circumstances, the Chief wonders if he should turn over the money to so unworthy a recipient. It is suddenly reported that the lady who left the money was suddenly struck down by the disease. "No quarter given there either," muses the Chief. He finally sends a policeman to turn the money over to the mother, directing the man to give both mother and son a good lecture. He marvels at the ability of the press to make black appear white.

Chief: That article in the morning paper sure had a quick effect. Imagine, these contributions turn-

[124] *Ibid.*, pp. 64-65.

ing up for "the old lady thrown out by her son." Isn't that a marvellous article. Oh! Ouch!

Policeman: Chief, it's terrible. At the hall where the election speeches are being delivered, the speakers have all collapsed.

Chief: Aha! Then this illness is not terrible at all! The pain is quite a beneficial one. We've never before suffered through such beneficial agony! I'm relieved, so relieved! There's no reason to feel any sympathy for those who are suffering. Say, you policemen, your work is going to be a snap from now on!

Curtain[125]

Leaving aside for a moment the ultimate artistic quality of the play, it is immediately apparent that Kishida was attempting here a whole new kind of satirical comedy very different from anything he had previously written. Like Beaumarchais (whom he mentions in the play), he resorted to comic exaggeration in order to analyze his age. In 1940 he wrote: "I am always attuned to psychology as it is revealed in individuals and to manners as they are revealed in a society. My interests are usually concerned with the way life is lived within a particular atmosphere, and to the way in which ideas are thus affected. The fact that I feel some skepticism about reality and retain a loyalty to my ideals in no sense represents a contradiction."[126]

The planning of the scenes in *A Commentary on Manners* certainly reveals Kishida's determination to pit his ideas against what he viewed as the degeneration of society; writing such a play at that time was surely an act of courage, even though specific political events are not directly touched on. (The play was probably written just prior to the attempted *coup d'état* in February 1936.) The early comic scenes of the play convey well the malaise of Japan at the time, while the longer, more serious scenes towards the end

[125] *Ibid.*, pp. 66-67. [126] *Ibid.*, ix, p. 317.

reflect Kishida's own responses to his milieu and something of his ideals.

In an essay published in 1936 Kishida stated that the writing of this play gave him a great deal of difficulty. He felt obliged to write draft after draft. "The first of my plays in which I try to 'say something' is my *Commentary on Manners*,"[127] he concluded, stressing how much importance he attached to the work. He was convinced that true satire required both intellectual strength and clear-mindedness on the part of its author, qualities he found lacking in the literary world of his period.

> Any poverty of thought in satire will be instantly revealed to our contemporaries. If only we could produce in this country satirical literature as sharp and yet as humane as that of Molière or Gogol, satire that could really take us all to task. Satire is not produced by an author settling down and braying like a stray dog. Those who write in this way will never gain back their artistic composure.[128]

He felt strongly that satire could have a cleansing effect on Japan; this belief determined him to write *A Commentary on Manners*. The play, in inspiration at least, was in keeping with Kishida's intentions; he aimed very high, and even if he did not fully succeed he must be given high marks for making the attempt.

The play begins well, with the juxtaposition of the short comic scenes. The core of the play is probably the scene in which the young man asserts that the "Golden Mean" is the most revolutionary doctrine of all. Here, as in the next scene between the doctor and his wife, Kishida seems to be appealing to the "honnête homme" of whom Molière speaks and to whom Kishida often referred to as his ideal potential audience.[129]

[127] *Ibid.*, x, p. 135.   [128] *Ibid.*, p. 136.
[129] See for example Kishida's comments in *zenshū*, ix, p. 311.

Yet, for all the author's strength of purpose, the play seems to suffer from the problem that crippled the dramaturgy of *Old Toys*: Kishida was so concerned with the seriousness of the issues that he failed to do more than state them. In the later major scenes especially, he failed to transmute his arguments into dramatic terms. Eric Bentley has criticized many modern ideological playwrights in terms that apply to Kishida as well: "dramatic dialogue must only present thoughts in the process of being thought. Which is another way of saying that the playwright must not be directly didactic."[130] Kishida may not be didactic in a political sense, but he had forgotten to keep his audience in any suspense while the "thoughts are being thought." The results are neither theatrical, nor, in the end, especially funny. The basic conception of the strange malady was a potentially effective theatrical device which actually anticipates the manner of the French Theatre of the Absurd.[131] If, artistically speaking, life had been something of a dream for Kishida, he now wanted to turn it into a cartoon, and it was the forces moving in his own society that forced him to this change of heart, this final compromise.

Of course the leftist theatre in Japan also wished to criticize society, although from a purely didactic, usually communist point of view. Thus Odagiri Hideo, a critic of

[130] Eric Bentley, *The Theatre of Commitment* (New York, 1967), pp. 170-171.

[131] By coincidence, Eugène Ionesco's play *Jeux de Massacre* (*Games of Slaughter*), which had its première in Paris in September 1970, made use of nearly the same theatrical device as that of *A Commentary on Manners*. Ionesco's play describes a whole town that begins to drop dead from a mysterious disease, and the author proceeds, in much the same manner as Kishida, to create a series of sketchlike scenes to satirize modern society. Needless to say, the purposes of the two plays are quite different (Ionesco's play is largely concerned with the nature of death), and there is no possible artistic influence involved, since Kishida's work is unknown in France; nevertheless, the similarities serve to illustrate how two very different authors might naturally choose a similar parable to create a moral or social satire.

246

Marxist persuasion, wrote of his disappointment in Kishida's dramas because "although they concern themselves with criticism of society, Kishida only framed his concerns in terms of the individual's loss of sincerity and purity."[132] Ironically, for the reader today, it is precisely because Kishida's plays are inhabited by individuals that they possess any kind of spiritual space and life.

At forty-seven, Kishida again decided to adopt a new course, this time in a compromise with the craftsmanship he had so painstakingly developed. Like many artists in this century, he found that the horrors of the new times demanded new techniques. A brave decision, and perhaps Kishida could have mastered a new aesthetic of playwriting. He had chosen one superb model, Molière. Had he known Brecht's work, he might have admired the way in which the German playwright could infuse his cool sense of irony into a theatrical setting.

Yet these last adjustments and compromises came too late. With one exception (a short play written on commission for a government travelling troupe in 1943), Kishida composed no new dramatic works until 1948, a period of twelve years. When he began to write again for the theatre he was fifty-six, sick, and discouraged. His postwar interests still lay in satire, and he tried to find some vantage point from which to view the vastly changing world of postwar Japan. His five postwar plays are competently written, but the general impression given by a reading of these works is of fatigue and a gradual withdrawal from contemporary concerns. In the years between 1923 and 1939, Kishida had become a respected figure, a *maître* in the world of the New Theatre, and the extent of his influence, as well as its limitations, had been established. In terms of the development of a literary theatre in Japan, Kishida's last period contains but one play, and a long silence.[133]

---

[132] Odagiri, *Kōza Nihon kindai bungaku shi*, IV, p. 412.

[133] Silence in terms of writing for the theatre. Kishida was active in the founding of the Literary Theatre, as noted above, and for

In a thoughtful article describing Kishida's activities at the beginning of the war in 1940 Nakajima Kenzō calls him "a sacrifice to the barricades" for his generation.[134] Nakajima was referring specifically to Kishida's activities on behalf of a government cultural committee, but the phrase is suggestive of the whole last phase of Kishida's writing career. Kishida himself recorded that he was concerned that the editors of *The Central Review* might refuse to publish *A Commentary on Manners*; after its publication he felt that he had nothing further to write for the theatre. Surrounded by an atmosphere of militaristic jingoism, he could do nothing but, like the boy in his last play, "look down at the ground."

I have pictured Kishida's career as a practicing playwright during the period 1923-1939 in terms of compromises. Had he written without reference to the standards of the performing theatre of his day in Japan, he might have developed into a Japanese Musset, a writer of precision and delicacy who could be fully appreciated half a century later, when the general public and the world of the theatre might have caught up with the literary world. Yet this was not his aim. Kishida wanted to raise the standards of the modern theatre in Japan in order to transform it into something that might provide some measure of spiritual reality, both in artistic and in Japanese terms, for his contemporaries. Kishida's compromises probably kept him from attaining any great heights of artistry; yet had he refused these compromises his plays would have been impossible to perform, and the New Theatre movement would have been unable to benefit from his insights and his craftsmanship.

---

several years with the government's cultural committees. A major novel, *Danryū* (*A Warm Current*), published in 1938, dealt with many of the questions of cultural conflict troubling Kishida at the time. He felt, however, that the theatre was closed to him because of the political atmosphere.

[134] See *Bungei*, May 1954, pp. 20-25.

CHAPTER VII

Kishida's Achievement

THE preceding considerations of Kishida's professional and literary work in the theatre have been presented principally in order to explain the discrepancies between his conception of the proper course for the New Theatre movement—a conception that, in the light of the ways in which the European movement had progressed, was substantially correct—and the compromises that he and others were forced to make with the prevailing situation in Japan. I have not attempted to subject the plays to any full literary analysis, nor, indeed, have I touched on all his works for the theatre. Nevertheless, perhaps enough has been said about the major plays to suggest Kishida's contributions to the development of the New Theatre movement and to the *corpus* of important Japanese modern drama.

The first was his use of a natural and rhythmic dialogue. Kishida was well aware of the difficulties in creating good stage dialogue in Japanese. The remarks he wrote in 1925 in an essay on Jules Renard serve to illustrate his sensitivity to the problem of writing Japanese that could be effectively delivered aloud.

There is a difference between learning and natural intelligence, between intellectual conceptions and ordinary thoughts. In Japan today, natural intelligence cannot manifest itself without recourse to a vocabulary gained through study and education. Without intellectual conceptions, individual ideas have no adequate means of expression in our language, because of tendencies long fostered in our society. In the west, a well-educated and a poorly educated man do not express themselves so very

249

differently. In Japan, however, the difference is enormous. A western dramatist can create a character who, even if he has no culture at all, can express individual, interesting ideas. Yet when such a passage is translated into Japanese, there is the danger of using a vocabulary available only to an educated person.[1]

Kishida was acutely aware of the difficulty of finding the right kind of language that could both place a character in his proper social setting and also permit the character to express his ideas and emotions with precision. Despite the fact that he felt ordinary Japanese was more limited for these purposes than French, he was able in the course of his career to create precisely the kind of dialogue he praised in Renard—speech attuned to the real language yet flexible enough to permit poetic insights into character. Ibaragi wrote that, along with Kubota Mantarō, Kishida was the first Japanese writer who brought individuality to dialogue on the stage. "Certainly no other writer up until that time had any such deep concern for the rhythm and tempo of stage dialogue. Such a skill is certainly not visible in such writers as Kikuchi Kan, Yamamoto Yūzō, or Osanai Kaoru."[2] Kishida's success in creating a genuine and personal stage language is an achievement even his detractors willingly grant him.

His second accomplishment was a successful fusion of theatrical and literary ideals in his work. Or, it might be said, he insisted on their unity, unlike some dramatists who aimed at nothing higher than scoring a momentary success, or others who totally neglected the demands of the theatre, so intent were they on Marxist sermonizing. Miyazaki Mineo singled out this aspect of Kishida when he wrote

[1] *zenshū*, v, p. 395.

[2] Ibaragi, *Shōwa no shingeki*, p. 131. On the same point, Endō Shingo adds that audiences were happily surprised to find that conversational Japanese on the stage could take on such nuances. Endō attributes this development in Kishida's skill to his living abroad. See "kotoba no bōrei," *Higeki kigeki*, July 1951, p. 6.

that "Kishida was a special case among Japanese dramatists. There was a great difference in literary quality between the work of most playwrights, who started with the ordinary Japanese notion of what constituted a play, and that of Kishida, who from the beginning had considered the drama as one form of literature."[3]

In this respect, Kishida's most obvious innovation was his rejection of complex plots typical of *kabuki*, *shimpa*, and earlier *shingeki*, and his attempts to create sustained poetic symbols to unify his dramatic conceptions. In the early plays, the symbols are quite obvious: the cherry trees in *The Cherry Tree in Leaf*, the chestnut tree in *The Tallest Chestnut in the Village*, or the swing itself in *The Swing*. The symbols are subtler and harder to detect in his longer, later plays; this fact itself suggests the superior level of the writing. *Ushiyama Hotel* is defined by the setting, the empty place where vagabonds and other wanderers collect. *A Space of Time* is closely structured around time itself so that its passing becomes a palpable presence in the structure of the drama. In *Mr. Sawa's Two Daughters*, the urge to divulge one's innermost secrets provides the rhythm of the play. The use of such devices to create and sustain a mood earn Kishida's plays the name of literature. His dramatic criticism also makes it evident how consciously he strove for the effects he achieved. The plays show not only considerable skill but a sophistication that marks Kishida as a specifically twentieth-century dramatist.

Charles Morgan defined the uniqueness of drama as a literary form in terms of what he called the principle of illusion.

> The hope of this illusion is the excitement, and the experience of it the highest reward of playgoing. . . . All that art can do in the way of imitation of a given natural subject is, first, to negate a spectator's own preoccupations of that subject so that he lies open to imaginative

[3] Quoted in Tanaka, *Gekibungaku*, p. 164.

251

acceptance of a different view, the artist's view, and secondly, to impregnate him with this fresh, this alien understanding. Illusion is the impregnating force—in masterpieces permanently fruitful, in lesser works of art, existent but without endurance, and from machine-made plays, however well made, absent.[4]

Kishida's relative success in the creation of illusion through the use of literary techniques saved his plays from the oblivion into which most of his predecessors in the New Theatre movement fell. His skill at matching style with content permitted him to achieve a sustained illusion, consistent and satisfying. *Diary of Fallen Leaves* is perhaps the most successful of his plays in this respect; each scene and incident in the scene seem chosen to shed light on the character of the old woman. In some plays, it is true, the style and the content do not match so well. *Mount Asama*, for example, may contain the ideas and characters requisite for a successful play, but Kishida's decision to create an emotional melodrama filled with the kind of overblown action most congenial to the actors and audience destroyed the consistency of his concept. The result was an artistic failure. Yet Kishida's best plays do create their illusions and establish in the reader (and presumably in the spectator) what Morgan calls "this alien understanding."

Some Japanese critics have raised objections to Kishida's work, perhaps because they were not prepared for his fresh view. For example, Yamamoto Shūji declared that "the world Kishida described in his plays did not exist in the Japan of his day. In a really fine play, illusion is more important than reality; yet the illusion must suggest real life as well."[5] Yamamoto seems here to indicate that Kishida's plays are too personal, too private, and not sufficiently representative of ordinary sentiments and responses to life. Unlike the works of the Marxist writers, Kishida's plays do not pro-

[4] Charles Morgan, "The Nature of Dramatic Illusion," in *Reflections on Art*, edited by Suzanne B. Langer (Baltimore, 1958), p. 94.

[5] See Tanaka, *Gekibungaku*, p. 262.

pound any program. Yet Chekhov, Ibsen, and Pirandello do not hold our attention because of the way they may typify Russian, Norwegian, or Italian reactions to contemporary society, but rather because in their best plays these writers establish their own individual worlds and maintain them against the pressure of ordinary spectator reactions. Yamamoto was wrong in attempting to make of a Kishida play a sociological event.

Sugahara Takashi, who directed the 1947 production of *A Space of Time* at the Bungakuza, wrote a perceptive article on his experience with the production.[6] He found the play beautifully written and psychologically sound, but too advanced in style for the actors with whom Sugahara was working. As a director, he himself had trouble with the play in trying to realize the subtle emotions of the text in a stage performance. Sugahara concluded that Kishida's plays had not yet been properly assimilated by the Japanese professional theatre. Each of Kishida's major plays, according to Sugahara, is an experiment describing Japanese psychological attitudes. He stated that most productions of Kishida's plays betrayed their author, because they failed to reveal how thoroughly Japanese they are, despite the techniques of dramaturgy Kishida borrowed from western models.

All the same, Kishida's use of poetic dialogue, his organization of a play around a central symbol, and his attempts to create illusion through literary technique created a dramatic genre that, at least since 1939, has dominated the serious theatre in Japan. His younger colleagues Morimoto Kaoru and Katō Michio both died young, before Kishida himself, but they achieved the first successes in a new poetic and literary theatre. Today Tanaka Chikao is no doubt the foremost exponent of this style.

Japanese critics have generally treated Kishida in terms rather different from mine. Many emphasize his role as a moralist; others take him to task for his lack of political

[6] See Sugahara Takashi, "Kishida gikyoku e no michi," *Nihon engeki*, July 1949, pp. 20-29.

consciousness. I thus append two short sections discussing these two lines of argument, and conclude with a brief analysis of Kishida's European literary sources.

Was Kishida a Moralist?

A surprising number of Japanese critics have insisted on the importance of certain aspects of Kishida's personality and upbringing in the creation of his plays. Indeed, this particular line of argument often takes precedence over all considerations of conscious artistry. For example, it is said that Kishida's upbringing in a military family was responsible for his strong set of moralizing attitudes towards life: Tanaka Chikao felt that this military background implanted in him a predisposition to "arrange everything point by point" in a clear definition of right and wrong;[7] Fukuda Tsuneari went so far as to find in him a perfect embodiment of the Japanese military spirit. For these men, Kishida was primarily a moralist.

Such statements are surprising in view of the contents of his plays: we find little reflection of doctrines of any kind in them; and although Kishida's critical writings are, it is true, sometimes sharp and opinionated, they are basically more graceful and humane than similar writings of his contemporaries (Osanai was the worst offender on this point). Surely it would never occur to anyone unfamiliar with Kishida's family background that the author of his plays and criticism was heir to martial traditions.

An understanding of the importance to the Japanese critics of such observations on the work of Kishida requires a few comments on the general nature of modern Japanese literature. Tatsuo Arima's recent study dealing with modern Japanese literature has characterized early twentieth-century writers thus:

> Realism mistakenly construed as the naturalist method becomes a synonym for fatalism. Man is perpetually

[7] See Tanaka, *Gekibungaku*, p. 167.

pained and defeated; and the description of such realities is the only genuine purpose of art.

There was, to be sure, nothing wrong about this method of writing in and of itself, or about the image of man it portrayed. Yet placed in a social context, the real man for the naturalists is a creature compelled to acquiesce in his fate, unable to affect it. More than any other intellectual group in their time, the naturalists suffered from the stifling of individual initiative and aspiration. Their social background and experience enabled them to expose with eloquence the dehumanizing pressure of social and family ties which characterized Japan's transition into the Meiji era. But that was all.[8]

Kishida dealt with similar problems, but he chose comic and not tragic forms of expression. *Mr. Sawa's Two Daughters* is a comedy, but Kishida's underlying ideas on human irresponsibility are quite serious. *Ushiyama Hotel* is a study in which Kishida criticizes the spiritual emptiness of those who cut their ties with their families and their friends. Even *Paper Balloon* could be interpreted as an examination of the problems between two people who have not yet learned to love each other.

The comic vision demands a consistent point of view on which the humor can be based. As a man, Kishida did maintain high standards in his conception of human relations, standards he held in his personal life and in his artistic conceptions.[9] These standards, no less important for being unexpressed, underlie all his writing. Humor and satire are conspicuously missing from the work of most first-rate

[8] Tatsuo Arima, *The Failure of Freedom* (Cambridge 1969), p. 96.
[9] All the critics seem united on the fact that Kishida led an exemplary, even austere, life. Disliking improper jokes and drunkenness, he earned a reputation among the more bohemian of his New Theatre colleagues of being too reserved, even cold, but Tanaka, Fukuda, Kon, and the others insist that he was not. Rather, they stress his natural sense of dignity and a strong sense of propriety.

Japanese modern writers—perhaps because the writers themselves, divorced from traditional religion and, with few exceptions, lacking any real interest in Christianity, can maintain no moral or intellectual perspective on man, "perpetually pained and defeated." Since Kishida, however, seems to have such a perspective, he may be called a moralist in the limited sense that the term is applied to Molière or to any other "serious" writer of comedy.

Yet is it possible that Kishida represented a manifestation of the Japanese military spirit as well? To this reader at least, he might conceivably do so only to the extent that he was willing to impose some kind of emotional logic on life in a search to define the nature of the Good. For it was his concept of the Good in human relations that ultimately provided the consistent point of view on which his comic vision was based. Yet Kishida's idea of Goodness was surely not closely related to the traditional Japanese ideas of self-sacrifice usually associated with the "military spirit." Nor were his ideas revealed directly in his plays; unlike Molière, he created no minor characters who directly explain the author's moral attitudes. The suggestion in the plays is that Goodness can be found in love and mutual respect. Such a conception makes Kishida a thoroughly modern writer, reflecting the most advanced spirit of his times.

Do these critics mean that without a "traditional military character," Kishida could not have become a modern playwright? Lacking a taste for paradox, I leave the matter at that.

Was Kishida an Intellectual?

Tatsuo Arima takes to task such prominent writers as Akutagawa, Arishima, Shimazaki Tōson, and others:

I believe that their novels and literary theories provide telling evidence of the various attitudes the Japanese intellectuals assumed toward society, of the kind of emotional and intellectual problems which post-Meiji Japanese had to cope with, of the conflict between old and new values—a constant theme in modern Japanese intellectual history—and above all of the prevailing image of man which is always crucial to the intellectual atmosphere of any age.[10]

Arima then finds fault with the writers for these reasons.

The fact is that the Taishō intellectuals were incapable of seeing the problems of their day in terms that would have enabled them to play a responsible and active social role. The primary purpose of this book is to analyze and explain the intellectual's inability to express abstract concepts in concrete social terms.[11]

In other words, an intellectual must have a political consciousness. Arima's analysis is compelling on several counts. Yet the charge of insufficient social awareness, by implication applicable to Kishida as well, falls rather wide of the mark.

The British music critic Ernest Walker once defended a composer by saying that, after all, he had set out to write a madrigal, not a symphony, and that any creative writer must be judged by what he tried to do, not for what he did not attempt. Many creative writers are "intellectuals," of course, in that they concern themselves directly with problems of pressing social concern. But much great art, and much morally great art, if I may be permitted the term, is not directly concerned with exploring the best means to "play a responsible and active social role." The question is certainly a real one at this time in the United States, where art for any sake other than social involvement may be suspect.[12] Yet judged even on this basis, Kishida does not

[10] Arima, *Failure*, p. viii.   [11] *Ibid.*, p. 1.

[12] Take, for example, the exchange of views between Robert Brustein and Arthur Miller in 1968. Reviewing Miller's play *The Price*, Brustein wrote in the *New Republic* of February 24, 1968 as follows:

"If Arthur Miller seems old-fashioned today to many seriously interested in the theatre, it is not because he has failed to keep abreast of the latest techniques in playwriting—nobody expects him to compete with La Mama—it is rather because his concerns are so

fail, for his later plays are strong in their condemnation of many elements of contemporary Japan, based on his own humanistic views.[13] It should surely be counted in his favor that, unlike the Marxists, he imposed no doctrinaire solutions.[14]

---

curiously insulated from the world in which we now live. The nation's cities are in total disarray, drowning in swill, torn by violence; our disgraceful involvement in Vietnam is making large numbers ashamed of being Americans; the Administration has systematically destroyed our confidence in its credibility and good intentions, perhaps in the democratic process itself; our young are either apathetic and withdrawn or inflamed with fury and frustration; our sense of reality is disintegrating, our illusion of freedom faltering, our expectation of disaster increasing—yet Arthur Miller, the most public-spirited of dramatists, continues to write social-psychological melodramas about Family Responsibility. . . . How can a new play fail to be affected, if only indirectly, by the events of its time?" (p. 39.)

Miller, stung to the quick, held a news conference at which he explained his point of view in writing the play. *The New York Times* of March 5, 1968, reported the event as follows:

Arthur Miller deprecated yesterday's criticism that his concerns as playwright, particularly as exemplified in his new work *The Price*, were divorced from the concerns of today.

The Price, the playwright said, "is right down the middle of our times. I haven't supplied the tags for the simple-minded to latch onto." Mr. Miller explained that since he was "a person committed to certain ideals, it was evidently expected of him that he should be a 'journalist' in the theatre. . . ."

Mr. Miller said that *The Price* dealt with two brothers trying to make "some concrete sense of their lives." One, a police sergeant, considers himself a failure because he chose not to finish college but to work and support his father, a victim of the depression. But, Mr. Miller explained, the policeman realizes at the end that his sacrifice represented an act of love. The point of the play, the playwright said, was that "certain things cannot be justified on a *quid pro quo* basis." The policeman's decision to support his father was "the price he paid for an act of love," Miller said. (p. 32.)

Without belaboring the point, the conflict between these two points of view seems to me difficult to reconcile. Miller's views are doubtless

My own view is that the issue of the "artist as intellectual" that has been of such importance in Japan is essentially false, at least so far as the theatre is concerned. Robert Brustein's view is surely the correct one.

> The revolt of the dramatist . . . is more imaginative than practical—imaginative, absolute, and pure. Dramatic art is not identical with reality but rather proceeds along a parallel plane; and dramatic revolt, therefore, is always much more *total* than the programs of political agitators or social reformers. The modern dramatist is essentially a metaphysical rebel, not a practical revolutionary; whatever his personal political convictions, his art is the expression of a spiritual condition.[15]

The work of a playwright is not to create any rational plan of action to redress specific social problems; his contribution comes in his ability to depict the human conditions that call for change. Such masterpieces of "committed theatre" as Georg Kaiser's *From Morn to Midnight,* Mayakovsky's *Opera Bouffe,* or Brecht's *Mahagonny* continue to hold our interest because of the fundamental humanity they

fully justified, but his arguments cannot succeed with those who demand a theatre of confrontation.

[13] Iwata wrote with some humor that Kishida had indeed done his best to read Marx but later confessed that it had no effect on him at all. See *Shingeki to watakushi,* p. 104.

[14] Endō Shingo commented that Marxist critics are mistaken when they criticize Kishida's plays as bourgeois; the criticism should rather be directed at the society he portrayed so accurately. (See "kotoba no bōrei," p. 6.) For a typical criticism of Kishida on political grounds, see Aoe Shunjirō, "Kishida engeki e no gimon." Aoe concludes his analysis of Kishida's work on a note of considerable vituperation: for him, the most that can be said of Kishida with his "air of the *salon*" and his "overly genteel love of the theatre" is that he is "posing in a fashionable swimming suit, afraid to take the plunge into history and get wet." See *Higeki kigeki,* April 1953, p. 63.

[15] Brustein, *Theatre of Revolt,* pp. 8-9. This was written some years earlier than his article on Arthur Miller and expresses a more temperate view than that of his invective against *The Price.*

express, rather than for the specific political theories or ideals of their authors.

Herbert Passin has written that there are three types of intellectuals who have developed in Japan since the Meiji Restoration: the progressive, politically oriented intelligentsia; the established intellectuals who work for the government; and, finally, a group he calls the "non-ideological intellectuals" who "regard their primary task as artistic and technical rather than moral or political."[16] Kishida no doubt falls into the third category. The very fact that his success as a playwright lay in portraying emotions behind ideas rather than in serving as an exponent for the ideas themselves is one mark of his excellence as a writer.

What Were Kishida's Literary Sources?

Despite Kishida's having spent several years in France and his later description of the importance to the New Theatre movement of an understanding of the modern European theatre, few Japanese critics have examined Kishida's possible literary sources. The few who have made the attempt generally lay emphasis on the translations of early twentieth-century French plays Kishida made for drama collections published in Japan in the 1920s. Several critics[17] make what I believe is a mistaken assumption that, since Kishida translated the plays, they must have been his favorites, and that the styles of their authors must therefore have influenced him. In many of these cases, however, such connections seem largely cases of guilt by association.

One possible influence often suggested is Georges Courteline (1860-1929), whose work represents the wit of *boulevard* comedy at its best. His one-act play *La paix chez soi*

[16] Jansen, *Attitudes*, p. 473.
[17] Among them Yamada Hajime (whose book *Kindaigeki* is considered the standard volume on the development of modern playwriting in Japan), Iwata Toyoo, and others.

(*Peace at Home*), first presented by Antoine in 1903, was revived by Jacques Copeau in 1918. Kishida published his translation of the play in the early 1920s and it was used for two Japanese productions, the first by the New Theatre Society in 1927 and the second, directed by Kishida himself, by the Teatro Comedie in 1932. He directed another short Courteline sketch, *Monsieur Badin*, for the same troupe in 1938.

Peace at Home presents an amusing argument between a hack writer and his loving but foolish wife, who has spent too much of the household budget on a lamp that does not work. Basically the play is a fine farce with a few notes of domestic emotion interjected into the rapid dialogue. In style, theme, and content, the play (like the others of Courteline's) provides a rapid look at the foibles of society, but Courteline shared few of Kishida's serious preoccupations. Kishida may have learned from him how to pace a scene for humorous effect, specifically for a play like *A Commentary on Manners*, which uses short scenes in quick juxtaposition to make its points. Courteline's formulas for a two- or three-character sketch may have suggested to Kishida the form for his early one-act plays. But he could certainly not have provided Kishida with much stylistic or thematic inspiration.

If Courteline seems an unlikely influence, then Georges de Porto-Riche (1849-1930), who has also been mentioned, seems even more improbable. Kishida did translate one of Porto-Riche's plays, *Le passé*, for a collection of modern European dramas published in 1930, but he had little to say about Porto-Riche in his introduction, and Kishida's work is quite out of sympathy with the *théâtre d'amour* of Porto Riche, the majority of whose plays, written in a Zolaesque "slice-of-life" style, often revolve around the emotional entanglements of mistresses and their lovers. To a modern sensibility the plays now seem heavy and even vulgar; as one modern critic put it, "the *théâtre d'amour* transformed the stage into an antechamber to the boudoir."[18] But when Antoine produced him, Porto-Riche was considered not only a daring but a highly significant dramatist. Copeau also produced one of his plays, *La chance de Françoise*, and Kishida may have seen it.

Two other writers translated by Kishida also seem remote from his style, although they too have been suggested as influences. Both were once considered major authors of the French stage, but time has dealt unkindly with them. Paul Hervieu (1857-1915) had plays produced by Jacques Copeau; and the play Kishida translated into Japanese, *La course de flambeau* (*The Trail of the Torch*), was praised by the writer and critic Brander Matthews in the introduction to the 1914 English translation, who found that Hervieu, "absorbed in the problems of human conduct which are the essential material of modern social drama, reveals his mastery in plays put together with implacable logic and almost the unadorned directness of a demonstration in mathematics." Today the arithmetic is unconvincing however, forcing the characters into extreme situations. If Porto-Riche represented an unhappy alliance between Zola, then Hervieu's marriage with Ibsen was equally lamentable. *Trail of the Torch* is grossly overplotted; by contrast, Kishida's plays, if anything, tend to suffer from inadequate plot structure and thematic materials.[19]

The second of these authors, Henri-René Lenormand, retained his reputation at least until the 1940s, when Harlan Hatcher included his work in a standard textbook on modern European drama with the admonition that he was an important spokesman for his era. Lenormand attempted to combine some of Freud's ideas concerning "the dark cave of the unconscious," as Lenormand phrased it, with

[18] See Clark and Freedley, *A History of Modern Drama* (New York, 1947), p. 281.

[19] Ironically, Iwata Toyoo found Kishida's only failure as a dramatist to be that he failed to write what Iwata called "strong pieces of the sort composed by Hervieu." See Iwata Toyoo *hyōronshū*, p. 252.

the more ordinary style of a drawing-room play. In their time his plays were considered well suited to the new psychology, daring and profound, but now they seem quite artificial in the light of further developments in *avant-garde* playwriting, and Lenormand's reputation has faded completely. Antoine and Pitoëff first produced his work in Paris, and his two major successes, *Le temps est un songe* (*Time Is a Dream*) (1919) and *Les ratés* (*The Failures*) (1920) were translated into English and successfully produced in New York. Kishida also translated these two plays into Japanese in 1924, and both were produced by a small troupe, the Kororoza, in the late 1920s. *Failures* was chosen by Kishida for a second Japanese production during the 1939 season of the Literary Theatre. Full of dark and suggestive innuendo, the texts of these plays are burdened with a heaviness and a vagueness totally at variance with Kishida's *esprit*.[20]

Kishida also translated on commission a play each by Tristan Bernard (1866-1947) and Saint-Georges de Bouhélier (1876-1947), but these minor comic writers had no significance for Kishida's own work.

[20] Even at his worst, Kishida was never responsible for any page of dialogue like the following:

[Nico, the hero, has a premonition that he will soon die. He is talking with his confidant, an older man from Indonesia with whom he has been intimate for years.]

Nico: My sister loves me too, and so does my fiancée. And yet for some time past I haven't been able to talk to them. Saidyah, do you know what space is?

Saidyah: It is the little road the ant travels between two blades of grass: it is the great empty road my eye travels on the way to the stars.

Nico: And time, do you know what that is?

Saidyah: It is a road also.

Nico: Saidyah, there is no such thing as either space or time.

Saidyah: If the master says so, it must be true.

Nico: I knew you would understand me.

(from Act Three of *Time is a Dream*, in Hatcher, *Modern Continental Dramas* (New York, 1941), pp. 599-600.

The question might more properly be raised as to whether or not Kishida was influenced by the two plays written by Jacques Copeau himself, but this also seems unlikely. Copeau's religious drama on the life of St. Francis, *Le petit pauvre* (*The Little Poor Man*), was not printed until after Kishida's death. Copeau's other play, a realistic drama entitled *La maison natale* (*The House into which We Are Born*), was not produced at Le Vieux Colombier until after Kishida returned to Japan. The play had a bad press when first presented but later came to be recognized as a genuine contribution to modern French theatre. It deals with death and its implications in a family already ravaged by greed and solitude; although an accomplished work, it draws on themes and techniques first introduced to the modern theatre by Ibsen, and was therefore unlikely to have influenced Kishida.

Only Iwata Toyoo, who knew Kishida well, has mentioned the obvious source of spiritual inspiration to Kishida, Jules Renard (1864-1910). Renard was one of the leading authors of his generation in France. Although his name is relatively obscure in the United States, Louise Bogan has reminded us that

> it is difficult to discover, given Renard's steadily augmented reputation in France and elsewhere since his death in 1910, the reasons for the almost total neglect of his work in England and America . . . for in France his early novel *L'Ecornifleur* is considered one of the great novels of the 19th century, and his *Journal* . . . [has been named], along with Gide's *Si le grain ne meurt*, as incontestably the greatest of the autobiographical masterpieces of the 20th century.[21]

Renard was not primarily a playwright; his reputation today rests largely on his *Journal* or *Notebooks* and a moving short novel *Poil de Carotte* (*Carrot Top*) (1894), which he dramatized himself in 1901 and which is now firmly

[21] Renard, *Journal*, p. 5.

fixed in the repertoire of the Comédie Française. Renard, active during a period of naturalism in literature, preferred to observe individuals without making comprehensive social judgments. His acute eye for human foibles, developed perhaps during the course of an unhappy childhood and nourished by a strong streak of pessimism, gave him an unparalleled ability to create characters about whom he was able to write with a wry and kindly humanity.

Renard's two most popular plays, *Le plaisir de rompre* (*The Pleasure of Separating*) (1897) and *Le pain de ménage* (*Daily Bread*) (1898), are each in one act. Antoine, when he first read them, acclaimed their superb quality. Copeau later produced *Carrot Top* and *Daily Bread*. Renard's plays may seem slight, perhaps because they are short, but he took the normal dreary fare of the *boulevard* theatre (adultery in the case of *Daily Bread* and the man leaving his mistress in *The Pleasure of Separating*) and, by giving the characters charm and spiritual reality, and especially through the creation of an extraordinarily rhythmic and psychologically effective dialogue, he managed to evoke a morally subtle and delicate set of responses in his audience. The materials of the plays belonged to the nineteenth century, perhaps, but he made of them works belonging to the best of the twentieth century's humanist traditions.

On several occasions Kishida wrote how impressed he had been by Renard's work, and he took great pleasure in trying to translate *Daily Bread* into Japanese while living in Paris. In 1925, Kishida revised this translation, adding to it his Japanese version of *The Pleasure of Separating*, and provided the plays with a long critical introduction on the accomplishments of Renard. The introduction makes good reading: Kishida clearly understood the technique and import of Renard's work. His comments on the problems of translating Renard's language into Japanese without distorting the nuances of French social distinctions, and the difficulties of conveying in Japanese the feelings of the individual characters when normal Japanese expression runs heavily to stereotyped polite language, are of particular interest.

Kishida wrote of Renard that "he gave me the hope, the inspiration, and the interest to write plays myself. Rather than speak of him, I would rather remain silent. I have inclined so much toward him, and I am so infatuated with his art."[22] He does not, however, single out the plots, character types, or even the themes of Renard: on this level, indeed, Kishida's work bears no more than a passing resemblance to that of the French writer. What Kishida admired in Renard was his ability to choose his words and to "respect the values of silence." From him, Kishida said, he learned that a character must have something to say before he speaks, and that a play in which characters continue talking all the time without artistic purpose is mere chatter. Kishida felt a close affinity with Renard's "reticence" as a writer. Renard did not choose to reveal his own feelings in any obvious or extravagant way. This reticence imparts a density of texture to the characters, and the same effect can be observed in Kishida's work. The old lady in *A Diary of Fallen Leaves* is perhaps the best example.

Another writer who owes something to Renard himself and whose work Kishida knew in France was Charles Vildrac (born 1882). His play *Le Pacqueboat Tenacity* (*The Steamship Tenacity*), written in 1920 and produced by Jacques Copeau the same year, was the single greatest success by a new playwright at Le Vieux Colombier. Contemporary criticism spoke of the theatre "effaced before life itself," as the audiences felt themselves at one with the characters on the stage and shared their emotions.

The play concerns two young French workers of no special distinction, Bastien and Ségard, who are about to sail to Canada on the *Tenacity* to start a new life and make their fortunes. Bastien is the stronger of the two psychologically, and although he knows how attached Ségard has

[22] *zenshū*, v, p. 392.

become to Thérèse, a waitress, he makes love to her and runs off with her, leaving Ségard to make the voyage alone. Vildrac, who was also an accomplished poet and novelist, wrote several other plays but never again achieved the phenomenal success of *Tenacity*. Like Renard's plays, *Tenacity* is noteworthy not for the ingenuity of its plot or the novelty of its views of life, but rather for Vildrac's evocative dialogue, so like ordinary conversation yet heightened to suggest eternal themes. *Tenacity* began a whole new genre of French theatre in the 1920s, the so-called "school of silence." Maurice Kurtz wrote of this genre that "emotions are usually evoked by the discreet means of subtle pauses and subconscious hints, never bombastic phrases or overt actions."[23]

Vildrac's play was first produced in Japan in 1933 by the Teatro Comedie (but in a translation not made by Kishida). In Japan, as in France, it is still considered a classic of modern theatre. Vildrac has never been cited as a possible influence on Kishida, possibly because he never translated any of the French author's works; yet he gave an enthusiastic approval to Vildrac's dramatic technique in a speech delivered at Meiji University, in which he called for similar plays by Japanese authors.[24] He may have suggested the production of *Tenacity* to the Teatro Comedie, since he was an informal adviser to the troupe. He included several of Vildrac's short plays in the repertoire of the Literary Theatre during its early years.

Kishida had seen the Copeau production of *Tenacity* and may have learned from it something about the techniques of writing dialogue. In addition, when he came to write his *Ushiyama Hotel*, he may have adopted the structure of Vildrac's play as a model. Both plays are set in a café-hotel, both develop involvements between those who travel and those who remain, and both end with a final voyage of departure for one of the major characters. By their at-

[23] Kurtz, *Copeau*, p. 100.   [24] See *zenshū*, IX, p. 88.

mosphere both plays suggest disorientation and a vague
nihilism. Yet Kishida's play is, thematically and otherwise,
quite distinctive, and his indebtedness to Vildrac is confined to the most general mechanics of *Tenacity*.

The question might also be raised as to why Kishida
chose to read, study, and emulate Renard or Vildrac when
the French theatre before 1940 could boast of such authors
as Claudel, Jules Romains, Montherlant, Anouilh, Giraudoux, and Cocteau. Kishida knew some of their work and
in several essays mentioned Claudel in particular. Perhaps
these writers failed to influence him because they did not
achieve their reputations until the late 1920s and 1930s.
Kishida had not seen these later works performed on the
stage and he was sufficiently absorbed in creating the kind
of drama perfected in France by an earlier generation of
playwrights that he continued to develop and define his
own aesthetic in their more conservative terms.

Jacques Copeau himself, although he was eager to seek
out new authors, represented the crest of the old wave; his
theatre accomplished much of its mission before World
War I, and during the 1919-1923 seasons the authors performed were for the most part mature writers. Copeau's
work as a stage director was advanced; indeed he can be
considered as indirectly responsible, as a result of his stress
on the importance of integrity in the theatre, for the development of a whole group of later writers who, inspired
by Copeau's ideals, chose the drama as their significant
means of expression. Their works, however, came slightly
later. Copeau staged the newest and best plays available to
him, but the offerings were to become incomparably richer
within a few years. Of all the writers mentioned above
whom Copeau produced, only Jules Renard has maintained
his reputation.

Kishida's work was by no means an imitation of any
French dramatist's; he had the good taste to choose, among
them all, Jules Renard as his chief inspiration, but he borrowed only those aspects of Renard's style pertinent to his

own artistic purposes. All in all, it might seem most accurate to say that Kishida had no direct models. When he wrote of the "southern European school of playwriting in Japan" that "it is not a question of taking inspiration from any particular French author," and "it is not even clear if such a movement exists in France itself,"[25] he was, perhaps more than anything else, showing that his debts to France were those of inspiration and not imitation.

[25] See above, p. 142.

269

CHAPTER VIII

Conclusion

> I felt that what I had seen in Paris was not
> so much the modernism of the theatre as a the-
> atricalization of the modern spirit.
>
> —*Iwata Toyoo*[1]

This account of Kishida and his relation to the New Theatre movement in Japan began with a quotation from Etō
Jun suggesting the importance of the difference between
modernization and westernization. In the case of the New
Theatre movement, the tendency toward adopting western
models, rather than attempting to adapt or modernize the
existing forms of Japanese theatre, provided a distinct pattern of development followed by the movement since its
beginnings. Its practitioners—playwrights, actors, and directors alike—all looked to Europe and for the inspiration of
their art.

Yet, examined more closely, the meaning of the word
"westernization" itself seems to differ slightly depending on
what aspect of the New Theatre movement is being considered. In the case of actors and directors, especially in
their experiments in staging western plays in translation,
imitation of the west was important in creating a new style
of acting. The actors and directors insisted that they had
to create the illusion of the reality of western life on the
stage before the spectators; the audiences, in turn, must
have considered most of these plays to be a glimpse of another world, an education in another set of emotions, actions,
speculations. To use Charles Morgan's phrase, these spectators actively sought an "alien understanding." But they

---

[1] Iwata, *Shingeki to watakushi*, p. 60.

sought it in sociological rather than in artistic or poetic terms.

Such a stage in the development of the drama was no doubt inevitable, but certain excesses of imitation could not be avoided. The following account by Klaus Mann, the son of Thomas Mann, who visited Japan in 1928 with his sister Erika, serves as an indication of this tendency. They saw there Osanai's production of Frank Wedekind's *Spring's Awakening* at the Tsukiji Little Theatre.

The contrast between the rigid ceremonial of the classic drama and the bold experiments of the modern stage is one of the most striking and characteristic phenomena in Japanese life. No doubt it is an unforgettable experience to see one of the great tragedians like the celebrated Ganjiro—a dynamic and disciplined artist on a classic scale. But even more bizarre than the odd, ritual apparatus of the Nipponese drama—which is perhaps the most conservative form of art still alive anywhere in the world— was a Japanese production of one of our favorite modern plays, Wedekind's *Spring's Awakening*. The little vanguard theatre where this stunning performance took place reminded us of those familiar institutions in Hamburg, Berlin, and Munich, where we had ventured on similar extravaganzas ourselves. We were delighted and bewildered to hear Wedekind's familiar sentences pronounced in the exotic idiom, and it was a charming queer experience to make friends with actors who tried so hard to imitate the gestures and the intonations of our own youth.[2]

Mann believed that the merits of the production stemmed from the actor's successful *imitation* of the west. They were not performing in accordance with any native acting style, however modified, but in as European a manner as possible. The Japanese actors had no desire to assimilate the play into

[2] Klaus Mann, *The Turning Point* (New York, 1942), pp. 154-155.

271

their own lives, but instead they sought to achieve exact fidelity to their models; their interest was less literary than sociological. It is the persistence of this viewpoint, which continues even today, that gives the New Theatre its reputation among many Japanese of being basically a foreign theatre, the purpose of which is chiefly to introduce western or, at any rate, western-inspired plays to Japan.

In the case of playwrights like Kishida, however, the word "westernization" by no means meant a mere copying of the western theatre. Kishida does not describe peculiarly western emotional situations in his plays; his characters are Japanese, their problems are Japanese, their outlook in life is Japanese. Kishida used what might be termed "poetic realism," a western technique of playwriting, to portray contemporary Japanese emotions that were wholly natural to him. They were not European. The traditional techniques of *kabuki*, which gave first place to the theatrical and the picturesque rather than to the psychologically true, were therefore not suitable to Kishida's purposes any more than the traditional techniques of the novel or of *waka* poetry were suited to the purposes of modern Japanese novelists and poets who wished to express certain new and urgent concerns. Indeed, Kishida's "borrowings" from European drama were no greater in quantity than, say, Eugene O'Neill's. Yet no American finds O'Neill excessively "foreign." Such borrowing and inspiration is a common, even desirable, part of the modern creative process in Europe and the United States. Writers of Kishida's generation in Japan, however, faced special difficulties when they attempted to participate in the same process, because the weight of the Japanese past was too heavy, the sense of difference in styles too great. And since their plays, when they were performed, were staged by groups that took a militantly "western" attitude towards all their activities, the prejudices which grew up concerning the artificiality of the New Theatre and its dramas seem natural. Yet such attitudes are at least partly erroneous, since they are largely based on considerations other than the texts of the plays themselves.

There are obviously no hard-and-fast rules as to how a foreign art form can be successfully naturalized. As a simple hypothesis, I might put forward the idea that an artistic form becomes generally accessible to and is absorbed by writers when it seems natural to them and to their readers, or, in the case of the theatre, to their spectators. In the case of a poem or a novel, the simple one-to-one relationship between writer and reader can permit this process to take place very quickly. As the theatre is a corporate art, however, the process of education for writer, actor, director, and audience is of necessity a much longer one.

When Ibsen began writing his important dramas of social conflict in the 1880s, he was attempting, in selective and artistic terms, to make the drama fit real life as he knew it, and to create a sense of intellectual and emotional actuality in his plays. He achieved what Iwata understood as "a theatricalization of the modern spirit." Osanai, on the other hand, succeeded in showing to Japan "the modernism of the theatre" only when he presented the same plays by Ibsen in Tokyo thirty years later; he was working with a different set of cultural sensibilities and a different audience. Thus, these same plays seemed remote from life rather than close to it. Even so, Osanai's groping for a new style and a new means to present an image of contemporary life on the stage was an important step toward establishing a genuine modern means of expression in the Japanese theatre.

Osanai considered the work of his own troupe to be *avant-garde*. In social terms, this judgment may have been correct. Yet the term *avant-garde* itself, implying a preference for the unconventional, requires the existence of a status quo, a set of rules, against which a revolt is made.[3]

[3] So it is, paradoxically enough, that many of the great directors of the west have studied Asian, specifically Japanese, theatre, in the hope of creating experiments of their own. Meyerhold, Brecht, Piscator,

Seen in that light, Osanai's real contribution to the New Theatre movement was to build a base of technique in his actors and of understanding in his audience for the principles governing emotional expression in the modern theatre. Judgments of the dramas themselves, however, must be made on a different set of considerations. Wedekind's *Spring's Awakening* is avant-garde in comparison with a melodrama by Arthur Wing Pinero; it is not *avant-garde* for a Japanese audience in relation to a *kabuki* play, because the principles of creation involved are too far apart to bear comparison. The potential spectators for the New Theatre and for *kabuki* were not the same, since audiences for the two art forms did not share the same interests. Kishida was surely right in his criticism of Osanai for having failed to teach his actors and his audiences how to appreciate a genuine dramatization of their own modern Japanese spirit.[4]

Reinhardt, and Copeau all showed great interest in *kabuki* and *nō*. Indeed, Copeau's last school production was a version in French of the *nō* play *Kantan*. (See Pronko, *Theatre East and West*, pp. 90-91 for details.) These men were anxious to expand the available means of expression and create a greater sense of poetry than was available in the western theatre, through a use of what were to them exotic techniques. But they had, of course, the whole accomplishments of Ibsen, Strindberg, Chekhov, Shaw, Pirandello, and the others on which to build.

Perhaps we are witnessing the beginnings of the same process now in Japan. Since Japanese writers have mastered their own methods for expressing emotion through realistic dialogue, they are now willing to seek similar expansions of technique and so are turning to the Japanese traditional drama for some of the same reasons that their western counterparts did. In particular, Kinoshita Junji's interests in *kabuki* and folk drama surely represent one important postwar manifestation of this tendency. See an article in French by Mori Arimasa in *Les Théâtres d'Asie*, pp. 185-199.

[4] On the other hand, Osanai's courage and fortitude in the face of constant criticism and financial difficulties cannot be overlooked. Indeed, as Iwata Toyoo has remarked, this spirit of being in the *avant-garde* helped sustain many writers, actors, and directors through financial and spiritual difficulties they could not avoid. See *Shingeki to watakushi*, p. 162.

274

Kishida, on the other hand, at least in the best of his plays, was creating a modern Japanese drama. Although he mastered the international style of playwriting, he wrote in his own way, as Lorca said a dramatist should, about the spirit of his own country; he was the first dramatist to succeed in putting into dramatic form the contemporary Japanese spirit. Judged by Etō's strictures concerning modernization and westernization, Kishida's work can be said to have modernized Japanese drama by finding a means to evoke the emotional life of his day. Kishida's plays are not to be dismissed merely as comedies in the French style; they are thoroughly Japanese stage works. And thoroughly modern ones.[5]

When questions of personalities and politics are finally put aside, as they surely must be, in any evaluation of the history of the theatre in modern Japan Kishida will take the important place he deserves.

[5] Kishida's personal experiences in Europe made him acutely aware of the problems of isolation and cultural confrontation that form an important theme in many of his plays. In this respect, Kishida's cosmopolitanism put him ahead of his period, since relatively few Japanese had shared the same processes of spiritual growth, certainly not theatrefuls of them, in any case. The urbane and sophisticated quality of his writing, so appealing to a foreign reader, may come to exercise a greater attraction to younger Japanese who now travel abroad with such freedom. The success of new works on similar subjects by writers like Endō Shūsaku (especially in his novel *Ryūgaku*, which deals with a Japanese discovering the complexities of European culture) show that the themes first selected by Kishida still retain their vitality in Japan today.

Herbert Passin has defined the concept of cosmopolitanism as "the assertion of a personal view and style without regard for the origin of the particular elements." (See Jansen, ed., *Changing Japanese Attitudes*, p. 477.) Kishida would seem a perfect example.

The New Theatre Movement Since 1939

THE efforts of Kishida's generation to improve standards of playwriting, acting, and direction managed to produce a marked improvement in the artistic endeavors of the New Theatre movement. A number of fine playwrights emerged (although none markedly more gifted than Kishida himself) and among writer, theatre company, and audience a healthier relationship has given the drama in postwar Japan a financial and artistic base far more solid than that of a generation before. The New Theatre can now be said to be a popular form of entertainment, although usually one for white-collar workers and intellectuals, as in most other countries.

As at the time of Kishida and Osanai, the major impetus for the production of modern drama remains today the theatrical company, rather than the system of independent production that is standard in the United States. During the war, only Kishida's Literary Theatre was permitted by the authorities to perform, but by 1945 a number of new organizations came into being. Those mentioned below remain the most influential groups at this writing. Most of these companies revolve around a leading personality, usually an actor or director.

By 1945 Kishida's Literary Theatre was finding great difficulties in continuing its productions. Most theatres had been destroyed during the war, and few patrons had the money for tickets. In April of that year, Kubota Mantarō chose a moving play by Morimoto Kaoru, *Onna no isshō* (*The Life of a Woman*), written earlier the same year, about the life of a self-sacrificing woman during the prewar and war years. Sugimura Haruko was chosen by Kubota, the director, to play the role of the heroine, and with the tremendous success of this production the artistic and financial success of the company was assured. With Kishida's death in 1954, Iwata's retirement from the company in 1963, and Kubota's death in the same year, Sugimura became the central figure in the company; her personality and political outlook have colored the newer public image of the Literary Theatre. Sugimura is usually considered to have considerable sympathies for the political left in Japan; nevertheless, she does not seem to believe in using the theatre as a political platform, and members of the company as a group have not participated in political activities, although many have done so on a personal basis.

The Literary Theatre has done a great deal to encourage the composition of good contemporary drama. Kishida himself lived to see the early plays of Mishima Yukio (1925-1970) staged there, and found them significant, a sign of hope for the future.[1] The Literary Theatre produced most of the work of Katō Michio (1918-1953), whose plays *Nayotake* and *Omoide-o uru otoko* (*The Man Who Sells Dreams*) remain, despite their debt to the work of Giraudoux, among the best of the dramas written in the early years after the war. Another dramatist the company encouraged was Tanaka Chikao (born 1905). He began his career as a young playwright under Kishida, and a number of his important postwar works, many of which owe their mystic and poetic qualities to his study of the modern French theatre, were first produced by the Literary Theatre. In dramas like *Maria no kubi* (*The Head of the Madonna*) and *Chidori* (*Plover*), both written in 1959, Tanaka can lay claim to being the finest serious literary playwright in Japan during the period; it is not surprising that he developed in an atmosphere created by Kishida and his associates.

Another prominent playwright and critic associated with the Literary Theatre until 1963, when he helped form a new

[1] For Kishida's comments on Mishima's early work, see *zenshū*, IX, pp. 204-206.

company, was Fukuda Tsuneari (born 1912).[2] His most influential play, *Kitty Taifū* (*Typhoon Kitty*), a recasting of Chekhov's *The Cherry Orchard* in satirical form as a basis for his own critique of Japanese society, was produced by the company in 1950. Several of his other works were also mounted, among them *Ryū-o nadeta otoko* (*The Man Who Stroked a Dragon*) in 1952.

The Literary Theatre also continued Kishida's practice of introducing contemporary western dramas of literary merit. Through its productions the Japanese public has become acquainted with the work of Sartre, Camus, Giraudoux, Anouilh, Ionesco, and, among American playwrights, Tennessee Williams, whose *Streetcar Named Desire*, both in its original production and in later revivals, was a considerable success. In the classical repertoire, Chekhov and Shakespeare are often presented; in particular, a 1956 production of *Hamlet* in a new translation by Fukuda Tsuneari was extremely distinguished.

In 1963, however, a dispute over artistic principles led a number of prominent members[3] to break away from the Literary Theatre and form a new group called Kumo (Cloud). According to the manifesto issued by the group, they wished to escape from involvement in any kind of politics, "separate the glamor of merely being western from that of the theatre," and gain a greater understanding of the whole range of the western theatrical tradition.[4] After a highly successful opening production of Shakespeare's *A*

[2] For an extended discussion of Fukuda, his plays, and his own attitudes toward the New Theatre movement, see "Fukuda Tsuneari: Modernization and Shingeki," by Benito Ortolani, in Donald Shively, ed., *Tradition and Modernization in Japanese Culture* (Princeton, 1971), pp. 463-499.

[3] Among them Fukuda, Kishida Kyōko, the daughter of Kishida Kunio, and Akutagawa Hiroshi, the actor son of the famous author Akutagawa Ryūnosuke.

[4] Portions of the manifesto are reproduced in Tanaka Chikao, *Shingeki kanshō nyūmon* (Tokyo, 1963), pp. 190-191.

278

Midsummer Night's Dream, again in a translation by Fukuda, the company continued a number of creative innovations such as using *kabuki* actors to play in Shakespeare and inviting foreign directors to stage Shakespeare, O'Neill, and Chekhov.[5]

Perhaps the most influential troupe in postwar Japan, however, is the Haiyūza (Actor's Theatre), led by Senda Koreya,[6] the *doyen* of Japanese New Theatre directors. Brother of the famous stage designer Itō Kisaku, Senda had an important career in the prewar proletarian theatre; he was arrested in 1940 and put in prison. At the end of the war, he joined Aoyama Sugisaku (one of the original directors of Osanai's Tsukiji Little Theatre) and founded the Actor's Theatre, which, as the name suggests, was organized to train and develop actors properly. The company set up a main company and a number of smaller "studios" where young actors and playwrights could practice and improve their craft.

Senda is certainly considered a political activist by the general public, but his approach to the theatre has been both catholic and eclectic. In foreign drama, his company has introduced a wide range of works to Japan, including plays by Molière, Kleist, Beaumarchais, Strindberg, and Brecht (his production of *The Threepenny Opera* was especially successful); among Japanese playwrights, he has produced several works by Tanaka Chikao as well as by such diverse talents as Hisaita Eijirō (born 1898), who wrote a number of plays for the proletarian theatre, Ishikawa Jun (born 1899), a leading novelist in the postwar period, and others. Senda's directing is rich and stylish, with considerable attention to the literary values of a text, but his earlier sense of theatre as

[5] For some details of these productions, see Ortolani, "Fukuda," pp. 476-477.

[6] For an account in English of Senda's career and views on the theatre, see David Goodman's interview with him in *Concerned Theatre Japan,* Vol. 1, #2, Summer 1970, pp. 48-79.

social protest has never deserted him, and these double concerns are visible in his productions at the Actor's Theatre.[7]

Another theatre company important in postwar Japan is the troupe called Mingei (The People's Theatre), also begun in 1945 through the efforts of Kubo Sakae, the most distinguished of the prewar Marxist dramatists. He was joined in his efforts by Uno Jūkichi (born 1914), an actor who performed in a number of prewar leftist productions. The group went through various political and artistic difficulties and did not take its present form until the early 1950s. Since the death by suicide of Kubo in 1958, the company has been led by Uno. The troupe has presented a number of distinguished Japanese dramas, including several early plays by Kinoshita Junji and his later masterpiece about the Soviet spy Richard Sorge and his Japanese counterpart, *Otto to iu Nihonjin* (*A Japanese Called Otto*), in 1962. Another modern Japanese drama of great importance, *Honō no hito* (*Man of Flame*), the finest work by the proletarian dramatist Miyoshi Jūro (1902-1958), is an account of the life and ideals of Vincent Van Gogh; in it the painter's life is given a complex and inspiring treatment.

The People's Theatre has produced foreign drama dealing with humanistic concerns, and the 1954 production of Arthur Miller's *Death of a Salesman* was one of the great theatrical successes of the postwar years in Japan. The People's Theatre has also been in the forefront of political activity among New Theatre troupes. It has participated in delegations taking theatrical performances to mainland China; in 1965, the group was led by Takizawa Osamu, the leading actor, who created the roles of Otto, Willy Loman, and Van Gogh. *Chinese Literature*, the official journal on literary concerns published by the Chinese communist government, reported that the dramas performed by the company showed "an emphasis for the need to struggle

[7] See, for example, Peter Arnott's account of Senda's production of a dramatization of Tolstoy's *Anna Karenina* in *Theatres of Japan*, pp. 241-246.

for freedom and resist oppression."[8] Takizawa's performances were described as played "with deep inner conviction and consummate artistry."[9] Activities of this sort, needless to say, continue to reinforce in the public mind an image of the New Theatre as politically far to the left. Along with a higher level of performances by the theatre companies has come an improvement in the taste of the audiences and in their number as well. To some extent, new elements in the audiences have been attracted to the theatre because of the popularity of New Theatre actors and actresses, who now appear regularly in films and on television, but the main impetus for increasing the size of the audience has come through the activities of organizations independent of the companies, which in effect subsidize certain performances for showings to their membership. The most influential of these organizations in the Rōdōsha engeki hyōgikai (Worker's Council on Theatre), usually abbreviated as Rōen, founded in the early 1950s by politically progressive labor unions who wished to give their membership access to cultural activities. Other competing organizations have since sprung up as well.

The principle employed by such groups is to sell tickets at reduced prices to worker audiences; the audiences, however, have turned out to be largely if not almost wholly white-collar, as might be expected, and much of the original political impetus of these organizations has been diluted, since the subscribers usually wish to see successful and entertaining productions, not necessarily political ones. The most positive effect of these subscription systems has been to decentralize the theatre; under the auspices of such sponsoring groups, New Theatre productions now tour the country and play fairly long runs in provincial cities and towns. The New Theatre may be moving closer to a national form of theatre rather than merely being limited to Tokyo.

[8] *Chinese Literature*, August 1965, p. 94.
[9] *Ibid.*, p. 95.

As audiences have improved, acting standards have certainly been raised. Kishida's idea that bright people with good modern educations would make the best actors has proved correct; now, indeed, the profession carries with it perhaps a greater suggestion of intellectual ability than it does in the west. Roundtable discussions printed in theatre magazines and other journals often include as participants New Theatre actors who seem able—indeed, determined—to unburden themselves on a variety of social, political, and artistic questions that would confound many of their counterparts in other countries.

Along with higher standards of education has come better acting technique. Certainly performances by New Theatre actors in films have contributed to their ever-increasing mastery of their voices and bodies. As Donald Richie remarks, "the best film actors, in Japan as elsewhere, have come from the stage and Japan's finest film actors have, almost without exception, had Shingeki training."[10] Television performances have also broadened the scope of their technique. And of course the new generation of actors has no connection with the older acting traditions of *kabuki* and *shimpa*, and thus has no learned traditions to break.

In literary quality too, as has already been suggested, the postwar period has seen the work of a number of distinguished dramatists emerge. In particular the plays of Tanaka Chikao and Kinoshita Junji have shown consistent distinction. In addition, several prominent novelists have written effective works for the theatre. Abe Kōbō (born 1924), known abroad for his novels, often written in a rather Kafkaesque style,[11] has written a number of striking dramas. His early efforts, such as *Doreigari (Slave Hunt)*, produced by the Actor's Theatre in 1962, contain certain Marxist ele-

[10] Donald Richie and Joseph Anderson, *The Japanese Film* (Rutland, Vermont, 1959), p. 392.

[11] Among those in translation are *Woman in the Dunes* (New York, 1964), *Face of Another* (New York 1966), *The Ruined Map* (New York, 1969), and *Inter Ice age 4* (New York, 1970).

ments; *Tomodachi* (*Friends*),[12] first produced in 1967, owes more to the Theatre of the Absurd. Whatever Abe's literary debts, however, the results always seem effectively his own creation.

Mishima Yukio, perhaps Japan's best-known modern novelist abroad, wrote a considerable number of plays for performance by New Theatre companies; he also experimented with *shimpa* in such plays as *Rokumeikan* (*Deer Horn Hall*), written in 1956, which deals with the political atmosphere during the Meiji restoration. He has made modern adaptions of medieval *nō* plays as well.[13] The work of professional dramatists has thus been buttressed by that of other serious writers who have turned, as have certain of their European and American counterparts, to the stage as a means to express their ideas. During Kishida's time, the acting companies and the audiences alike would have been ill-equipped to serve the needs of such writers, but no similar disparity exists today.

Needless to say the New Theatre movement is not without its current problems; indeed, as Tsuno Kaitarō has pointed out, many of the younger generation feel that the New Theatre has in itself become static and must be superseded by a new *avant-garde*.[14] Nevertheless, the problems seem those of healthy growth and a genuine maturity. From our contemporary point of view, Kishida seems to have anticipated many of the steps necessary for the New Theatre to take in order to succeed artistically. History has, so far, proved him right.

[12] *Friends* has been translated by Donald Keene and published by Grove Press in 1969.

[13] Several of these plays are available in English, translated by Donald Keene, in *Five Modern nō Plays* (New York, 1957).

[14] See his article "Biwa and the Beatles," in *Concerned Theatre Japan*, Special Introductory Issue, October 1969.

Biographical Notes on Kishida's Life

THE general outlines of Kishida's career are well known: his early military training, his trip to France, his return to Japan, his marriage, and the birth of his two daughters. Intellectually, his love of France and French literature remained so powerful that his last plans, made during his final illness, were to take his two daughters to visit France. Physically, his weak constitution and almost constant illness certainly gave him an introspective turn of mind. Yet the kind of documentation that would permit any extended discussion of the relation of his artistic work to his own emotional or intellectual life has so far remained unrecorded.

Various writers and other associates of Kishida have sketched their impressions of him, and most of these comments are reproduced elsewhere throughout the book. Kishida was generally considered to be very kindly but extremely reserved. Few speculated at all on the relation between his own emotional life and the dramas he created.

The writer who has come closest to establishing this association is Fukuda Tsuneari, in an essay written in 1955.[1] Fukuda, a disciple and friend, found Kishida a man who always showed love and respect for others, qualities that stemmed from the character of one who was himself disciplined and austere. Fukuda concluded that Kishida manifested the kind of military spirit associated with the *samurai* warriors of his ancestors: in the modern and international milieu in which he lived, however, aesthetic consideration replaced moral ones.

Fukuda finds that in the early plays, such as *Paper*

[1] See Fukuda Tsuneari, "Kishida Kunio," in *Gendai Nihon bungaku zenshū* (Tokyo, 1955), Vol. 33, pp. 402-406.

Balloon or *Roof Garden*, the real dramatic issue lies in the destruction of the proper order of things (in both cases a marriage) by an outside force: poverty. Kishida's characters are well-educated, graceful, "modern" people, and Fukuda concludes that Kishida may permit them too easy an emotional escape from their economic situation. Nevertheless, the fear of a threat to order, according to Fukuda, seems typical of Kishida's whole psychology.

The attempt to use Kishida's own comments as the basis for a psychobiography may be tempting, but despite the fact that Kishida wrote two volumes of essays, he recorded virtually nothing about himself after his return from France. He was married in 1927 to Murakawa Tokiko and remained a dedicated father and husband. Several commentators testified that Kishida never fully recovered from the death of his wife in 1942. Despite, or perhaps because of, their closeness, he wrote nothing at all about her. Aside from a few indications that she may have done occasional work in journalism, it seems that she had no profession. Any details concerning the nature of her relationship with her husband remain, as far as I have been able to ascertain, completely unrecorded.

Kishida's two daughters have both had independent careers. The elder, Eriko, born in 1928, has had some success as a writer of poetry and children's stories. The younger daughter, Kishida Kyōko, born in 1930, made her debut as a professional actress in 1950, at the age of twenty, in Fukuda's *Typhoon Kitty*.[2] Kishida saw the première and wrote an article in response to questions about his reactions to his daughter's performance.[3] Despite the title of the article—"Oya no joyū" ("The Parent of an Actress")—it tells nothing of significance whatsoever about his relationship with his own daughter.

[2] For a comment on the play, see Appendix I, p. 278.

[3] *zenshū*, IX, pp. 204-206. A second article, "Shingeki to musume Kyōko" (The New Theatre and my Daughter Kyōko) on p. 207 is no more revealing.

285

Kishida Kyōko has been, in print at least, only slightly more informative about her father. In a series of articles commemorating the republication of several of her father's plays, she contributed a short essay on her impressions of him.[4] Her remarks are more or less what might be anticipated. She indicates that he gave the impression of being strict yet was surprisingly gentle; when he did reprimand her, it was usually, impeccable stylist that he was, for sloppy speech. Commenting on her mother's death, she remarks that when she and her father looked at the body together, it was the first and only time she saw him cry. All these details confirm the general outline of his character but do not provide any deeper insights.

Kishida Kyōko has continued to keep the family name prominent in theatrical circles. She has had a distinguished career as a stage actress, first as a member of the Literary Theatre, then with the Cloud troupe. She is well known to foreign audiences through her performances in films, notably in *Woman in the Dunes* (taken from the Abe Kōbō novel), for which she won a number of national and international awards.

Without a proper biography of Kishida, the plays must stand on their own. Nevertheless, we are not left without some insight into the nature of the man who created them. Indeed, as Kishida wrote himself, "comedy . . . is a mirror in which the author himself is reflected."[5] Even without any connections established between Kishida's own life and his art, the plays seem to me, at least, sufficiently rewarding on their own, largely public terms.

[4] Inserted pamphlet to *Gendai Nihon bungaku zenshū*, Vol. 33, p. 5.

[5] See p. 143, above, for the full citation.

Bibliography

WORKS BY KISHIDA KUNIO

All Japanese text citations are from the *Kishida Kunio zenshū*, Tokyo, 1955.

Asamayama (*Mount Asama*). Vol. II.

"Bungaku ka gikyoku ka?" ("Literature or Drama?"). Vol. IX.

Buranko (*The Swing*). Vol. I.

Chiroru no aki (*Autumn in the Tyrols*). Vol. I.

"Engeki honshitsuron no seiri" ("Some Amendments to the Essence of Dramatic Theory"). Vol. VIII.

"Engekiron no ippōkō" ("One Direction for Dramatic Theory"). Vol. VIII.

"Engeki tōmen no mondai" ("Current Problems of the Theatre"). Vol. VIII.

Furui Omocha (*Old Toys*). Vol. I.

Fūzoku Jihyō (*A Commentary on Manners*). Vol. III.

"Gekidan ankoku no ben" ("Some Words on the Gloomy State of the Theatre Companies"). Vol. VIII.

"Gekidō kyūsai no hitsuyō" ("The Need to Reclaim the Art of the Theatre"). Vol. VIII.

"Gekijō to kankyakusō" ("Theatres and Spectators"). Vol. IX.

"*Gekisaku* ni tsugu" ("Concerning *Playwriting* magazine"). Vol. IX.

"Gekiteki dentō to gekiteki inshū" ("Theatrical Tradition and Theatrical Custom"). Vol. VIII.

"Gendai engekiron ni tsuite" ("Concerning Contemporary Dramatic Theory"). Vol. IX.

"Gikyoku izen no mono" ("Before the Play"). Vol. VIII.

"Gikyoku no seimei to engekibi" ("The Life of the Drama and the Beauty of the Theatre"). Vol. VIII.

287

"Gikyoku oyobi gikyoku sakka ni tsuite" ("Concerning Drama and Dramatic Writers"). Vol. VIII.

"Gikyokushū *Asamayama* ni tsuite" (Concerning the drama anthology *Mount Asama*"). Vol. IX.

"Gikyokushū *fūzokujihyō* ni tsuite" ("Concerning the drama anthology *A Commentary on Manners*"). Vol. IX.

"Gikyokushū *saigetsu* ni tsuite" ("Concerning the drama anthology *A Space of Time*"). Vol. IX.

Hazakura (*The Cherry Tree in Leaf*). Vol. I.

"Ichigon" ("One Word"). Vol. IX.

"Iwademo no koto" ("It Goes without Saying"). Vol. IX.

"Joyū no oya" ("The Parent of an Actress"). Vol. IX.

"Kabuki geki no shōrai" ("The Future of *kabuki* Drama"). Vol. VIII.

Kamifūsen (*Paper Balloon*). Vol. I.

"Kankyakusō to shingeki no shukumei" ("Audiences and the Destiny of the New Theatre"). Vol. IX.

Karai hakase no rinjū (*The Last Moments of Doctor Karai*). Vol. III.

"Kishida Kunio shū ni tsuite" ("Concerning a Collected Volume of My Work"). Vol. IX.

"Kokaijō" ("An Open Letter"). Vol. IX.

"Kore kara no gikyoku" ("The Drama from Now On"). Vol. VIII.

Mama sensei to sono otto (*Professor Mama and her Husband*). Vol. II.

"Mikansei na gendai geki" ("The Incomplete Modern Theatre"). Vol. VIII.

Mura de ichi ban no kuri no ki (*The Tallest Chestnut in the Village*). Vol. I.

Ochiba nikki (*Diary of Fallen Leaves*). Vol. I.

Okujōteien (*Roof Garden*). Vol. I.

"Osanai kun no gikyokuron" ("The Dramatic Theory of Osanai"). Vol. IX.

"Pommes cuites o nageru" ("Throwing Cooked Apples"). Vol. IX.

Saigetsu (*A Space of Time*). Vol. III.

Sawa-shi no futari musume (*Mr. Sawa's Two Daughters*). Vol. II.

"Sendōsei bannō" ("Almighty Agitation"). Vol. VIII.

"Serifu toshite no nihongo" ("The Japanese Language in Dramatic Dialogue"). Vol. IX.

"Shanhai de senshi shita Tomoda Kyōsuke kun" ("The Death of Tomoda Kyōsuke, fallen in battle in Shanghai"). Vol. IX.

"Shibai to boku" ("The Drama and Me"). Vol. IX.

"Shibai to kenbutsu" ("The Drama and Entertainment"). Vol. IX.

"Shibai to seikatsu" ("The Drama and Our Daily Life"). Vol. IX.

Shiitake to yūben (*Mushrooms and Eloquence*). Vol. III.

"Shimpa geki to shimpa haiyū" ("*Shimpa* drama and *shimpa* actors"). Vol. VIII.

"Shingekikai no bunya" ("Types of New Theatre"). Vol. VIII.

"Shingeki kyōkai no butai keiko" ("A Rehearsal of the New Theatre Society"). Vol. IX.

"Shingeki no kankyaku shokun e" ("To my Friends, the New Theatre audiences"). Vol. IX.

"Shingeki no kara" ("The Husk of the New Theatre"). Vol. VIII.

"Shingeki no shimatsu" ("The State of the New Theatre"). Vol. VIII.

"Shingeki no tame ni" ("For the Sake of the New Theatre"). Vol. VIII.

"Shingeki no undō no futatsu no michi" ("Two Roads for the New Theatre Movement"). Vol. IX.

"Shingeki to musume Kyōko" ("The New Theatre and my daughter Kyōko"). Vol. IX.

"Shingeki undō no ikkōsatsu" ("One Consideration for the New Theatre Movement"). Vol. VIII.

"Shinkokugeki no *okujōteien* o mite" ("*Roof Garden* in a Performance by the Shinkokugeki troupe"). Vol. IX.

Shokugyō (*Vocation*). Vol. II.

289

Shu-u (*Sudden Shower*). Vol. I.

"Tsukiji shōgekijō no hataage" ("The Launching of the Tsukiji Little Theatre"). Vol. IX.

"Tsukijiza no *mama sensei*" ("*Professor Mama* at the Tsukijiza"). Vol. IX.

Ushiyama hoteru (*Ushiyama Hotel*). Vol. II.

"Watakushi no engekiron ni tsuite" ("Concerning my Dramatic Theory"). Vol. VIII.

"Zoku kotoba kotoba kotoba" ("More Words, Words, Words"). Vol. X.

Adoration. Translated by Richard McKinnon. *The Literary Review*, Autumn, 1962.

It Will Be Fine Tomorrow. Translated by Eiji Ukai and Eric Bell. In *Eminent Authors of Contemporary Japan*, Vol. II. Tokyo, 1931.

"New Movements on the Stage," *Contemporary Japan*, IV (1935-1936), 350-356.

Roof Garden. Translated by Noboru Hidaka. In *The Passion by S. Mushakoji and Three Other Japanese Plays.* Honolulu, 1933.

General Works in Japanese

Akiba Tarō. *Nihon shingekishi* (*A History of the New Theatre in Japan*). Tokyo, 1956.

Akita Ujaku. *Akita Ujaku jiden* (*The Autobiography of Akita Ujaku*). Tokyo, 1953.

Aoe Shunjurō. "Kishida engeki e no gimon" ("Doubts concerning the Dramas of Kishida"), *Higeki kigeki*, August 1953, 44-64.

———. "Some demo gimon wa kaishō shinai" ("Even so, the Doubts Do Not Resolve Themselves"), *Higeki kigeki*, October 1953, 68-71 and November 1953, 46-52.

Endō, Shingo. "Kishida Kunio shi no omoide" ("Recollections of Kishida Kunio"), *Higeki kigeki*, April 1954, 6-10.

———. "Kotoba no bōrei—Kishida Kunio no gikyokuron to sono eikyō," ("The Apparition of Words—the Dramatic Theory of Kishida and its Influence"), *Higeki kigeki*, July 1951, 2-13.

Fukuda Tsuneari, "Kishida Kunio ron" ("Views on Kishida Kunio"), *Toyoshima, Kishida shū*, Tokyo, 1955. (Vol. xxxiii of *Gendai Nihon bungaku zenshū*).

————. *Watakushi no engeki hakusho* (*My White Paper on Drama*). Tokyo, 1958.

Hasegawa Nyozekan. *Ethyl Gasoline*. In Vol. xli, *Nihon gendai bungaku zenshū*. Tokyo, 1930.

Hijikata Yoshi. *Enshutsusha no michi* (*The Path of a Theatre Director*). Tokyo, 1969.

Hisamatsu Sen'ichi, ed. *Gendai bungaku daijiten* (*Encyclopedia of Modern Literature*). Tokyo, 1968.

Ibaragi Tadashi. "Ajita Ujaku kaishaku" ("An Interpretation of Akita Ujaku"), Vol. viii. *Gendai Nihon gikyoku senshū*. Tokyo, 1955.

————. *Nihon shingeki shōshi* (*A Short History of the New Theatre Movement in Japan*). Tokyo, 1966.

————. *Shōwa no shingeki*. (*The New Theatre in the Shōwa Era*). Tokyo, 1956.

Igayama Masahi. "*Ushiyama hoteru* no ishoku" ("Local Color in *Ushiyama Hotel*"), *Shingeki*, June 1954, 79-89.

Ito Kisaku. *Butai bijutsu* (*Scenic Art*). Tokyo, 1963.

Iwata Toyoo. *Higashi wa higashi* (*East is East*). In Vol. 1 of *Nihon gendai gikyoku shū*, edited by Iwata Toyoo. Tokyo, 1963.

————. *Iwata Toyoo engeki hyōron shū* (*The Collected Theatre Criticism of Iwata Toyoo*). Tokyo, 1963.

————. *Shingeki to watakushi* (*The New Theatre Movement and Me*). Tokyo, 1956.

Kawamori Yoshiro. "Kishida Kunio kaishaku" ("A Commentary on Kishida Kunio"), *Toyoshima, Kishida shū*. Tokyo, 1955. (Vol. xxxiii of *Gendai Nihon bungaku zenshū*.)

Kawatake Shigetoshi, ed. *Engeki hyakkajiten* (*An Encyclopedia of Drama*). Tokyo, 1963.

Kawatake Shigetoshi. *Gaisetsu Nihon engekishi* (*A Brief History of the Theatre in Japan*). Tokyo, 1966.

———. *Nihon engeki kenkyū shomoku kaidai* (*A Bibliography of Materials for Research on the Japanese Drama*). Tokyo, 1966.

———. *Nihon gikyoku jiten* (*A Dictionary of Japanese Drama*). Tokyo, 1964.

——— and Shimomura Masao, ed. *Nihon no engeki* (*Japanese Theatre*). Tokyo, 1959. (Vol. VI of *Gendai engeki kōza*).

———. *Ningen Tsubouchi Shōyō* (*Tsubouchi Shōyō the Man*). Tokyo, 1959.

Kitami Harukazu. *Bungakuza zashi* (*A History of the Literary Theatre Troupe*). Tokyo, 1963.

———. "Kishida, Iwata kara bungakuza e" ("From Kishida and Iwata to the Establishment of the Literary Theatre"), Vol. V, *Gendai no engeki*, edited by Kawatake Shigetoshi and Kurahashi Takeshi. Tokyo, 1966.

Kon Hidemi. "Kishida Kunio ron" ("Views on Kishida Kunio"), *Kaizō*, April 1939, 44-50.

———. "Moraristo Kishida Kunio," *Bungei*, May 1954, 34-36.

Kōno Toshio. "Kishida Kunio kaishaku" ("A Commentary on Kishida Kunio"), *Kishida, Serizawa, Toyoshima shū*. Tokyo, 1966. (Vol. LXII of *Nihon gendai bungaku zenshū.*)

Kubo Sakae. "Mayoeru riarizumu" ("Realism Astray"), *Kubo Sakae zenshū*, Vol. VI. Tokyo, 1962.

Kubota Mantarō. Miscellaneous essays on the New Theatre Movement in *Kubota Mantarō zenshū*, Vol. XIII. Tokyo, 1967.

Kurabayashi Seiichirō. *Shingeki nendaiki (senchūhen)* (*A Chronicle of the New Theatre*) (*The War Years*). Tokyo, 1969.

———. *Shingeki nendaiki (sengohen)* (*A Chronicle of the New Theatre*) (*The Postwar Years*). Tokyo, 1966.

Matsumoto Kappei. *Nihon shingeki shi: shingeki binbō monogatari* (*A History of the New Theatre: A Tale of Poverty*). Tokyo, 1966.

Mizushina Haruki. *Osanai Kaoru to tsukiji shōgekijō* (*Osanai Kaoru and the Tsukiji Little Theatre*). Tokyo, 1954.

Murayama Tomoyoshi. "Engeki" ("Drama"), in *Kindai no bungaku* (*Modern Literature*), edited by the Nihon bungaku kyōkai. Tokyo, 1952. (Vol. vi of *Nihon bungaku kōza.*)

Nakajima Kenzō. "Kishida Kunio no shōgai" ("The Life of Kishida Kunio"), *Bungei*, May 1954.

Odagiri Hideo. *Kōza Nihon bungaku shi* (*A Course on the History of Japanese Literature*). Tokyo, 1957.

Okakura Shiro. "Shōwa jūnendai no shingeki" ("The New Theatre in the Second Decade of Shōwa") *Bungaku*, Feb. 1955, 114-125.

Oki Naotarō. "*Gekisaku* sakka kaishaku" ("A Commentary on the writers for *Playwriting*"), *Gendai Nihon gikyoku senshū.* Tokyo, 1955.

―――. "Kishida, Kubota kaishaku" ("A Commentary on Kishida and Kubota"), *Gendai Nihon gikyoku senshū.* Tokyo, 1955.

―――. "Kume Masao kaishaku ("A Commentary on Kume Masao"), *Gendai Nihon gikyoku senshū.* Tokyo, 1955.

Osanai Kaoru. *Osanai Kaoru engekiron zenshū* (*The Collected Dramatic Criticism of Osanai Kaoru*). Tokyo, 1965.

Ozaki Hirotsugu. "Kindai geki to kindai gikyoku" ("Modern Theatre and Modern Drama"), Vol. ii, *Kōza Nihon Bungaku.* Tokyo, 1969.

―――. *Shingeki no ashiato* (*New Theatre: Footprints Left Behind*). Tokyo, 1956.

―――. *Tsubouchi Shōyō.* Tokyo, 1965.

Shimomura Masao. *Shingeki* (*New Theatre*). Tokyo, 1956.

Shinkyō gekidan, ed. *Engekiron (Dramatic Theory)*. Tokyo, 1936.

Sugahara Takashi. "Kishida gikyoku e no michi" ("The Path to Kishida's Dramas"), *Nihon engeki*, July 1949, 20-29.

Sugai, Yukio. "Osanai Kaoru kaishaku" ("A Commentary on Osanai Kaoru"), *Osanai Kaoru engekiron*, Vol. 1, Tokyo, 1964.

——. *Shingeki: sono butai to rekishi (The New Theatre: Its Stage and Its History)*. Tokyo, 1967.

——. "Taishōki no engeki zasshi" ("Drama Magazines in the Taishō Era"), *Bungaku*, March 1960. 325-338.

Tanaka Chikao, ed. *Gekibungaku (Drama as Literature)*. Tokyo, 1959. (Vol. xxii in *Kindai bungaku kanshō kōza*.)

——. *Shingeki kanshō nyūmon (An Introduction to an Appreciation of the New Theatre)*. Tokyo, 1963.

Tanaka Eizō. *Meiji Taishō shingekishi shiryō (Materials for The History of the New Theatre in the Meiji and Taisho Periods)*. Tokyo, 1964.

Tanizaki Junichirō. *Seishun Monogatari (A Tale of Youth)*. Vol. xxi, *Tanizaki Junichirō zenshū*. Tokyo, 1958.

Teatro henshūbu, ed. *Shingeki benran (A Manual of the New Theatre)*. Tokyo, 1965.

Toita Yasuji. *Engeki gojūnen (Fifty Years of Drama)*. Tokyo, 1950.

——. *Shingekishi no hitobito (People in the History of the New Theatre)*. Tokyo, 1952.

Tsubouchi Shōyō. *Shōyō gekidan (Theatre Writing of Shōyō)*. Tokyo, 1919.

Tsuji Hisakazu. "Kishida engekiron o megute—Aoe ronsetsu e no gimon" ("Concerning Kishida's dramatic theories —Doubts about Aoe's Remarks"), *Higeki kigeki*, July 1953, 9-15. August 1953, 8-13.

Yamada Hajime. *Kindai geki (Modern Drama)*. Tokyo, 1951. (Vol. xii of *Nihon bungaku kyōyo kōza*.)

Yamamoto Shūji. "Gekibungaku ni okeru kindaiteki shu-
juso" "Various Modern Elements in Theatrical Literature," *Gekibungaku*, edited by Tanaka Chikao, Tokyo,
1959.
Yoshida Seiichi, ed. *Nihon bungaku kanshō jiten (A Dictionary for the Appreciation of Japanese Literature).*
Tokyo, 1960.

WORKS ON JAPAN AND THE JAPANESE THEATRE
IN WESTERN LANGUAGES

Anderson, Joseph, and Richie, Donald. *The Japanese Film:
Art and Industry.* Rutland, Vermont, 1959.
Arima Tatsuo. *The Failure of Freedom: A Portrait of Mod-
ern Japanese Intellectuals.* Cambridge, 1969.
Arnott, Peter. *The Theatres of Japan.* London, 1969.
Barrault, Jean-Louis. *Journal de bord: Japon, Israël, Grèce,
Yougoslavie.* Paris, 1961.
Bowers, Faubion. *Japanese Theatre.* New York, 1952.
Ernst, Earl. *The Kabuki Theatre.* Oxford, 1956.
Etō Jun. "An Undercurrent in Modern Japanese Literature,"
Journal of Asian Studies, XXIII (May 1964), 433-445.
Goodman, David. "An Interview with Senda Koreya,"
Concerned Theatre Japan, I, 2 (Summer 1970), 48-79.
Iwasaki Yozan and Glen Hughes, trans. *Three Modern
Japanese Plays.* New York, 1923.
———, trans. *New Plays from Old Japan.* New York, 1930.
Jansen, Marius, ed. *Changing Japanese Attitudes toward
Modernization.* Princeton, 1965.
Japan UNESCO Commission, ed. "Shingeki Drama," *Japan,
its Land, People, and Culture.* Tokyo, 1954.
———, ed. *Proceedings of the International Symposium on
the Theatre in East and West.* Tokyo, 1965.
———, ed. *Theatre in Japan.* Tokyo, 1963.
Kikuchi Kan. *Tojuro's Love and Four Other Plays.* Translated by Glenn Shaw. Tokyo, 1956.

Komiya Toyotaka. *Japanese Music and Drama in the Meiji Era.* Translated by Donald Keene and Edward Seidensticker. Tokyo, 1956.

Kōri Torahiko. *The English Works.* Tokyo, 1936.

McClellan, Edward. "The Impressionistic Tendency in Some Modern Japanese Writers," *The Chicago Review,* XVII, 4 (1965), 48-60.

Mori Arimasa. "Le dramaturge Japonais: Kinoshita Junji." *Les Théâtres d'Asie,* edited by Jean Jacquot. Paris, 1961.

Morrison, John W. *Modern Japanese Fiction.* Salt Lake City, 1955.

Nakamura Mitsuo. *Modern Japanese Fiction,* translated by Donald L. Philippi and others. Tokyo, 1968.

Ortolani, Benito. "Shingeki: the maturing New Drama of Japan." *Studies in Japanese Culture,* edited by Joseph Ruggendorf. Tokyo, 1963.

Sansom, Sir George. *The Western World and Japan.* New York, 1950.

Satō Toshihiko. "Ibsen Parallels in Modern Japanese Drama," *Yearbook of Comparative and General Literature,* XI (1962), 183-190.

Shea, George Tyson. *Leftwing Literature in Japan.* Tokyo, 1964.

Shively, Donald, ed. *Tradition and Modernization in Japanese Culture.* Princeton, 1971.

Sieffert, René. "Le Théâtre Japonais." *Les Théâtres d'Asie,* edited by Jean Jacquot. Paris, 1961.

Takaya, Ted Terujiro. *An Inquiry into the Role of the Traditional Kabuki Playwright.* Columbia University Ph.D. dissertation, 1969, unpublished.

Tsubouchi Shōyō. *L'Ermite,* translated by Yoshie Takamasu. Paris, 1920.

Tsuno Kaitarō. "Biwa and the Beetles: an Invitation to Modern Japanese Theatre." *Concerned Theatre Japan,* Introductory Issue (October 1969), 6-32.

Ueda Makoto. "Japanese Literature since World War II." *The Literary Review,* VI, Autumn 1962, 6-22.

Yamagiwa, Joseph K. *Japanese Literature in the Shōwa Period: A Guide to Japanese Reference and Research Materials.* Ann Arbor, 1959.

Yamamoto Yūzō. *Three Plays.* Translated by Glenn Shaw. Tokyo, 1957.

WORKS ON THE WESTERN THEATRE

Albee, Edward. *Box and Quotations from Chairman Mao.* New York, 1969.

Bentley, Eric. *The Playwright as Thinker.* New York, 1946.

———. *The Theatre of Commitment.* New York, 1967.

Braun, Edward. *Meyerhold on Theatre.* New York, 1969.

Brustein, Robert. *The Theatre of Revolt.* Boston, 1964.

Clark, Barrett and Freedley, George. *A History of Modern Drama.* New York, 1947.

Chekhov, Anton. *Swan Song.* Translated by Theodore Hoffman. In Chekhov, *The Brute and Other Farces*, edited by Eric Bentley. New York, 1958.

Cole, Toby and Chinoy, Helen K., ed. *Directors on Directing.* New York, 1963.

———, ed. *Playwrights on Playwriting.* New York, 1961.

Copeau, Jacques. *The House into which We are Born.* Translated by Ralph Roeder. *Theatre Arts Monthly*, VIII, July 1924.

———. *Notes sur le métier de comédien.* Paris, 1955.

———. *Le Petit Pauvre.* Translated by Beverley Thurman. *Port-Royal and Other Plays*, edited by Richard Hayes. New York, 1962.

Corrigan, Robert W. *Theatre in the Twentieth Century.* New York, 1963.

Courteline, Georges. *Monsieur Badin.* Translated by Albert Bermel. *The Plays of Courteline.* London, 1961.

———. *Peace at Home*, translated by Virginia and Frank Vernon. *Modern One Act Plays from the French*, edited by Virginia and Frank Vernon. New York, 1933.

———. *Théâtre complet.* Paris, 1961.

Dickinson, Thomas H. *Theatre in a Changing Europe*. New York, 1937.

Fowlie, Wallace. *Dionysus in Paris: A Guide to the Contemporary French Theatre*. New York, 1960.

Garten, Hugh Frederick. *Modern German Drama*. New York, 1962.

Gassner, John. *Directions in Modern Theatre and Drama*. New York, 1965.

Ghéon, Henri. *The Art of the Theatre*. New York, 1961.

Goering, Reinhard. *A Sea Battle*. English translation made in 1958 of the play *Seeschlacht* by June Falcone and Bayard Morgan, available on microfilm at the Columbia University Library, N.Y.

Gorchakov, Nikolai. *The Theatre in Soviet Russia*. New York, 1957.

Gorelik, Mordekai. *New Theatres for Old*. New York, 1962.

Gorky, Maxim. *The Lower Depths*, translated by Alexander Bakshy. In *Seven Plays of Maxim Gorky*, edited by Alexander Bakshy. New Haven, 1945.

Harvey, Paul and Heseltine, J. E., *Oxford Companion to French Literature*. Oxford, 1959.

Hatcher, Harlan, ed. *Modern Continental Dramas*. New York, 1941.

Hervieu, Paul. *The Trail of the Torch*, translated by J. A. Haughton. New York, 1915.

Ibsen, Henrik. *Last Plays*, translated by Arvid Paulson. New York, 1962.

Ionesco, Eugène. *Jeux de Massacre*. Paris, 1970.

Kaiser, Georg. *From Morn to Midnight*, translated by Ashley Dukes. New York, 1922.

Knapp, Bettina Liebowitz. *Louis Jouvet, Man of the Theatre*. New York, 1957.

Kurtz, Maurice. *Jacques Copeau: Biographie d'un théâtre*. Paris, 1950. (The book was originally written as a Columbia University Ph.D. dissertation. Quotations used in the present dissertation are taken from the original English-language manuscript, not from the published French adaption.)

Lenormand, Henri-René. *Failures*, translated by Winifred Katzin. New York, 1923.

———. *Time is a Dream*, translated by Winifred Katzin. *Modern Continental Dramas*, edited by Harlan Hatcher. New York, 1941.

Ley-Piscator, Maria. *The Piscator Experiment*. New York, 1967.

Lunacharsky, Anatol Vasilevich. *Three Plays*, translated by L. A. Magnus and K. Walter. London, 1923.

McGowan, Kenneth and Melnitz, William. *The Living Stage*. Englewood Cliffs, N.J., 1955.

Mann, Klaus. *The Turning Point: Thirty Five Years in this Century*. New York, 1942.

Martinet, Marcel. *La Nuit*. Paris, 1921.

Mayakovsky, Vladimir. *The Complete Plays*, translated by Guy Daniels. New York, 1968.

Mazaud, Emile. *The Holiday*, translated by Ralph Roeder. *Theatre Arts Monthly*, VI, January 1922.

Miller, Anna Irene. *The Independent Theatre in Europe*. New York, 1931.

Morgan, Charles. "The Nature of Dramatic Illusion." *Reflections on Art*, edited by Suzanne B. Langer. Baltimore, 1958.

Piscator, Erwin. *Le théâtre politique*. Paris, 1962.

Porto-Riche, Georges de. *Le passé*. Paris, undated.

Pronko, Leonard Cabell. *Theatre East and West*. Berkeley, 1967.

Renard, Jules. *The Journal*, translated by Louise Bogan and Elizabeth Roget. New York, 1964.

———. *Le pain de ménage*. Jules Renard, *Oeuvres complètes*, Vol. VII. Paris, 1926.

———. *Le plaisir de rompre*. Jules Renard, *Oeuvres complètes*, Vol. VII. Paris, 1926.

———. *Poil de Carotte*. Jules Renard, *Oeuvres complètes*, Vol. V. Paris, 1926.

Rolland, Romain. *The People's Theatre*, translated by Barrett Clark. New York, 1918.

———. *The Wolves*, translated by Barrett Clark. New York, 1937.

Romains, Jules. *Dr. Knock*, translated by Harley Granville-Barker. *From the Modern Repertoire*, Vol. III, edited by Eric Bentley. Bloomington, Indiana, 1956.

Sinclair, Upton. *Prince Hagen.* In Upton Sinclair, *Plays of Protest.* New York, 1911.

Tretyakov, Sergei Mikhailovich. *Roar China!*, translated by F. Polianovska and Barbara Nixon. London, 1931.

Valency, Maurice. *The Flower and the Castle: An Introduction to Modern Drama.* New York, 1963.

Vildrac, Charles. *The Steamship Tenacity*, translated by John Strong Newberry. *Chief Contemporary Dramatists*, Third Series, edited by Thomas H. Dickinson. Boston, 1930.

Waxman, Samuel. *Antoine and the Théâtre Libre.* Cambridge, 1926.

Wedekind, Frank. *Spring's Awakening*, translated by Eric Bentley. *The Modern Theatre*, Vol. VI, edited by Eric Bentley. New York, 1960.

Young, Stark. *The Theatre.* New York, 1954.

Index

In order to assist those readers who do not know Japanese, main entries for titles of literary works, organizations, magazines, etc., are given under the English translations used in this book. Cross-references are provided for the same information in Japanese. Japanese names are listed under the family name. In the case where commonly used artistic names are employed in the text (for example, "Shōyō" for "Tsubouchi Shōyō"), cross references to the proper full name are provided.

Library of Congress Cataloging in Publication Data

Rimer, J. Thomas.
   Toward a modern Japanese theatre.
   Bibliography: p.
   1. Kishida, Kunio, 1890-1954.   2. Theater—Japan—History.
I. Title.

PL832.I8Z85   895.6′2′4   73-16747